Approaches to Teaching
the Poetry of John Gower

Approaches to Teaching World Literature

For a complete listing of titles,
see the last pages of this book

Approaches to Teaching
The Poetry of John Gower

Edited by

R. F. Yeager

and

Brian W. Gastle

The Modern Language Association of America
New York   2011

© 2011 by The Modern Language Association of America
All rights reserved. Printed in the United States of America

MLA and the MODERN LANGUAGE ASSOCIATION are trademarks
owned by the Modern Language Association of America. For
information about obtaining permission to reprint material from
MLA book publications, send your request by mail (see address below),
e-mail (permissions@mla.org), or fax (646 458-0030).

Library of Congress Cataloging-in-Publication Data

Approaches to teaching the poetry of John Gower /
edited by R. F. Yeager and Brian W. Gastle.
p. cm.—(Approaches to teaching world literature; 117)
Includes bibliographical references and index.
ISBN 978-1-60329-099-9 (hardcover : alk. paper)
ISBN 978-1-60329-100-2 (pbk. : alk. paper)
1. Gower, John, 1325?–1408—Study and teaching.
2. Gower, John, 1325?–1408—Criticism and interpretation.
I. Yeager, Robert F.   II. Gastle, Brian W.
PR1988.S78A67 2011
821'.1—dc22   2011006671

Approaches to Teaching World Literature 117
ISSN 1059-1133

Cover illustration for the paperback edition:
Gower shooting an arrow at the world, from Gower's
Vox clamantis. MS HM150, fol. 13v. Huntington Lib.,
San Marino, California. Reproduced by permission of the Trustees.

Published by The Modern Language Association of America
26 Broadway, New York, New York 10004-1789
www.mla.org

CONTENTS

Introduction: Gower in Context

John Gower (d. 1408) was, during his lifetime and into the Enlightenment, considered the father of English poetry. A contemporary and friend of Chaucer's (who entrusted Gower with his power of attorney when he traveled to Italy in 1378 and who famously placed *Troilus and Criseyde* under the corrective scrutiny of "moral Gower and philosophical Strode"), Gower invariably—and deservedly—appears alongside Chaucer in early laudatory accounts of the birth of English letters.

Everyone read him: Thomas Hoccleve and John Lydgate praised his language and his narrative skills; Edmund Spenser probably based his parade of the sins (in book 1 of the *Faerie Queene*) on a section from Gower's French poem the *Mirour de l'omme*; William Shakespeare took the plot of *Pericles* from the "Tale of Apollonius of Tyre" in book 8 of Gower's *Confessio Amantis* and included "Ancient Gower" himself as the chorus; Ben Jonson, in his *Grammar*, drew more examples of "good English" from Gower than from any other writer, including Chaucer, and named Gower "father of our language"; John Milton seems to have borrowed his portrait of Sin in *Paradise Lost*—with her wolfish offspring swarming in and out of her loins—from Gower; Samuel Johnson employed a bit of Gower here and there, for illustration, evincing little concern that either the name or the reference would go unrecognized. Indeed, not to know Gower was, for centuries, the exception among educated readers rather than the norm.

All this changed after Johnson. Gower fell victim to shifting tastes both social and literary, the more so because, as English-speaking readers became increasingly monolingual, the roughly two-thirds of his poetry composed in Anglo-French and Latin was no longer within their reach. All pendulums nonetheless swing two ways. Editorial and scholarly efforts, especially over the last several decades, have restored Gower's reputation and commensurately extended our appreciation of his achievement—even as students, exposed to his poetry in increasing numbers, have discovered its many merits: the readability of his clear, no-nonsense manner of expression (often compared with the "plain style" of the later English Augustans); his economical depiction of emotion; the punch he can deliver, even with the briefest sketch of a tale. Few medievalists today would fail to recognize John Gower for the significant literary presence he clearly was—a uniquely original writer in his way as accomplished, and as vital to our comprehending the English late Middle Ages, as Chaucer, Langland, or the poet of *Sir Gawain and the Green Knight*.

This volume is intended to assist instructors as they address the particular challenges—and reap the benefits—that teaching Gower's poetry brings to the classroom. Gower shares with Chaucer profound curiosities—about marriage, classical authors, narrative theory, and love as it was practiced in the Middle Ages, at once so alien to our students and yet so reassuringly familiar. Like the poet of *Gawain* and *Pearl*, he is troubled when realities of chivalry, fidelity, and religious faith fall short of the ideal. Like Langland, he has an acute interest in, and an urgency to debate directly, the big issues—public and private morality, the establishment church, national governance, law and justice (not always in Gower's mind the same things), war and peace, heresy, social class in the form of the three estates, and behaviors appropriate to each. More than any of his fellow poets, Gower was also politically engaged, addressing poems of advice to two kings (and all others who could read!), a great deal of it polemical in the extreme. Of the "big four," Gower's commentary on Richard II and Henry IV is the most trenchant, and the most observably informed, stemming, apparently, from a close relationship with the Lancastrian house and an involvement (even from across the Thames in Southwark, where he lived for thirty years) with the politics of court. Further, his portrayals of power, both national and local, draw on his demonstrable connections with the church and on his firsthand involvement with the mercantile element in London—as historians have long recognized through their recourse to Gower for details of contemporary life and attitudes.

For teachers, such writing poses special problems, more than offset though they are by special opportunities. The background materials students need to understand the shape of church and state, or even relations between women and men, in late medieval England are significant. One purpose of this volume is to supply such background and to indicate successful methodologies for bringing it into the classroom when Gower is the focus. Other sorts of background are needed for teaching Gower too, since his reading was both unusually deep and wide-ranging. All his works are rich with reference to multiple sources, including the Bible, confessional and penitential literature, the classics (Ovid in particular, but also Vergil, Statius, Horace), and contemporary literatures of all types, from poets of *fin amour* (Guillaume de Lorris and Jean de Meun, and especially Guillaume de Machaut and Eustache Deschamps) to anonymous French and English romances to native folktale collections. Gower was, moreover, a thoughtful historian, concerned to place in context the advances (and recursions) of human societies; he also shared a keen interest with Chaucer in matters scientific, and his uses of astrological, astronomical, and alchemical materials are extensive—simultaneously rewarding and challenging to the teacher and the student.

There is also the fact that Gower wrote two-thirds of his verse in languages other than English. That he took great pride in having done so is vividly evident from the three large tomes naming his major works in Anglo-French, Latin, and English that support his head on his tomb in Southwark Cathedral. For him, and doubtless in the eyes of his contemporaries, this was a great achievement. For us as teachers of medieval literature, Gower's trilingual oeuvre represents an unusually accessible opportunity to help our students recognize how characteristically medieval it is, how more than the single English of any of his contemporaries it so accurately reflects the nature of late medieval English literature and its interactivity with Continental forms and fashions. The present availability of translations of Gower's shorter poems in Latin and French, and their value as poems and as artifacts, in addition to their brevity, renders them attractive vehicles for the classroom. Gower's unique trilinguality can act as a basis for exciting cross-cultural teaching: it makes a point about life in late medieval London not even Chaucer's writing can match.

Responses to our survey of instructors who currently teach Gower's works or who would like to introduce the study of Gower into their classrooms raised these pedagogical issues along with a number of others that the essays in this volume have been assembled to address, including the following: locating Gower within the larger context of medieval literature, both English and Continental, and providing a cultural and historical backdrop for his works; evaluating and selecting appropriate editions, texts, readings, and media (especially electronic materials); positioning Gower in relation to schools of contemporary literary theory and to scholarly research in the field; teaching Gower's poetry in the context of other commonly anthologized pieces—in comparison with Chaucer, alongside work of women writers, and so forth; integrating Gower's multilingual works into an otherwise English syllabus and teaching his languages in general. Since Gower's poetry is most often taught in four-year colleges and universities, in undergraduate medieval literature survey classes (90% of survey respondents), graduate medieval literature seminars (81% of survey respondents), undergraduate sophomore survey of early British literature (60% of survey respondents), and the undergraduate Chaucer seminar (55% of survey respondents), the essays in this volume focus on approaches that relate to these classes. We have, however, also included essays that suggest how Gower can be taught in community college survey courses, composition courses, and courses devoted to literary theory.

The volume begins by delineating the rich textual tradition of and scholarly context for Gower's poetry, including an overview of editions available in print and online, a comprehensive discussion of salient secondary studies for students and instructors, and a survey of online and other digital resources useful in the classroom. The specific approaches to teaching Gower that follow are organized into five main categories. Essays in the section "Historical Approaches and Context" suggest how Gower's work can fit within the historical milieu of his time and, to some extent, the literary tradition that follows. Included under "Language, Literature, and Rhetoric" are essays offering instructors ways to focus on Gower's mastery of form, aural effect, rhetoric, and diction, in order to address survey participants' desires to become more familiar with his languages. Essays in "Theoretical Approaches" profile successful experiments with Gower's texts as subjects for theoretical engagement. The section "Comparative Approaches," taking into account that Gower frequently is taught alongside Chaucer, includes essays on ways to teach major sources, narratives (the stories of Florent and

Constance), and milieus shared by both. And finally, "Specific Classroom Contexts" discusses the teaching of Gower in a range of specialized classroom experiences, from the community college to the graduate school.

RFY and BWG

NOTE

Unless otherwise noted, translations of the *Mirour* cite Wilson's edition, and citations to Gower's works in their original languages are to *The Complete Works*; the *Confessio Amantis* appears in volumes 2 and 3 of this edition, with volume 3 beginning at book 5, line 1971.

Part One

MATERIALS

Texts for Teaching
Russell A. Peck

The John Gower canon is trilingual. With one exception (*In Praise of Peace*), Gower's earliest and latest writings are in French and Latin: his first French work and his greatest, the *Mirour de l'omme* ("The Mirror of Man," over 30,000 lines), was written in the mid-1370s; and his first and greatest Latin opus, the *Vox clamantis* ("Voice of One Crying," 6,266 lines), was begun in the late 1370s, though it was finished shortly after 1381.

But in fact, Gower appears to have written in both Latin and French throughout his life. His *Cinkante balades* ("Fifty Ballades") was perhaps begun early on, when Chaucer was also writing ballades in French, and continued to be expanded sporadically up to the end of the century. If R. F. Yeager is right, the ballades were mainly written circa 1390–93, after Gower had essentially finished his first draft of the *Confessio Amantis*; they were then recopied for presentation to Henry IV in 1399–1400, presumably shortly after the coronation (Introduction to *Cinkante balades* 11–14). Another sequence of eighteen ballades, called the *Traitié selonc les auctours pour essampler les amantz marietz* ("Treatise following the Authorities as an Example for Married Lovers") in the headnote to the poems, was perhaps copied in anticipation of his marriage to Agnes Groundolf in 1398, though, according to Yeager (Introduction to the *Traitié* 7–9), the ballades may, given the kinds of exempla they use and the mirror reversals of themes in the *Confessio*, have been drafted at about the same time as the *Confessio* (i.e., 1385–90). Gower's return to composing primarily in Latin later in life is evidenced by his writing of shorter moral and political Latin pieces from about 1394 to 1401, poems that reflect his disenchantment with the reign of Richard II, a disenchantment that culminated in his scabrous political allegory against Richard called the *Cronica tripertita* ("Tripartite Chronicle"), which he linked as an eighth book to his *Vox clamantis*, written two decades earlier.

But during the years between 1385 and about 1393 Gower wrote primarily in English, and it is the *Confessio Amantis* that establishes him as a major figure in the history of English poetry. The first recension of the *Confessio*, dedicated to Richard II, with friendly remarks about Chaucer, was finished about 1390, though Gower continued to add to it and adjust passages over the next two or three years, possibly even later. A second recension, citing the year as 1392, changes the dedication from Richard to "a bok for Engelondes sake" (prologue, line 24) in honor of "myn oghne lord, / Which of Lancastre is Henri named" (86–87). This version, referred to as the Lancastrian recension, also alters the conclusion to the poem (8.2942–3178), removing Richard's name and praise to pray instead for good governance and the welfare of the state. This carefully crafted poem of 33,444 lines of English verse, along with 396 lines of Latin epigrams and hundreds of lines of Latin marginal commentary in the Lancastrian recension of 1392, is one of the truly great books of the English Middle Ages.

The English Works of Gower

Confessio Amantis

The twenty-first century is a good time to be teaching Gower in that more teaching texts are available now than ever before. Although Gower's influence on other English writers was considerable even into the seventeenth century with the writings of Shakespeare and Jonson, knowledge of his work was sparse from the Restoration until the latter part of the nineteenth century. But with G. C. Macaulay's four-volume edition, *The Complete Works of John Gower* (1899–1902), Gower began to be studied again in earnest. Macaulay's edition immediately became the standard scholarly basis for all Gower studies and still will, for generations to come, enjoy that position of preeminence. All four volumes of his complete works are consistently precise in quality of editing. His detailed glossaries, his linguistic introduction, his knowledge of the manuscripts reflected in his extensive textual notes, and, especially, his learned explanatory notes that frequently deal with possible sources, linguistic quirks, historical circumstances that are alluded to, and wise observations on the poem's ideas and craft, set this edition apart from all others as a scholarly resource.

In 1900–01 Oxford University Press reprinted volumes 2 and 3 of Macaulay's *Complete Works* as *The English Works of John Gower*, under the auspices of the Early English Text Society (EETS), thus guaranteeing that it would remain available in print over a long period of time. With its detailed textual and explanatory notes and 96-page glossary, the EETS edition of the *Confessio Amantis*, now distributed by Boydell and Brewer–University of Rochester Press, has served scholars especially well for research and courses in philology. But because of the high cost of the volumes and the reluctance of university bookstores, particularly in America, to order books that don't have a manageable return policy, the EETS books have been little used for literature courses at the undergraduate level, where readers are likely to be concerned primarily with literary issues and are less prepared for or interested in the expertise that characterizes Macaulay's achievement. One consequence of this lack of a less specialized readership was that during the twentieth century Gower was seldom included in anthologies of Middle English literature. His work was scarcely read at all except for occasional comparisons with Chaucer, where his poetry was usually taken out of context and used to demonstrate the superiority of Chaucer's literary genius.

The situation of Gower studies changed somewhat in 1968 with the publication, in England, of J. A. W. Bennett's *Selections from John Gower* and, in America, with the Holt Rinehart edition of a generous selection of the *Confessio*. The selections for both editions are based on Macaulay's text. The Holt Rinehart edition includes the complete prologue, most of book 1, and complete narratives of forty tales taken from all eight books of the poem. This 525-page volume served for the next thirty years, especially in America, as the main access to Gower for college students. The edition glosses difficult words in the right margins and provides prose summaries of what is missing between selections. Users of the volume could thus have a reasonable sense of the whole poem. The marginal glossing is sparse, however, and the edition includes only two of the Latin epigrams (the first for the prologue and the first for book 1) and none of the Latin marginalia. The general introduction places the poem within its literary and philosophical context. This abridgment of the poem has had a dozen reprints and is still available in the Medieval Academy Reprints for Teaching series from the University of Toronto Press.

For the twenty-first century, however, the difficulty of finding an adequate, inexpensive complete edition of *Confessio Amantis* has been considerably alleviated by the publication of Peck's three-volume edition of the complete poem in the Middle English Texts Series (METS), sponsored by the Consortium for the Teaching of the Middle Ages (TEAMS). This edition includes the complete English text of the 1392 recension found in the Fairfax 3 manuscript in the Bodleian Library, Oxford; all the Latin epigrams and marginal Latin paraphernalia of the manuscript along with English translations by Andrew Galloway; and extensive marginal glossing of words that are likely to be difficult for modern readers. Each of the three volumes has a comprehensive introduction, bibliography, selected textual notes, and explanatory notes to introduce readers to current scholarship and discussion of central critical issues. The contract between TEAMS and Medieval Institute Publications guarantees that the volumes will remain in print indefinitely and that they will be reissued (with corrections and updated scholarship) when current printings are depleted.

All METS editions are available online free to individual users. This access makes it possible to include Gower in courses where he is used for purposes of illustration or comparison, rather than featured as a major unit in the syllabus, since assigning specific passages is now an affordable option. The METS three-volume edition of the *Confessio* is designed for classroom use. In recognition that not many courses will study the complete poem, especially at the undergraduate level (though the three-volume edition works well for a major authors course), volume 1 includes the prologue, book 1, and book 8—that is, the frame of the poem. This beginning–ending layout enables the study of the poem's genre and organizational ideas, namely, (1) the setting up of a confessional structure into which tales and other kinds of exempla are placed; (2) a sense of Gower's ideas about audience along with theories of reading for purposes of enlightenment and therapy, though he acknowledges in the end the limitations of such theories, all of which depend on the ability of the audience itself to comprehend problems of self and society rationally; (3) the comic debate between the poem's two primary dramatis personae, Amans (the lover) and Genius (his complex father-confessor); (4) the complex conclusion, with its deconstruction of the dramatic voicing established in book 1 along with its poignantly disenchanted view of one's personal sense of self (whether inside or outside the poem); and (5) the disappointing failure of practical and theoretical politics due to the fragile ability of the state to govern itself reasonably. The poem's confessional plot, given the preoccupations of the lover and his ambiguous confessor (is he Venus's priest or Reason's?), is dichotomous in its exploring of social issues pertaining to good rule and the more personal concerns of a devoted lover who wants to read everything in terms of his own narcissistic desires. This dichotomy, especially evident in the first and last books of the poem, creates an open-ended effect that is crucial to understanding the poem.

The layout of volume 1 of Peck's edition attempts to get at these ambiguities in voicing: book 1 on Pride and book 8 on misguided love include several of the most memorable tales in the *Confessio*, namely, The "Tale of Mundus and Paulina" (a study of rape, religious and political corruption, and the restorative power of good family and positive social dynamics), the "Tale of Florent" (the loathly lady story out of which Chaucer's Wife of Bath builds her tale), the "Trump of Death" (an epitome of the need for humility when faced with the inevitable), the "Tale of Narcissus" (a retelling of Ovid's demonstrating how one may be destroyed by the mistress of one's imagination), the "Tale of Albinus and Rosemund" (a tale of mental cruelty and retaliation), the "Tale of the Three Questions" (a celebration of female intelligence, the shaping of a socially viable identity, salvation of family through the daughter, and lessons in mutual profit), and the "Tale of Apollonius of Tyre" (Gower's ultimate romance of alienation, loss, and recovery of all aspects of the communities of self). This final tale serves as a summary exemplum for the whole of the *Confessio* and becomes the basis of Shakespeare's late romance, *Pericles*, where "Gower" appears as a Pirendello-like character/author trying to keep a handle on his sources and his own sense of being, a truly Goweresque topic that is present throughout the *Confessio*.

Finally, like Macaulay's edition, volume 1 of the METS edition includes the contrasting versions of the beginning and conclusion to the 1390 and 1392 recensions, which can lead to excellent discussion of the growth of a poet's understanding of his own work, problems of finding a right ending, the intricate relationship between Chaucer and Gower, discussion of historical social and political issues in the last decade of the fourteenth century, and so on.

Volume 2 of the METS *Confessio* presents books 2–4. The introduction to the volume focuses on Gower as dramatist, exploring his skills at staging exemplary ideas in the brain of his reader. All three books in this volume focus on performative aspects of Gower's ingenious narratology. Book 2, organized around the topic of envy, features the "Tale of Constance," which Chaucer also uses as his Man of Law's Tale. This story is one of the principal "accused queen" narratives in English (variants on calumniated women are found in several other Middle English romances — *Emaré*, *Octavian*, *The Earl of Toulouse*, and *Sir Eglamour of Artois*). Gower's telling of the story is more straightforward than Chaucer's (where all agency is attributed to "Criste, sanz faille" [line 501]). Gower's queen is more personally empowered — a heroine oppressed but clever in her strategies of self-defense.

Other memorable tales in book 2 include the "Tale of the Travelers and the Angel" (a fable illustrating one of Envy's five children — "joy over another's grief," according to the Latin marginalia at line 224) and a lively account of the mythical "Tale of Deianira, Hercules, and Nessus" that demonstrates the dangers of, and the horrendous results that may ensue from, "Falssemblant" ("False-Seeming"). Several of the stories in this book are "historical" and work well to demonstrate Gower's notion of the interconnectedness of history and fiction. The book ends with accounts of Pope Boniface as a supplanter and the story of Constantine, whose charity (the antidote to Envy) heals many of the problems of the state, but whose "donation," endowing Christianity as the official religion of Rome, leads to disastrous abuse by greedy churchmen in years to come.

Book 3, on Wrath, includes the poignant "Tale of Canace and Machaire," the incest narrative that Chaucer mocks in the introduction to The Man of Law's Tale. Students find the tale remarkably affecting in its sympathy toward Canace, the victim of an angry father and the patriarchy that supports him. The "Tale of Pyramus and Thisbe" is likewise a fine retelling of Ovid's narrative as a study in sentiment, a more likely source for Shakespeare's treatment of the story in *Midsummer Night's Dream* than Chaucer's or Ovid's. Book 3 concludes with a sequence on the evil of war and the mentality that supports crusades and other forms of political aggression. Book 4, on Sloth, includes several of the most remarkable adaptations from Ovid in the English language. Some have identified this as their favorite book in the *Confessio*, partly because of the lively debate between Amans and Genius that ensues and the ingenuity of the lover, who is so busy in his futile love labors that his mentor enters into a discourse on the history of labor, inventors, and alchemy as a rational antidote to Amans's besottedness.

Volume 3 of the METS *Confessio* includes books 5–7. The introduction to this volume focuses on Gower's attitudes toward history and law and the importance of those topics for reading and teaching the poem. Book 5, on Avarice, is the longest in the poem — longer by far than the prologue and books 3 and 6 combined. Students interested in the rise of capitalism and economic structures based on money will find Gower's concerns here to be particularly relevant. Greed and covetousness have, in Gower's eyes, become the dominant sin of the times. His view is closely akin to that of Chaucer, Langland, or the *Castle of Perseverence* poet in this regard. Covetousness contagiously infects all aspects of social behavior. Book 5 introduces new structural principles quite different from the first four books, principles that enable Genius to develop shorter historical or biblical exempla as part of his analysis of the social malaise of greed. At the outset of book 5 Genius provides a history of world religions to illustrate the implosive affect of greed in spiritual matters. Several of Gower's finest, tour de force narratives are found here: the brief classical fable of Vergil's mirror, the folkloric "Tale of Adrian and Bardus," the Ovidian "Tale of Tereus, Procne, and Philomena," and the comical "Tale of Hercules and Faunus," all of which provoke stimulating discussion and thoughtful essays. But, for me, the crowning achievement of book 5 is Gower's deeply considered study of Medea.

Book 6, on Gluttony, is brief, focusing on only two aspects of the sin—drunkenness and delicacy, though with amusing applications of both to the delicately insatiable sensibilities of the lover. The subtlest strategy of book 6 is its examination of sorcery and witchcraft as a concluding assessment of gluttony, which becomes a means for Genius to explore how a gluttonous will uses fantasy and make-believe to shape fantastic destinies to pleasure itself. The story of "Ulysses and Telegonus" demonstrates how little we understand of present actions whose consequences revisit us in later years; the "Tale of Nectanabus" makes the same point, but in a more complex way as Nectanabus deliberately manipulates people's minds to effect what he presumes will be to his benefit. But, ultimately, he, like Ulysses, is destroyed by his own brainchild, namely the future king, Alexander.

Book 7 takes off from book 6 to demonstrate how Aristotle instructed Alexander after Nectanabus's death. This book, which is essentially an educational treatise on good kingship (whether of state or self), is in some ways the hardest to teach. If students have become interested in the central issues of law and governance in the poem, they will be impressed with Gower's encyclopedic view of what is essential in educating the prince—from theology, physics, and mathematics to astronomy, rhetoric, and policy. Law and the making, understanding, and keeping of contracts are prominent topics from the prologue on. Defined here as categories, they apply to nature, social policy, and personal behavior. The books Gower most frequently goes to for exempla in book 7 are Vincent of Beauvais's *Speculum naturale*, Giles of Rome's *De regimine, principium*, Godfrey of Viterbo's *Pantheon*, Ovid's *Fasti*, and the Hebrew Bible. The stories of Lycurgus, Tarquin, Aruns and Lucrece, Virginia, and Sara and Tobit may not be initially as pleasing as some of the earlier stories, but they set up well book 8 with its "Tale of Apollonius" and the final pleas of the lover before Venus rejects his suit and gives him a mirror for self-study. Poor Amans comes to recognize that he is an aged John Gower who must put the world behind him, look to the welfare of his own soul, and pray for the state of England—a sorrowful ending indeed. Volume 3 of the METS edition includes a subject index to all three volumes that is helpful to students wishing to research specific topics, particularly students working in special areas such as women's studies, classical literature and its influence on the Middle Ages, religious studies from saints' lives to theology, or projects that require comparisons with other medieval writers and historical documents.

In Praise of Peace

In Praise of Peace seems designed to follow the conclusion to the *Confessio*, though it was written nearly a decade after Gower had completed his first draft of that poem. As its most recent editor points out, the poem is a kind of enchiridion (Livingston 89), a summary work on the political themes of Gower's earlier poetry—more arguments against war, a strong appeal to the king to rule well over his rightful domain, to make peace between factions within Parliament that led to the crises between the throne and Parliament in 1387–88, and to uphold peace as if it were a sacramental right.

The poem may be found in volume 3 of Macaulay, *Complete Works of John Gower*, under the title "To King Henry the Fourth in Praise of Peace" (481–94), and in two METS editions, one by Michael Livingston and another by Kathleen Forni, both of which are available on the METS Web site. This 395-line poem is of interest to courses dealing with late-fourteenth-century politics, kingship, governance, conscience, and social welfare.

Gower's Latin Works

Vox clamantis

Macaulay's edition of Gower's Latin works is no longer in print, though *Google Books* has put all of volume 4 of *The Complete Works*, *The Latin Works*, online. Eric W. Stockton's translation, *Major Latin Works*, includes the complete *Vox clamantis* and the *Cronica tripertita*, but it too is now out of print. The *Longman Anthology of British Literature* includes a couple of snippets from book 1 of the *Vox* to illustrate Gower's response to the Uprising of 1381 (Braswell and Schotter 463–66; this is the only bit from Gower in the anthology). But although Gower is somewhat conservative here in his attitude toward social mobility, the *Longman* selection distorts the dramatic purpose of book 1 and Gower's general attitude toward the third estate, whose virtuous members often displace those of higher estate who are unvirtuous. To understand Gower, especially his political views, readers need to consider the larger contexts of his pointed remarks, particularly when the settings are dramatic, as in book 1. The whole *Vox* is worthy of intensive study, especially for students interested in English estates theory and the weaknesses of social and political behavior in the latter half of the fourteenth century. *Vox*, book 1 (what has been called the "Visio") and the whole of the *Cronica tripertita* offer an interesting pairing of two Latin political allegories that are strikingly different in their modes of exemplification: *Vox*, book 1, is a kind of symbol allegory that dramatizes a nightmare of the "self" trapped in a violent diegesis of wilderness, where everything familiar seems transformed into bewildering monstrosity; the *Cronica*, on the other hand, is a personification allegory that voices the action from a nondiegetic position outside the events of the previous decade as an admonition against the criminal follies of Richard's indulgent rule. In both the *Vox* and the *Cronica*, Gower's discussions of knights and kingship engage astute consideration of chivalry, office, and duty and stand in contrast to the methods of social analysis through narrative exempla that Gower uses in book 7 of *Confessio Amantis*.

Cronica tripertita

Neither Macaulay's edition of the *Cronica* nor Stockton's 1962 translation is in print, so, as with the *Vox*, *Google Books* is the best option for retrieving the Latin text. The whole of the 1,055-line poem (or, at least, excerpts) is worthy material in courses dealing with politics, satire, or allegory. In their excellent discussion of the poem, A. G. Rigg and Edward S. Moore link the *Cronica* with *Vox*, book 1, in terms of well-crafted satire that adjusts history to suit the demands of the occasion. The first part of the *Cronica* presents the fall of Richard to the appellants, a section Gower labels "Opus humanum" ("work of man"), indicative of Richard's role in his own demise. Gower names part 2, on Richard's systematic revenge against his opponents of a couple of years earlier, "Opus inferni" ("the work of hell"). Part 3, which depicts Richard's final undoing, is labeled "Opus in Christo" ("work in Christ") which argues that Richard is, in the end, destroyed by Christ.

The Shorter Latin Works

The minor Latin works, on the other hand, are readily available both in Yeager's edition and online on the METS Web site. These fifteen poems, ranging from four-line prayers for the soul of John Gower ("Orate pro anima") to poems about the many types of love as Gower prepares in his old age to approach "the marriage bed in the order of husbands" ("Est amor," line 27), about the celebration of God's vision that oversees all human actions ("O Deus immense"), and a long diatribe (321 lines) about the manifold plague of vices that infected the reign of Richard II ("Carmen super multiplici viciorum pestilencia"). The poems are rich in biblical citations and forthright in their political critique. Yeager has included in his edition an image from the Cotton Tiberius manuscript, A.iv, folio 9r, of Gower the satirist shooting an arrow at the world. That image is not available in the online versions of Yeager's volume, though it is available widely elsewhere online (www.luminarium.org; www.johngower.org).[1] The image provides a good starting point for consideration of political satire not simply in Gower but in Chaucer and the host of satirists writing in English or Latin in the later fourteenth and fifteenth centuries, a topic supported by texts available in two METS editions by James Dean (*Political Writings*; *Ecclesiastical Satires*).

The French Works of John Gower

Mirour de l'omme

The *Mirour de l'omme* is Gower's earliest major work. It is found in a single manuscript and is not known to have been recopied. It too is out of print, though available online through *Google Books*. The *Mirour* is a treasury of Gowerian ideas, to which Gower returned repeatedly in his later writings. I have taught the poem several times in graduate seminars using William Burton Wilson's translation. Although the *Mirour* is long (over 400 pages, including notes), students come away with a sense of amazement at the subtlety of Gower's text, whether it be the opening metaphysical discussion of sin as nothingness or the account of the incestuous rape of Sin by her son Death to produce the seven deadly daughters of Sin, who are then married to the World ("Siecle") to produce fivefold further offspring (students like to compare Milton's genealogy of Sin in *Paradise Lost* and also to juxtapose the violent genealogy of Sin and her children with the comely espousing of Reason to God's seven virtuous daughters as studies in a weird kind of domestic drama).

Likewise of great interest is Gower's elaborate discussion of medieval estates theory in the *Mirour* and the falling off of behavior "nowadays." Priests "farm out prostitution as if it were property of land and tillage," and for the first estate "a dozen whores are worth more than a thousand chaste women" (269). With regard to the first estate, Gower observes the vast falling off from "The Worthies" to lazy knights these days, who buy off their duty in order to stay at home as "hedgerow" knights, making profit off the dilemmas of the unfortunate, and turn themselves into avaricious murderers who go abroad to plunder innocent people and destroy Christian communities that feel the distress of such "chivalry" everyday (315). "Nowadays" in the third estate judges, men of law, sheriffs, bailiffs, and even jurors use their offices to get rich by afflicting their neighbors and the rest of the Commons with their greed. Following the example of the other two estates, they gladly engage in war for personal advantage: "Christian cruelty, so full of lawlessness, that makes common slaughter pitilessly among men as if they were beasts in the market" (316). These days Christians blame the world for the evils they perpetrate. Gower ends his *Mirour* with a meditation on the birth and life of the blessed Virgin Mary, whose compassionate mediation on humankind's behalf seems the best hope. Gower's *Mirour* has ample energy to provide a wealth of research materials on virtually any medieval topic.

The *Cinkante balades* and the *Traitié*

Like the *Mirour*, the *Cinkante balades* and the *Traitié* are available in French in Macaulay's *The Complete Works of John Gower.* Volume 1, *The French Works*, is digitized online by *Google Books*. Yeager's edition of both ballade sequences in French with facing-page translation is now available in a METS volume. Tamara O'Callaghan and Brian Merrilees likewise have an edition and translation of the *Traitié* available online. The "Online Texts" section of *The Gower Project*, an online hypertext program that, though still in its infancy, shows great promise for teachers of Gower, also links to this edition. The French text in Yeager's edition is from Macaulay, though he includes a linguistic introduction to the French by Brian Merrilees; the French text in O'Callaghan and Merrilees's edition lacks discussion of Gower's Anglo-French.

Gower's French ballades are of use to the teacher in three key ways: for study of medieval *forme fixe* poetry; for study of the English court and aristocratic literary practice; and for comparison with the presentation of love in the *Confessio* itself, where the futility of Amans's impetuous love is different from issues of married love explored in the *Traitié*. Yeager points out the likeness of these ballades to "treatises" on married love (*traitié* means "treatise" [Introduction to the *Traitié* 5]), noting that the *Traitié* ballades do not follow an implied love narrative, the way the *Cinkante balades* or the Middle English ballades of Charles of Orléans do, but, rather, are more like Chaucer's moral ballades in their topicality, except that, unlike Chaucer's (which are solitary), Gower's are arranged carefully according to a thematic coherence (Yeager, *French Balades* 7–9). The *Cinkante balades*, on the other hand (of which there are fifty-four), offer a vague story of love akin to what we find in the Renaissance in a sonnet sequence such as Sidney's.

Yeager's METS volume, along with James Wimsatt's *Chaucer and the Poems of "Ch,"* will be useful to students of French literature in tracking French influences on the fourteenth-century English court. The French poet Oton de Granson was in residence in London in the latter years of Edward III and may have been a factor in teaching Gower as well as Chaucer the merits of French poetry, particularly the poetry of Guillaume de Machaut and Eustache Deschamps. Peter Nicholson's *Love and Ethics in Gower's* Confessio Amantis offers an excellent introduction to Machaut's influence on the French side of Gower's vision. Nicholson is currently editing the works of Granson as an adjunct text to METS.

NOTE

[1] Variations on the image in Cotton Tiberius are also found in Glasgow, MS Hunter 59, and Huntington, HM 150.

The Instructor's Library

Peter Nicholson

As the essays in this book demonstrate, the *Confessio Amantis* is taught in many different contexts and for a wide variety of purposes, but, whatever the situation, the best advice for further reading, not just for the instructor but also for the student who wishes to deepen his or her understanding of Gower, is simply more Gower. Those studying a single tale will want to read the entire book in which the tale is found. Those doing a whole book (a far better choice than a selection of excerpts for an appreciation of the unique structure of the poem) should also look at the frame in which the confession is set by reading (at very least) the prologue, book 1, and book 8 (which compose vol. 1 of Peck's edition). And every reader of the *Confessio* can benefit from some acquaintance with Gower's other major works, the *Mirour de l'omme*, the *Vox clamantis*, and the two cycles of *balades*, the *Cinkante balades* and the *Traitié pour essampler les amantz marietz*.

The first recommendation for the instructor's library, then, is at least one of the two complete editions of the poem. These are discussed more fully in Russell A. Peck's "Texts for Teaching," in this volume. Each has its advantages for this purpose: Peck's edition (2000–04) is more accessible; it is more up-to-date; it offers complete translations of the Latin apparatus; and it contains helpful same-page glosses for beginners in Middle English. G. C. Macaulay's (1900–01) has a page layout that gives a clearer sense of how the poem appears in the early manuscripts; it has the only complete glossary; and it presents the eight books of the poem in the correct order. It is also the point of reference for all serious scholarship. An instructor may well want to make use of both.

For Gower's other works, we have good translations of the *Vox clamantis*, by Eric Stockton, and of the shorter Latin poems, by R. F. Yeager, and a serviceable translation of the *Mirour de l'omme*, by William Burton Wilson. The *Traitié pour essampler les amantz marietz* and the *Cinkante balades* are available in a TEAMS edition with facing-page translations by Yeager, as well as in their original French in Macaulay's edition of the complete works. And for speakers of Japanese, the *Confessio* is available in a translation by Masayoshi Itô.

With few exceptions, critical examination of Gower's works has focused almost exclusively on the *Confessio*. Exceptions can be found in Maria Wickert's groundbreaking study of the *Vox clamantis* and in Kurt Olsson's "John Gower's *Vox clamantis* and the Medieval Idea of Place." The lyrics have received some overdue attention recently, particularly in the work of Yeager (see his essay in this volume). Otherwise, what commentary there is on the *Vox* and *Mirour* is generally to be found within broader discussions of Gower's entire career. John Hurt Fisher, in *John Gower: Moral Philosopher and Friend of Chaucer*, which is cited again below, discusses all three of Gower's longer poems as constituents of a single major work. Yeager (*John Gower's Poetic*) includes all of Gower's works within his discussions of the poet's style and of his transformation of his sources. Shorter, somewhat different overviews of Gower's literary career are provided by Peck ("John Gower" [1994]) and Winthrop Wetherbee ("John Gower"). And introductions to Gower's French and Latin works can be found in the essays by Yeager, Rigg and Moore, and Ardis Butterfield in Siân Echard's indispensable *A Companion to Gower*, which also includes chapters by other distinguished Gowerians on the poet's life, his language, the manuscripts of his works, his reputation and influence, his sources, and some of the major interpretive issues in the *Confessio*.

Gower is well provided with bibliographies. Yeager's *John Gower Materials* offers a topical arrangement of material on Gower up to 1979. My own *Annotated Index* lists references to particular passages or tales in the *Confessio*, each with a brief summary, in the published criticism up to 1987. And the bibliography in Echard's *Companion* is arranged chronologically and covers material on all of Gower's works through 2003. These are to be supplemented by the semiannual reviews of current scholarship that appear in the *John Gower Newsletter*. For Gower's language, J. D. Pickles and J. L. Dawson's *Concordance* (1987) is a valuable companion to Macaulay's glossary, and there is a concordance to Gower's French works by R. F. Yeager, Mark West, Robin L. Hinson, and Hollifield.

The Confessio Amantis: *Gower's Sources*

Sources or analogues for the vast majority of the tales in the *Confessio* are identified in Macaulay's notes. The very few additions can be found in the notes to Peck's edition or in my *Annotated Index*. A comparison of Gower's tale with its sources might seem to be an obvious classroom exercise, but unfortunately it is not as easy as an instructor might hope. Because of his freedom with his material, it is not always clear which text Gower was working from, and his reading included many works that are virtually unknown today. And, while many of his tales are clearly derived from Ovid (as Beidler's collection, *John Gower's Literary Transformations*, suggests), he also knew and used other medieval versions of the same tales, which are much more difficult to find. The most easily accessible materials are for the tales also told by Chaucer, in *The Book of the Duchess* (Ceix and Alceone), in *The Legend of Good Women* (Dido, Lucrece, and several others), and especially in the *Canterbury Tales* (Constance, Florent, Phebus and Cornide), not only because Chaucer's version is readily at hand but also because the texts that have been made available for the study of Chaucer's poem (e.g., in Correale and Hamel's *Sources and Analogues*) are equally useful for the study of Gower's.

For the sources and models for the overall design of the poem and for the figures in the frame, we are better off. The *Confessio Amantis* stands at the confluence of several different generic traditions. For the dialogue of instruction the most important source is Boethius's *Consolation of Philosophy*; for the dis-

cussion of the place of human love in a divinely created universe and for the figures of Nature and Reason, the most important texts are Bernardus Sylvestris's
Cosmographia, Alan of Lille's *Plaint of Nature*, and Guillaume de Lorris and
Jean de Meun's *Roman de la Rose*; and for the discussion of the moral qualities
of a good lover, Gower drew on the *dits amoureux* of Guillaume de Machaut,
notably the *Dit dou Vergier* and the *Remede de Fortune*. All these are available
in good translations.

The Critical Tradition I: Major Studies

Despite the strong critical interest that he has won in the last couple of decades,
the volume of book-length studies on Gower remains relatively small, especially
in comparison with a figure like Chaucer. Taking them up in chronological order: the earliest, Wickert's *Studien zu John Gower*, is most concerned with the
Vox clamantis, but in its final chapter it includes a sensitive reading of Gower's
tales of Actaeon, Pygmaleon, and Florent in comparison with their analogues
in Ovid and in Chaucer. Fisher's *John Gower: Moral Philosopher and Friend
of Chaucer* offers a readable and learned survey of Gower's life and work,
emphasizing the single-mindedness of his three major poems and the poet's reaction to the political and historical events of his time. Götz Schmitz's
The Middel Weie (in German) analyzes how the style and structure of the *Confessio* reflect and complement the moral themes of Genius's instruction. Patrick
Gallacher, in *Love, the Word, and Mercury*, finds a unifying theme for the poem
in its many different references to speech, including the lover's pleas to his lady,
his confession, and the perfect blend of truth and love found in God's words as
manifested in the Annunciation. Peck, in *Kingship and Common Profit*, finds
the poem unified around a different analogy, that between the governance of a
kingdom and the individual's proper rule of his personal "domain." Alexandra
Hennessey Olsen, in *"Betwene Ernest and Game,"* applies linguistic and struc-
turalist terminology to the study of the form and language of the poem. Yeager
takes a broader view in *John Gower's Poetic*, treating all three of Gower's major
works in separate chapters on the poet's style, on his self-conscious use of the material he drew from his predecessors, on his tales, on the nonnarrative portions
of the *Confessio*, and on the coherency of moral purpose and design in Gower's
final major poem. Kurt Olsson, in *John Gower and the Structures of Conversion*, offers a close reading of the entire *Confessio*, analyzing how the underlying
moral argument on the relation of nature, reason, and grace emerges from the
clash of discordant and partial views (including Genius's) that are presented
during the course of the long dialogue. María Bullón-Fernández, in *Fathers and
Daughters in Gower's* Confessio Amantis, describes Gower's use of the relationship between father and child as a device for exploring issues of power and
authority not only in a family context but also in the political and textual realms.
Diane Watt, *Amoral Gower*, invoking, among others, both queer and feminist

theory, argues that the *Confessio* not only destablilizes conventional and accepted categories of gender and sex but also offers a sustained critique of the possibility of any consistent moral principles. Ellen Shaw Bakalian, in *Aspects of Love in Gower's* Confessio Amantis, offers a more traditional view of the moral lessons of the poem, analyzing the relation between *kinde* and reason and the attribution of moral responsibility in a group of selected tales. In *Love and Ethics in Gower's* Confessio Amantis, I offer another close reading of the entire poem, emphasizing the unity of each book and the coherency of Genius's lessons as he instructs Amans not on the need to abandon his love but on how he might become a more virtuous lover. And most recently, Elliot Kendall, in *Lordship and Literature*, posits that the structures and practices of the late medieval aristocratic household provide the governing metaphor of the poem.

In addition to these book-length studies, Gower has been well served by published collections of essays, including A. J. Minnis's *Gower's* Confessio Amantis: *Responses and Reassessments* and five collections edited by Yeager. Three of these derive from the annual sessions of the John Gower Society at the International Congress on Medieval Studies at Kalamazoo: *John Gower: Recent Readings*; *Re-Visioning Gower*; and *On John Gower: Essays at the Millennium*. *Chaucer and Gower: Difference, Mutuality, Exchange* originated with the Gower session at the 1990 International Congress of the New Chaucer Society, and the fifth was a special issue of *Mediaevalia* (vol. 16). In *Gower's* Confessio Amantis: *A Critical Anthology*, I have gathered together some of the more influential studies on the poem from before 1983. And finally, two Japanese scholars have collected their studies published over many years and reprinted them in English: Masayoshi Itô's *John Gower, the Medieval Poet* and Masahiko Kanno's *Studies in John Gower*.

The Critical Tradition II: Major Issues

A brief map of the critical terrain will help place these individual works in context and can also provide a guide to some of the interpretive issues that are likely to arise in teaching the poem. Three major landmarks dominate the early criticism of the *Confessio*: Macaulay's introduction to his edition, a brilliant half-chapter in C. S. Lewis's *Allegory of Love*, and Fisher's monumental *John Gower: Moral Philosopher and Friend of Chaucer*. These three not only define the terms of later critical debate; they still provide a valuable starting point for those who are beginning their study of the poem. Macaulay finds little value either in the framework of the poem or in its ostensible moral purpose. Its real achievement, he declares, lies in its tales, and he singles out specific examples to praise for their "simple directness" and for the technical skill and naturalness of Gower's verse (Introduction 2: xiv), an approach to the study of the *Confessio* that is still encouraged by the editions of excerpts from the poem and by the reprinting of isolated tales in student anthologies. Lewis, while echoing Macaulay's praise of

Gower's storytelling, takes a very different view of the poem as a whole, calling Gower "a poet of courtly love" (213). Looking to the *Le roman de la Rose* as Gower's model, he finds a continuity and consistency between the poem's moral lessons and the instruction of the lover, and he finds the confession frame to be not a clumsy contrivance but a perfectly chosen device for linking the two. He also accords especially high praise to the poem's moving conclusion. Fisher, on the other hand, dismisses the love allegory of the frame as a mere sugar coating to its moral and political themes. Emphasizing the continuity with the *Mirour de l'omme* and the *Vox clamantis* and placing his focus on the prologue and book 7, he describes Gower's major poems as three parts of a single continuous work and the *Confessio Amantis* as the conclusion to a grand argument linking individual virtue, legal justice, and the responsibilities of the king.

Fisher's view of the poem continues to be reflected in the many writers who plumb Gower's work for evidence of his social and political stance or who use his works as a source of information about fourteenth-century English social and political history, an approach to the study of the *Confessio* found in several of the essays that follow in this volume. A selection of examples illustrates the range of the scholarship on this aspect of the poem. David Aers, in "Representations of the 'Third Estate'" and in "Reflections on Gower as '*Sapiens* in Ethics and Politics,'" cites evidence of Gower's unreflective conservatism; Yeager, in "Pax Poetica: On the Pacifism of Chaucer and Gower," looks at the evidence for his pacifism; and Judith Ferster, in *Fictions of Advice*, situates book 7 within the *Fürstenspiegel* tradition and examines the commentary on contemporary issues that it offers. And the most detailed and challenging study, Larry Scanlon's *Narrative, Authority, and Power*, finds in the *Confessio* a close examination of the relation between political and clerical authority and of the interdependence between prince and poet. Among those who emphasize Gower's political themes, not everyone feels that Genius's instruction of the lover is as insignificant as Fisher presumes. Peck (*Kingship*) finds not only a causal link between individual virtue (as reflected in Amans) and the harmony of society as a whole but also a complex structural analogy between "proper rule" in the lover and the restoration of proper rule in the kingdom. Elizabeth Porter, in "Gower's Ethical Microcosm and Political Macrocosm," focuses on the causal link, citing Giles of Rome and *Secretum secretorum* as the sources for Gower's doctrine that all harmony in society depends on the ethical health of its individuals and of the king, and she sees Amans not just as a model for private individual reform but also as a surrogate for Richard II, whose ethical health is a prerequisite to order in his realm. And James Simpson, in *Sciences and the Self in Medieval Poetry*, reverses the emphasis, arguing that Amans's instruction in politics (e.g., in book 7) is the model for the restoration of his own ethical self-rule.

The heirs of Lewis are to be found in those who focus on Genius's instruction of Amans without regard to its political consequences, but they provide some important qualifications of Lewis's account of the poem. J. A. W. Bennett, in "Gower's 'Honeste Love,'" offers an important restatement of the theme of the

Confessio, setting aside Lewis's notion of "courtly love" in favor of a doctrine of "honeste love" that has its proper culmination in chaste marriage. In "Gower's Narrative Art," another classic essay in the same year, Derek Pearsall describes the poem in terms very similar to Bennett's and shows how both Gower's compassion and his moral discrimination are most fully revealed in his tales. H. A. Kelly, in two lengthy chapters in his *Love and Marriage in the Age of Chaucer*, demonstrates the compatibility between sexual love and virtue in Gower's poem, and he also explains some of the apparent inconsistencies in Genius's instruction. Minnis, in a series of essays but most notably in "Moral Gower and Medieval Literary Theory," investigates the background in medieval literary theory for Gower's treatment of love within a moral frame and for his mixture of "lust" and "lore." J. A. Burrow, in "The Portrayal of Amans," provides a sensitive and illuminating examination of Gower's combination of the analytic confession frame with the conventionalized portrait of the lover drawn from the *dits amoureux* of Machaut and Jean Froissart. And in my *Love and Ethics*, I return to Machaut for the sources of Gower's notion of love as virtuous service without regard to rewards, and I examine some of the paradoxes that result from the application of ideals drawn from poetry to the realities of Amans's world.

For all of these, the goal of the moral instruction of Amans is to improve his conduct in the sense of making him a more virtuous lover. Others, pointing in particular to one passage near the end of book 8, have defined the goal rather differently, as getting Amans either to abandon his love as sinful or to transcend human love entirely. Peck (in *Kingship*) argues the former case most vigorously, referring repeatedly to Amans's "love fantasy" and to his loss of self-rule. A similar if milder view is adopted by Michael Cherniss in *Boethian Apocalypse* and by Olsson in *John Gower and the Structures of Conversion*, and it also appears as an unspoken assumption in the work of a great many others. Such a view of the moral purposes of the poem makes a considerable difference in the understanding of many of its lessons. It also makes a difference in the assessment of Genius's role, since Genius doesn't consistently advocate this position and can often be seen as encouraging that which (by this view) he should decry. Thus where Pearsall can declare that Genius "becomes something akin to Conscience" ("Gower's Narrative Art" 476) and Minnis can refer to him as "a sort of universal priest" ("Moral Gower" 61), there are many who do not accept that he speaks so transparently for the poet or that the moral lessons of the poem are in any way so straightforward. Genius comes into the poem, of course, with a long history, as George Economou describes in his 1970 essay. For one small group of critics, notably David Hiscoe in "Heavenly Sign and Comic Design" and Thomas Hatton in "John Gower's Use of Ovid in Book III of the *Confessio Amantis*," Gower's Genius is a comic figure, a completely unreliable teacher, as guilty of concupiscence as Amans himself. Others have seen him as limited though not wholly unreliable. Peck (*Kingship*) suggests that he be equated with *ingenium* (or as Langland terms it, *Ymaginatyf*), a faculty capable of offering images for consideration but without the powers of intellect and reason. Some version of faculty allegory is also adopted by Kathryn Lynch (*The High Medieval Dream Vision*) and James Simpson (*Sciences and the Self in Medieval Poetry*). Olsson (*John Gower*), without labeling Genius so precisely, also attributes to him a limited role in a dialogue that is meant to enact the discovery of a moral truth. Like Peck, Lynch, and Simpson, he sees each lesson as tentative and incomplete, a partial step to the truth that is only fully revealed with the triumph of reason in the conclusion.

Not everyone, however, is persuaded either of the possibility or of the necessity of constructing a coherent morality from the poem, even in so dispersed a form. For one group of critics, the *Confessio* contains contradictions that cannot so easily be reconciled, and the failure should be attributed to Gower rather than to Genius. Cherniss, in *Boethian Apocalypse*, for instance, describes the conclusion of the poem as both arbitrary and unsatisfactory since the release of Amans from Venus's court because of his age, while optimistic about the eventual triumph of reason, does not address the issue of personal responsibility that is expressed with such clarity and force in the prologue. Hugh White, in *Nature, Sex, and Goodness in a Medieval Literary Tradition*, now the best survey of the depiction of nature in the medieval texts most closely associated with Gower's, finds an inherent and irresolvable conflict between Nature and Reason in the *Confessio* itself, a conflict in which Nature is usually the victor, and he declares that Genius's effort to find some accommodation between sexual love and morality ends in failure and "division." And Winthrop Wetherbee, in his chapter in *The Cambridge History of Medieval English Literature* ("John Gower"), finds tension at many different levels: between the Latin marginalia, the Latin epigrams, and the vernacular text; between the tales and their morals; and between the framework of the poem and Genius's natural sympathy for his characters. In this "radically dialogic structure," he proclaims, the synthesis at which Gower aims "may finally be beyond the ordinary power of Genius and his poet" (604).

Others have embraced the poem's paradoxes and inconsistencies, especially as those elements engage the readers' participation in the construction of the poem's meaning. Theresa Tinkle, for instance, in her discussion of the multiple appearances of Venus in the poem in *Medieval Venuses and Cupids*, denies the poet's intention to grant final authoritative status to any of its competing discourses. "The poem does not offer a single meaning, but, rather, engaging invitations to reflect on the perspectives that create meaning and on the discourses that construct sexualities" (196–97). The challenge to the reader to supply the interpretation that is implicit or explicit in the discussion of the limitations of Genius's role is foregrounded by Peck in his essay "The Problematics of Irony." Simpson, in *Sciences and the Self*, arguing from the lack of any stable authoritative figure in the poem, describes the construction of meaning as a process of "information" that is enacted in the reader. And Olsson, in "Reading, Transgression, and Judgment," describes the reading of the poem as a moral act intended to sharpen our capacity for moral judgments. In *Ethics and Exemplary Narrative*, J. Allan Mitchell draws on medieval ethical theory to argue for the tentative and partial nature of every moral lesson in the poem, because of the way in which it may be contradicted or limited by other lessons and because it must be submitted to the judgment of the reader's own conscience before it can find application in the reader's life. Elizabeth Allen, in *False Fables and Exemplary Truth*, explores the possible disruptions among purpose, form, and response in all exemplary literature and the contingency of all interpretation. And Watt, in *Amoral Gower*, finds the multiple disruptions of order in the poem to be not a failure but a deliberate challenge on Gower's part to the possibility of any universal morality.

Another very different way of approaching the underlying moral structure of the *Confessio* has been to examine its construction of gender and sexuality. An opening for such an approach is offered by Carolyn Dinshaw, who, in "Rivalry, Rape and Manhood," describes the "violent obliteration of the feminine" (149) in Gower's treatment of the rape of Philomene and in the discourse of courtly love in both the *Confessio* and Chaucer's *Troilus*. One very productive avenue has been provided by Gower's treatment of incest. Georgiana Donavin, in *Incest Narratives and the Structure of Gower's* Confessio Amantis, finds incest at the moral foundation of the poem in two aspects: as represented in Venus's relation with Cupid, as the model for the moral failings of all who serve in the "court of love"; and as represented in such episodes as Apollonius's reunion with his daughter, as a vehicle for spiritual emancipation. Scanlon, in "The Riddle of Incest," examines the three father-daughter pairs in "Apollonius of Tyre" and credits Gower with an awareness of "the essential injustice . . . of the patriarchal law of exogamy" (123) and of the historical and social dimensions of incest that even modern psychoanalysis has managed to repress. Bullón-Fernández, in *Fathers and Daughters in Gower's* Confessio Amantis, examines the father-daughter relations in eleven tales; she sees Gower exploring the "gaps and fissures," particularly in the contradictions in the father's role, in patriarchal ideology. Donavin returns to the incest theme in "Taboo and Transgression" to examine the "discursive genesis of prohibited desire" (102), the way in which the incest taboo serves to perpetuate the activity that it prohibits. Taking a somewhat broader view, Karma Lochrie, in *Covert Operations*, focuses on the contradictions in Genius's use of the "natural" and the "unnatural" in order to explore the instability and incoherence of all Western heteronormative ideologies. Watt, particularly in her chapter "Transgressive Genders and Subversive Sexualities," examines how Gower "destabilizes accepted categories of gender and sex" (xii) as part of his sustained critique of all established ethical structures. And Donavin, in " 'When Reson Torneth into Rage': Violence in Book III of the *Confessio Amantis*," examines the relation between sexuality and violence in the poem and describes how the taboo against acknowledging the link results in the perpetuation of violence against women.

Like all major works of literature, the *Confessio Amantis* has served as a mirror of the preoccupations of its readers. Some extol its complex but coherent plan, others celebrate its fractures, but all find it worthy of study and explora-

tion. One recent group of critics has argued that the burden lies on the reader
to choose among the sometimes contradictory voices in the poem, in the hope
that by that very exercise he or she might become more wise. Such too is the
duty imposed on both student and instructor by the variety of ways of reading
the *Confessio* that have been offered by its commentators.

Electronic Resources

Brian W. Gastle

Medieval studies, and the teaching of medieval literature specifically, has benefited greatly from the recent proliferation of multimedia and online resources.
But as most teachers know, getting students to find appropriate and dependable material is now more of an issue than ever before. A simple *Google* search
for "John Gower" elicits over 100,000 hits (from the John Gower Society Web
site to *Google Books* of Gower editions and studies to remarks made by West
Ward candidate John Gower at the Hamilton City, New Zealand, town council
meeting). Furthermore, the ephemeral nature of electronic publishing makes
any discussion of sources always already out of date: Web pages come and go;
materials are often added, updated, or deleted without clear notification of the
change; and technologies change so quickly and dramatically that, in a decade
or two, it may be pointless even to talk about static Web pages or URLs. Fortunately, there are a manageable number of online and electronic resources that
can provide, or lead the student (and instructor) to, authoritative, dependable,
scholarly, and pedagogical materials, and a number of these resources are being
supported in such a way that they should remain available through technologi-
cal advances of the foreseeable future.

John Gower Society and Professional Organizations

One place to start with an exploration of online materials is the John Gower
Society (JGS) Web site (www.johngower.org). JGS, which publishes the *John
Gower Newsletter*, has been in existence for over twenty-five years and is dedicated to offering support for scholarly and pedagogical endeavors related to
Gower. The site links to, describes, and evaluates online materials at other sites
such as editions, translations, scholarship, pedagogical materials, images, and
other media. It also publishes some original materials, including scholarship,
lesson plans, and audio files, that have been reviewed by either the JGS board
or members. The JGS Web site includes (and updates) references and links to
many of the resources described in the following sections.

Apart from JGS, there are a number of long-standing academic and professional organizations that offer materials useful for students and teachers
of Gower and his times. The New Chaucer Society (http://artsci.wustl.edu/
~chaucer), which publishes *Studies in the Age of Chaucer*, does not publish
original material on its site, but it does maintain a list of links to currently available material on medieval studies. Like the JGS site, the New Chaucer Society
site is maintained and overseen by a board of scholars who ensure the academic
quality of its materials and support its continuance. Similar organizations include the Medieval Academy of America (www.medievalacademy.org) and the

Lollard Society (www.lollardsociety.org). Since these sites do not depend on the support of a single person or institution, they are good bets as long-term sources for materials online.

Editions, Dictionaries, and Manuscripts

The area in which the Internet has perhaps most helped scholars and students of Gower is in the availability of texts. While Gower's works are available in print, they are available online much more widely and in a wider array of formats, and the ability to work on and with the language has never been more readily available. Since Macaulay's great scholarly edition of all of Gower's works is now in the public domain, excerpts are available widely online, including at the Online Medieval and Classical Library (www.omacl.org), and the entire edition is available from *Google Books.*

Individual texts are also available online in a number of venues. The *Confessio Amantis* is most commonly available, since it is the text most often taught and studied. The recent TEAMS (Consortium for the Teaching of the Middle Ages) Middle English Texts Series edition, edited by Russell Peck, is available on the TEAMS Web site. While TEAMS began as a part of the Medieval Academy of America, it now enjoys independent status as a nonprofit educational organization supported, in part, by the University of Rochester and the National Endowment for the Humanities. TEAMS also publishes (in print and online) editions and translations of *In Praise of Peace* and other Latin works by Gower (www.lib.rochester.edu/camelot/teams/tmsmenu.htm). Excerpts of Gower's works are even more widely available, from individual course sites maintained by scholars in the field, such as the Harvard Chaucer page (www.courses.fas.harvard.edu/~chaucer/), to pages maintained by Gower aficionados in the general public. These editions and texts are supported by an increasing number of materials for the study of Gower's texts and language, including manuscript images and language aids.

Many of Gower's manuscripts are held by university libraries and museums, and as these institutions have begun to digitize their collections, more and more of Gower's manuscripts are becoming available online. Selections from University of Glasgow MS Hunter 7 and MS Hunter 59, with their iconic images of Gower shooting his arrow at the world, are both available from the University of Glasgow as part of the "Contemporaries" section of its online *World of Chaucer: Medieval Books and Manuscripts* site (http://special.lib.gla.ac.uk/exhibns/chaucer), and a teaching site sponsored by the University Glasgow, *Reading the Past: From Script to Print* (http://special.lib.gla.ac.uk/teach/manuscripts/literary.html), offers high-resolution images of pages. The Pierpont Morgan Library allows access to whole folio images as well as select miniatures from the *Confessio Amantis* in Pierpont Morgan MSS M125 and M126 (http://corsair.morganlibrary.org). Such primary materials can be invaluable for teaching teaching (see esp. Kelemen's essay, in this volume).

Bibliographies and Scholarship

Apart from providing a variety of primary materials, electronic resources also offer teachers and students easy access to scholarship and research aids related to Gower. Of these aids, the *Online Gower Bibliography* (http://gowerbib.lib .utsa.edu/) is the most directly related to Gower research; it is a joint effort of the John Gower Society and the University of Texas Library, at San Antonio, and includes bibliographic information printed in the *John Gower Newsletter* covering the years 1980 to the present. Similar bibliographic aids, as well as the occasional original essay or other secondary material, appear on a variety of medieval studies Web sites such as Georgetown University's *The Labyrinth: Resources for Medieval Studies* (www8.georgetown.edu/departments/medieval/ labyrinth/) and *ORB: Online Reference Book for Medieval Studies* (http://the-orb.net/). The University of Michigan's *Middle English Compendium* and *Middle English Dictionary* (http://quod.lib.umich.edu/m/mec/) provide invaluable information for close reading and etymological work on Gower's language. Most libraries also subscribe to databases and services, such as JSTOR (www.jstor .org) and Project Muse (http://muse.jhu.edu), that contain searchable, full-text, peer-reviewed scholarship about Gower and other medieval authors.

Of course there are a host of Web pages and Web sites devoted to medieval literature and medieval studies, but students must be careful to evaluate the authoritativeness and professional worth of much of this material, since there is no guarantee, given the many personal Web pages that are self-published, that material online has been peer-reviewed or vetted for accuracy. For example, Siân Echard, a contributor to this volume, maintains a useful Web page that includes information about Gower's tomb, manuscripts, and later works (http://faculty .arts.ubc.ca/sechard/gower.htm). But students are far more likely, because of its high ranking on the results pages of online search engines, to access Gower materials online on *Luminarium* (www.luminarium.org), a site created and maintained by a private individual, not affiliated with any organization or university, supported by advertising and book sales. Some material on this site has been contributed by scholars, but other material is student work; *Luminarium* does take pains to explain which material on the site was contributed by students and which by scholars and teachers, but not all Web sites do so. Since there is relatively little material online devoted to Gower (compared with what is available for Chaucer), using Gower to teach evaluation of online sources is a manageable and fruitful focus in a variety of classroom settings.

Part Two

APPROACHES

Teaching Gower's Reception:
A Poet for All Ages

Derek Pearsall

John Gower, an almost exact contemporary of Chaucer, has suffered through-out the centuries from his proximity to the greater poet and from the inevi-table diminution by comparison. If it were not for Chaucer, one might hazard, Gower would be much more highly regarded and certainly more widely read and taught. Chaucer thus poses a challenge to the teacher of Gower, particularly one who seeks to teach Gower by placing him in the context of contemporary and near-contemporary poets. Not only did Chaucer do everything Gower did, and much better, but he also stapled to him, in the epilogue to his *Troilus and Criseyde*, the label "moral Gower," which has shaped his reputation more power-fully than any experience of actually reading his poetry. It is not that the label is in any way ironic or undeserved: the moral and didactic impulse is strong in Gower, and his great poem, the *Confessio Amantis*, has been justly admired as an account of the renovation of the self through inward examination and through the wisdom embodied in the stories of the past. Not only that, there are parts of the *Confessio* where the main subject, the lover's "confession" and the stories that his confessor Genius tells to instruct him in the right way of moral loving, is held suspended while larger issues of moral and social renovation are foregrounded. Book 7, which in itself almost constitutes a "mirror for princes," stands as a statement of the political and social theory that underpins the poem, while both books 5 and 7 introduce encyclopedic accounts of astronomy and mythology as part of a systematic program of humane learning.

Even so, "moral Gower" is not all there is, or even the most important of his claims upon us. For it is above all as a poet of human feeling that readers will remember Gower, both in the portrayal of the delicacy of love's courtesy and the fineness of love-feeling in the confessional "frame" and also in the deep engagement with the conflicts of love's experience in the exemplary stories that make up the bulk of the poem. He follows out with unwavering sympathy the enigmatic tangles that love makes of honor, propriety, virtue, and justice and is ungrudging in the humanity with which he draws out the consequences—the sad suffering of Medea made mad with jealousy, of Philomene driven mad with grief, of the incestuous brother and sister Machaire and Canace, of those who gave too much in love (Ariadne) or not enough (Rosiphelee). At times the pressure of feeling behind a story, the exactness and comprehensiveness of Gower's human sympathy, will set up a conflict with the moral of the story expounded by Genius or, more explicitly and brutally, in the Latin marginal summary that accompanies it. Such dilemmas, as with the "love and honor" or "love and duty" conflicts of Thomas Malory's *Morte D'Arthur*, of William Shakespeare's "problem plays," of novels by Jane Austen and George Eliot, are the greatest pleasures for the student and reader of Gower. Juxtaposing Gower's poetry with works of this kind makes for engaging, enlightening teaching—of Gower, no less than of other writers.

Admiration of Gower, however, was for long straitjacketed in the academic vocabulary of approbation that Chaucer had authorized. Gower was not only the elder statesman of English poetry, he "that first garnished our Englysshe rude," as John Skelton put it in the *Garland of Laurel* (387), but also the poet above all of a virtuous morality. The echo of Chaucer is apparent in John Lydgate, who speaks of his "moral mateer ful notable" in the *Fall of Princes* (9.3410), while William Caxton characterizes Gower's poetry as "ful of sentence set ful fructuosly" in his *Book of Curtesye* (line 327). Admiring expressions such as these can be turned fruitfully to hand as ways into Gower's writing or used to start a discussion about works of a later period.

Much of this dutiful eulogizing comes nevertheless from writers who seem, from the absence of evidence of direct allusion and imitation, to have read little Gower. But Thomas Hoccleve, it has been argued, absorbed a subtle reading of Gower; Lydgate had consulted Gower's beautiful story of Canace for his version of her sad story in the *Fall of Princes*; and Caxton's comments may reflect the direct experience of preparing the *Confessio* for the press. Also, in the context of this set rhetoric of stereotyped praise, in which sententiousness and eloquence are what a poet must be praised for, whatever the nature of his writing, it is worth remembering that there were a very large number of owners of Gower manuscripts (there are over fifty manuscripts of the *Confessio* surviving, suggesting perhaps some hundreds once extant), who must presumably have read something of what they possessed. Sometimes, the evidence of reading is clearly there in their marginal comments, where they note tales that particularly caught their attention—Tereus, Florent, Lucrece—or remark on some aspect of women's behavior, usually in a sardonic and stereotyped antifeminist vein that is at odds with Gower's more humane sympathies.

Caxton's 1483 print of the *Confessio*, and the much better and more widely disseminated 1532 edition, printed by Thomas Berthelette, brought Gower to a much wider audience, though among the admiring references there is little evidence of reading or use. There was as always the deterrent of length: with over 36,000 lines, the *Confessio* would have been as forbidding to the untutored reader in the early modern period as it is to students today. There was also the increasing antiquity of his language; thus the difficulty of reading becomes another inducement to praise vaguely. Robert Greene (1594), speaking of the duties of poets in his *Vision*, praises Gower's "visage graue, sterne and grim—Cato was most like to him" (line 7)—a judgment surely based on his reputation alone—and uses him as a witness for morality against Chaucer, which is a kind of unpoetic justice, we might think. But there were more discerning readers, such as Philip Sidney and Edmund Spenser, the latter of whom was surely influenced by Gower in his use of pictorial allegory, and Ben Jonson, who considered Gower a model of good English and cites him more frequently than Chaucer in his *English Grammar*.

Shakespeare's witness to Gower, however, is exceptional. Shakespeare uses the story of Apollonius from book 8 of the *Confessio* as one of his sources for *Pericles, Prince of Tyre* and introduces Gower as a kind of chorus to speak the prologue:

> To sing a song that old was sung,
> From ashes ancient Gower is come.   (act 1 [prologue], lines 1–2)

He also speaks linking passages before each act and before some further scenes (4.4, 5.2) and then winds up the matter with the morality of "Virtue preserv'd from fell destruction's blast" (5.3.105). The purpose of introducing Gower may be to give a semblance of coherence to the ragged plot but also to claim indulgence for this play of strange reversals, coincidences, supernatural interventions, and uncomplicated morality by associating it with an older and simpler world of storytelling. Old Gower is there to be humored as he transports us to a fairy-tale world where the usual rules do not apply. Whether this was Shakespeare's idea is not clear, for the playwright is usually held to be not responsible for acts 1 and 2. When he takes over, in act 3, the language of Gower becomes at first more ostentatiously archaic, and then, as Shakespeare grows interested in the possibilities of using the chorus as a form of imaginative stimulation, as in *Henry V*, hardly archaic at all, while the jog-trot of the imitation octosyllabic gives way to a vigorous pentameter. There is little similarity between Gower and Shakespeare in their treatment of the story, but the influence of Gower's narrative, of patient virtue ultimately blessed by providence, on Shakespeare and the movement toward the last plays, should not be underestimated. Similarities and contrasts of these kinds offer practical opportunities for teaching.

In the seventeenth and eighteenth centuries Gower fell into a steep decline, though there is evidence that a few bright spirits, such as Thomas Warton and

Samuel Johnson, saw good in him. His reputation took an undeserved blow when he was accused by Thomas Hearne of being a political turncoat because of his switching of allegiance from Richard II to Henry IV in the prologue and apparatus to the *Confessio*. Chaucer scholars were happy to contrast Gower's self-serving maneuvering with Chaucer's stalwart loyalty to Richard II (itself another myth). When Thomas Tyrwhitt, the great editor of the *Canterbury Tales*, suggested that the mock-scandalous allusion to the telling of stories of incest in the introduction to The Man of Law's Tale might be a playful satiric aside at Gower's expense, and that Gower responded spitefully by removing Venus's eulogy of Chaucer in the epilogue to the *Confessio*, the stage was set for the famous Chaucer-Gower "quarrel." Gower was always the loser in this contest — less witty, less generous, less humorous — but the myth of the quarrel has persisted as an element in the inevitable comparison of the two poets. Despite its fabrication — or perhaps because of it — the "quarrel" also can be approached as a tool for teaching.

Gower remained a byword for tedious moralizing throughout the nineteenth century, even though it is difficult to believe that pictorial narrative poets like John Keats and Alfred, Lord Tennyson, did not read him to advantage, and it wasn't until after G. C. Macaulay's magisterial edition of Gower's works came out in 1899 that a truer estimate of Gower's poetic ability began to emerge. It is the independent tales, extracted from their context, that have generally attracted the greatest praise, but Gower's most eloquent critics, such as C. S. Lewis and J. A. W. Bennett ("Gower's 'Honeste Love'"), have always spoken for the integrity of the *Confessio* and the function of both the stories and the frame in the creation of a wise and generous "morality of love." Christopher Ricks, and Lewis too, in *The Allegory of Love*, has given close attention to Gower's skill with the short couplet, to his gift for the smooth-running paragraph and his daring use of enjambment and the abrupt, caesural break to bring variety.

The greatest rewards for the reader and teacher of Gower are likely to be in the independent stories, and more might be claimed for them than their wise sympathy. They are often to some degree painfully unresolved, hung suspended in some abyss between the moral indecipherability of Ovidian paganism (most of the hundred-odd exemplary stories are from Ovid — they provide, incidentally, a painless education in classical history and mythology) and the hard-won equilibrium of Christian moralism. That students are puzzled at these stories, even outraged — at, say, the lack of vehemence in the condemnation of Tereus — is not undesigned, for the stories mean to test and strain ideas of moral certainty. In this students may appreciate how close these stories are to Chaucer's most finely wrought narratives, in which likewise ancient myths and folktales will be told in ways that test their capacity for meaningful resolution to the breaking point and beyond. Some of the richest experiences of study and teaching are in the comparison of the two poets' narrative techniques — of the tale of Florent with The Wife of Bath's Tale, the tale of Constance with The Man of Law's Tale, and the tale of Appius and Virginia with The Physician's Tale.

The story of Gower's political opportunism has also taken an unexpected turn. The historicist movement of the past thirty years, the greater emphasis on the deep historical contextualization of literary works, has had fruitful consequences for the reader of Gower. The poet who is responsive to the pressure of public events and who incorporates that response in subtly imaginative ways in his poetry is exactly what critics and readers now want. Teaching Gower from this perspective can be very successful. It is not just the shifting dedications of the *Confessio*, the political theorizing, the allusions to the Lollards, the idea of the just war that contribute new vitality to reading, but the whole political context of the *Confessio* in Gower's Latin poems and prose writings, such as the *Vox clamantis*, the *Cronica tripertita*, and the shorter Latin poems. (All can be found in translation.) What is imprecise and allusive and "literary" in the *Confessio* is spelled out with more vehemence and clarity in these Latin writings. The distinction usefully enforces the recognition (one point of a stimulating class) that historical poetics is not just a matter of detecting Gower's opinions and relating them to historical events but of trying to understand the "undisentanglability" of those opinions and events and the processes through which they are re-created in different forms of discourse, none of them simply "true."

Social Class in the Classroom:
Gower's Estates Poetry

Scott Lightsey

Few English writers of the later Middle Ages discuss the mutually supportive roles of medieval social structure with the clarity and moral forthrightness of John Gower. His work can therefore serve well as an introduction to medieval attitudes about social order and the measure by which we can better understand how his contemporaries represented their society. Presented on their own, Geoffrey Chaucer and William Langland can leave students with an incomplete or unbalanced sense of what medievals found important in their social order. Chaucer's General Prologue to the *Canterbury Tales* offers a playful "show— don't tell," and Langland's view in *Piers Plowman* is veiled in the allusive allegorical terrain of his fair field of folk, whereas Gower's measured verse is clear and straightforwardly didactic. For this reason, Gower can play a vital role in providing students with a solid base in the underlying concerns upon which estates literature is founded.

One way that medieval society reveals its difference from the modern is in the pervasive attention to the individual's place in the social order, his or her "degree," or "state." To our students, this concern equates with their modern ideas of social class, but the equivalence with medieval estate does not really hold. Today the term *social class* carries a variety of meanings, from simple hierarchies of income, education, and socialization to complex negotiations involving the subtler inequalities of, for example, gender, ethnicity, income, and family structure. Social class is therefore an issue of great moment to our students, who find themselves subject to myriad expectations of social order in a modern society with often conflicting lines of class division, even as the cultural ideals of much of Western society tell them they are largely unbound by deeply ingrained notions of position. Here we can use contrast to bring them to an understanding of the rigid expectations and historical mores of medieval culture by using the literature of the estates, a literature of satire and complaint known most often to students of medieval literature only through the works of Chaucer and Langland.

Fortunately, alongside these and other poets writing on themes of social import, we have the works of John Gower, whose poetry unambiguously frames the roles, relationships, and mutual responsibilities of society's different classes. Gower's estates material provides an opportunity to explore with students the difference of a class system based on stability and ingrained beliefs about birthrights, bloodlines, and immutable rank while also illuminating his more experimental contemporaries in ways that reflect back positively on Gower's treatment of the estates. That his measured diction and careful consideration of form make these judgments beautiful, as well as thoughtful, compounds the idea of difference that drives most students' understanding of the estates. When his approaches to social position are incorporated into larger discussions of medieval social hierarchy, his work shines in mutual illumination among the other great poets of his time, such as Chaucer and Langland, with whom he is frequently anthologized. Gower's estates material is therefore an ideal teaching tool for introductory efforts, comparative study, and even more advanced work as graduates seek to frame Gower's poetry in the larger context of his milieu.

Of course, most students who are likely to encounter Gower's poetry are already somewhat familiar with Chaucer or the basic idea of *The Canterbury Tales*, and it is there that we can begin when introducing Gower through contrast. The portrait of the estates in the *Confessio Amantis* is comprehensive and conventional, forming a stately contrast to the entertaining (but ambiguous), uneven, and—by the standards of their day—even somewhat outré version of estates portraiture offered in Chaucer's General Prologue. Gower's estates are not the tripartite model's three types masquerading as a gamut of personalities; his work maintains an adherence to form and a dignity of pace and proportion that makes his representation of the estates seem basic, fundamental, formal, and thus highly accessible to students who feel unsure of their ability to read through the ambiguities of Chaucer's personifications or Langland's allegory.

Whether through anthologized selections from the prologue of the *Confessio Amantis*, handouts based on Eric W. Stockton's translation of the *Vox clamantis* (in *Major Latin Works*), or selections from Burton Wilson's translation of the *Mirour de l'omme*, Gower's consistent and measured approach to ideas about societal roles and rank and their relation to the greater good he called "common profit" can be presented to students with relative ease. I teach this material alone in courses where Gower can be treated in depth, but most often Gower's poetry makes an appearance as part of a survey unit on Middle English or otherwise in concert with the other major Middle English writers of his time. I find this latter arrangement works best with students interested in gaining a general knowledge of the period. It helps them build a lens through which to analyze a fairly wide range of contemporary material, from shorter lyric complaints easily brought to students through James M. Dean's TEAMS volume, *Medieval English Political Writings*, to the social concerns evident in longer verse.

The estates represent more than a rigid notion of social order. As put forth in the prologue of the *Confessio Amantis*, we find this important framework for understanding medieval culture and poetry in lines 93–584 as Gower outlines the relative positions of state, church, and Commons (helpfully set out in sections in Russell Peck's accessible TEAMS edition). In simple terms, the *estates* can be defined as a way of classifying people according to their relative social positions and the work they do within the prevailing social and political hierarchy, and Gower offers students the clearest grounding in the true stakes behind this working hierarchy by framing it in terms of a former age of amity and love, contrasted with the faults of a decayed present. Ruth Mohl, in *The Three Estates in Medieval and Renaissance Literature*, has characterized the genre of estates literature according to four basic functions:

1. The intent of showing the range of social order through a list of the estates or classes, organized by rank.
2. The subjecting of the list to complaint or lament as the shortcomings of each class are enumerated.
3. The demonstration that one's place in this framework is dependent on acceptance of one's station and that station's place in the social order, which is ordained by divine decree; in other words, God wills the individual's place in society.
4. The offering of remediation for the shortcomings of these classes.

Of course few poets follow this form perfectly, but the basic intent is clear in Gower's *Confessio Amantis* and in the *Mirour*, in which a significant aspect is the temporal frame; for Gower, the world is the *senectus mundi*, the world grown old as the ages of man have progressed since the expulsion of Adam and Eve from the Garden of Eden. He uses this framework to put forward the idea of a flawed society whose parts, as encapsulated in the idea of the estates, do not work properly:

> If I schal drawe into my mynde
> The tyme passed, thanne I fynde
> The world stod thanne in al his welthe.
> Tho was the lif of man in helthe,
> Tho was plenté, tho was richesse,
> Tho was the fortune of prouesse,
> Tho was knyhthode in pris be name [esteemed by reputation],
> Wherof the wyde worldes fame —
> Write in cronique [chronicle] — is yit withholde.
>   (*CA*, prologue, lines 93–101)

For Gower, the site of complaint is his contemporary society, which never measures up to an idealized past when "al the baronie / Worschiped was in his astat" (104–05) but now "love is falle into discord" (121) as the nobility and elite clergy have failed to execute their social responsibilities properly, forming a cascading effect in which all society is disordered. Students quickly pick up on the temporal rhetoric, following Gower's understanding that

> Tho was ther unenvied love,
> Tho was the vertu set above
> And vice was put under fote.   (115–17)

It helps students frame the estates as a way that medieval people conceived of an ideal version of their society. The estates can be taught to students through analogies such as the image of the American cowboy, in which a mythologized ideal stands for the ruggedness, lone accomplishment, and self-sufficiency that Americans feel is part of the national character. Similarly, the tripartite framework of the estates, with its three mutually supporting branches, is an idealization of a social order reflective of the perfect structure of the heavenly hierarchy and is not necessarily applicable to the lived existence of most medieval people. It was their shorthand for how society should work, each layer of the populace supporting the others in a mutually integrated loop: the nobility protected Christendom and its people, the clergy looked after the souls of all, and the peasants fed everyone. As long as everyone did as expected, the system worked, but in the "modern" world of the Middle Ages, poets like Gower looked across their society and found it wanting. The literature of the estates was their vehicle for addressing the problems they saw in the practice of the social order, and through it we have the perfect vehicle for introducing students to the poetry and its social context.

In the undergraduate classroom, I like to introduce Gower as part of a unit on Ricardian authors, which I begin by assigning the prologues from the *Confessio Amantis*, the B text of *Piers Plowman*, and *The Canterbury Tales*. This approach lightens the burden of emphasis on the individual authors, placing it instead on the larger matter of how all three authors introduce and set up their work. By looking across these three great prologues of Ricardian poetry, students are given an opportunity to apprehend how all these authors variously employ the estates model to establish their individual projects.

I usually sketch the tripartite model of the estates on the board, using a triangle equally anchored in the nobility, clergy, and peasantry, noting that medievals believed in an idealized notion of this simple model of social interdependence. Then, on first opening the poetic matter for discussion, I ask the students to characterize each author's broad view of society. They almost invariably begin with Gower, whose schematic style (emphasized or perhaps simply echoed by Peck's headings in the TEAMS edition) lends itself to clear and easy exposition. They naturally follow Peck's headings delineating the state, clergy, and Commons and quickly equate Gower's political divisions with the corresponding groups they understand in terms of social class; it is from there that we make the matter of medieval social order and its poetic framing more complex and meaningful.

Gower helpfully prefaces his approach to the estates in the *Confessio* with the notion of the aging world and its decayed moral condition, offering clarity to students who are already struggling with the barriers presented by reading verse in Middle English. In effect, among undergraduates I have found that Gower's directness naturally rises above the barriers usually felt by more experienced readers, who might find his rigid first-person address somewhat artless or even oppressive in contrast with the deftly controlled light satire of Chaucer or Langland's artful swerves among the sketch-portraits in his allegorical landscape. To these newcomers, Gower is a handhold they can use to pull themselves into a fuller understanding of Ricardian verse.

Once we establish the basic shape of Gower's societal image, I ask for details about how Gower represents each class in turn, and it is here that students usually begin to work by analogy with the other authors' estates material. Students can read about greed among the estate of clerks (in *CA*, prologue 198–211) and compare it with the priests in *Piers Plowman* seeking leave to work where the money is, in London (prologue 83–86). Similarly, students find in Chaucer's portraits of the Monk and Friar a more personalized but no less compelling image of clerical avarice, desire, and gluttony. Through these comparisons, Gower's straightforward complaint against the clerical class shows Chaucer's clever portraits for the paradigmatic representations they truly are, shielding students from the tendency (so common among newcomers to Chaucer's works) to think of the pilgrims as real people.

The conversation can then evolve into a discussion of contrasting styles, and it is here that students probably benefit most from Gower's straightforward complaint. Asking students why they tended to begin with the *Confessio* elicits an awareness of the power of Gower's direct address, which tells them exactly where he stands. They find his openness reassuring in the face of the ambivalent manner in which Chaucer shows moral failures but refuses to tell them exactly what he thinks. Chaucer's narrator's games force students to apprehend a semiotic system they are often not yet equipped to interpret. Similarly, while Langland's first-person address appears direct, the allegorical setting and sense of urban crowding leave them unsure simply because of the unfamiliarity of allegory.

As this sketch of an approach indicates, Gower's presence among his contemporaries naturally inclines toward a Gower-based teaching approach, since his estates material serves well as the basis for discussion and elicits comparisons that can lead to establishing an effective basis for understanding more generally the concerns of medieval culture and poetics. The same approach can be taken with graduate seminars, but when introducing graduate students to Gower's work, I assign not only the prologue of the *Confessio Amantis* but also selections from the Wilson translation of the *Mirour de l'omme*, as well as the first ten books of the Stockton translation of the Latin *Vox clamantis*. In the graduate environment, I strive to acquaint the students with the individual author's politics as well as the wider view of medieval culture made available through the estates. In the case of John Gower, the complaints in the *Vox clamantis* amply demonstrate his loyalist distrust of the Commons in the events around the Peasants' Revolt of 1381, giving students an additional anchor in contemporary politics and authorial approach.

Additionally, Gower's adroit shifts between the generalized condition and personal implication offer a level of subjective analysis and self-reflexivity unavailable in the other prologues. In his complaint on the Commons, Gower starts with the objective sense of third-person analysis, as seen here:

> And eche in his compleignte telleth
> How that the world is al miswent.   (*CA,* prologue 516–17)

He then implicates himself—and all humanity—by shifting to the first person while addressing the greater condition of fallen humanity's responsibility for our earthly and moral condition, only a few lines later:

> So moste it stond upon ousselve
> Noughte only upon ten ne twelve,
> Bot plenerliche upon ous alle,
> For man is cause of that shal falle.   (525–28)

In upper-level classes and in graduate seminars, where there is more room for students to assimilate the nuances of individual style, there is still much to gain in reading closely Gower's carefully managed lesson in the state of the human condition.

Ultimately, we have to ask what it is we want students to come away with as they encounter Gower's poetry and estates framework. Is it a sense of his attention to form, the customary nature of his content, the measured quality of his verse, or the didactic moral intent that makes his poetry such a positive tool for introducing students to the vital notion of the estates? To understand Gower's approach is to understand what was typical of the time, to have a baseline from which to measure the many other approaches to the genre of estates literature, especially those that are more familiar but that should be understood as experimental, as in Chaucer, or more loosely framed, as in Langland's *Piers Plowman*. It can be hard to get students to sink their teeth into Gower's commentary on social status and duty specifically because Gower is so close to the mean, his moral perspective pushed forward, ahead of the art he brings to its expression. However, close attention to Gower's profound, clear-eyed, and openly didactic approach to this poetic vehicle for social commentary offers students perhaps the best opportunity in Ricardian literature to develop an understanding of how the complexities of social thinking play out in Middle English verse.

Teaching the *Confessio Amantis* as a Humanist Document of the First English Renaissance

Russell A. Peck

I have found it useful in British and medieval survey courses to teach John Gower as a protohumanist writer who, more than any of his contemporary fourteenth-century writers, addresses what we have come to think of as topics of the English Renaissance — topics that anticipate the voicing concerns of Thomas More and, later, William Shakespeare and Ben Jonson, writers who often refer to Gower for literary, linguistic, and methodological examples. I have divided the essay into five parts: (1) At the heart of Gower's prenatal humanism is his reassessment of the ancients on their own terms in an attempt to feel the pulse of humanity through "olde bokes" (the phrase occurs in various forms dozens of times in the *Confessio*), books that may be read as models for behavior, both good and bad. This ancient heartbeat creates for Gower and later humanists a quintessential ambiguity, since reading the ancients as exempla on "their own terms" requires translation of ethical and moral issues into "our language," which is never easy to do. But, as a humanistic endeavor, it alerts Gower and his audience to the complexity of reading processes and relativities of understanding through the staging of images, personifications, and dramatic in-character voicing. (2) Through this bookish staging of intuited phenomena, Gower explores the subtleties of reading as a mental, incorporative process. Every reader functions as an individual perpetually making choices and drawing conclusions according to a combination of past experience and memory, strongly overshadowed by personal biases. This thinking process involves a political, ethical, and social individualism that may be more frustrating and alienating than progressive and ameliorating. (3) A focal feature of thirteenth- and fourteenth-century English philosophical development is the rapid advancement of empirical thought, what Chaucer speaks of as "this newe science" (*PF* 25), that figures prominently for Gower in humanist issues. In the *Confessio* Gower's strong interest in empirical science is at play not simply in book 7 with its discussions of the arts but throughout in a science of perception whereby he would "wryte of newe som matiere" (*CA*, prologue, line 6). His insights into how the human brain works in conjunction with the senses (especially the eyes and ears) to construct images (mental "facts"), plots ("facts" in action), and conclusions (mental resolutions, such as they seem to be) define the *practique* of his scientific theory of reading (i.e., thought). Gower keeps us perpetually aware of how the human brain works to effect both literary production and readerly reception. (4) For Gower the human individual is part of a human estate; she or he is a social entity within a political and legal nexus for which he or she has an innate responsibility — a kingdom to justify outside oneself as well as within (see 8.2111–21). (5) Finally, given that these mental phenomena are essentially linguistic and rhetorical, the conclusions — the processes of making a good end — are the most difficult of all, requiring a transformational shift relative to another place, but, nonetheless, all the more deeply engrained in this place, an adjustment that requires a different kind of voicing.

1. Gower and the Ancients: A Humanist Exercise in Learning to Read

Perhaps no single feature of humanism is more important than the writings of the ancients, whose books make possible rediscovery of an otherwise lost human history so crucial to the recovery of a functioning sense of self. Gower's humanist instinct is encyclopedic, seeking out ancient authors, directly if possible, but, if that is not possible, then whatever compilation he can lay his hands on. Here's his beginning:

> Of hem that [those who] writen ous tofore
> The bokes duelle [remain], and we therfore
> Ben tawht of that was write tho [written then]:
> Forthi good is that we also
> In oure tyme among ous hiere [us here]
> Do wryte of newe som matiere [matter]
> Essampled [Exemplified] of these olde wyse [wise men/books],
> So that it myhte in such a wyse [way],
> Whan we ben dede and elleswhere,
> Beleve to [Be left behind for] the worldes eere [ear]
> In tyme comende [coming] after this.   (*CA*, prologue 1–11)

This opening passage, with its brilliant use of inversion—did the ancients "write us" before we were or simply "write before us"—makes clear the ambiguous value of books whose recovery through study serves through perpetual renewal as a defense against an ever-dying present and future. The ancient narratives help people reconnect themselves to human history in constructive ways that define purpose and basic obligations. The key is not simply the books themselves but, rather, how one reads them; for Gower the therapeutic processes of reading and the individuality of every reader and writer are corollary topics.

The whole of the *Confessio* is an allegory on how to read, along with the dangers of misreading or manipulation of others through skewed reading practices. The prologue sets up theoretical propositions on what reading entails that apply throughout the poem. Its opening exemplum, Nebuchadnezzar's dream of the statue of time, establishes a paradigm of the problematic of reading. The king, unable to understand the images his brain has incepted (i.e., his vision), tells Daniel his "swevene" ("dream"),

> And preide him faire that he wolde
> Arede [Interpret] what it tokne may,
> And seide, "Abedde wher I lay,

> Me thoghte I syh [looked at] upon a stage
> Wher stod a wonder straunge ymage. . . .   (prologue 600–04)

What Gower has given us is the basic workings of a thought process that is, in itself, a study in reading. An idea comes to the thinker as if from nowhere — "me thoghte" — where the subject does not act but is the recipient of action (the thought comes to him). As the image is realized in his mind, it seems to be played on a stage to which the dreamer/reader is audience. Then, spontaneously, a next step in the process results: as he looks on the image, the dreamer/thinker immediately desires to know what this image that has materialized in his dream means. He would "arede" it to determine what it "tokne may" ("signifies"). That is, he instantaneously is caught up in an exegesis, for which he calls upon young Daniel for help. Daniel serves as *imaginatif*, an intellectual function in the second lobe of the brain that can explicate images inducted through the senses as he explains that the dream of the monster of time signifies the ages of time past, from the golden age to the present time of the fourteenth century, which God's judgment could destroy in an instant, a reading that Nebuchadnezzar, even with Daniel's explication, cannot understand fully.

In this exercise in reading cognition, for Nebuchadnezzar, for Daniel, for all readers, including us in the concurrent audience, the idea happens twice — first through the senses as *imaginatio* records the idea in the first lobe of the brain ("I syh upon," i.e., "I looked upon"), and again in the second lobe ("me thoghte"), as the image, once incepted into the brain, becomes idea, affected by memory and motives that are resident in the third lobe of the brain (see the figure of the brain diagram in part 3 of this essay). This pattern of inception, apprehension, and comprehension recurs throughout the poem. Amans perpetually attempts to "read" Genius's tales and instructions according to his own private interests, even as Genius attempts to read Amans according to his pedagogical assignment, a familiar dilemma to every teacher of reading and writing, as well as every reader of the poem.

In brief, the *Confessio Amantis* is a basic exercise in pedagogy — the study of old books and ways of reading them for personal profit. Stories from the past are called on to instruct future generations. It is easy to love Gower the poet through the dozens of tales he incorporates into his poem. But the stories and other widely diverse kinds of exempla — from proverbs, epigrams, and parables to lists of data from the phenomena of nature and categories within political structures — cannot be fully appreciated without the prologue that opens up to the reader the richness of Gower's visionary complex of sociological, political, and physical milieu. It is not easy for modern readers to begin study of the *Confessio* with the prologue. To do so is like starting a Chaucer class with The Parson's Tale. But the prologue is where Gower begins, and with good reason. It enables him to establish the basic structures of society, that human domain that his argument perpetually critiques — the three estates and such topoi of human behavior as deceit, greed, corruption of law for singular profit, the degeneration of time, and, from an individual point of view, life in a desert of one's own making. Conversely, it establishes the value of that most fundamental human invention, poetry, that can inaugurate, if properly measured, a countermovement against the world's chaos, as the "Tale of Arion" at the conclusion of the prologue asserts. Though the prologue is difficult, its utopic use of estates theory helps readers understand human circumstances. To study such conditions Gower explores causes, and for that one needs a means. The confessional device in book 1 supplies that means. The prologue locates problems within a Christian humanist ideology.

2. Humanism, the Individual, and Pragmatic Choice

One reason reading is so difficult is because we live in a fallen world where all perception is fragmented by time, place, and intention. In the prologue Gower defines the divisions and disconnections in human behavior as the primary effect of sin. Sin is a divisive crime against God, self, and society perpetrated by individuals: "For man is *cause* of that schal falle" (528); "Bot al this wo is *cause* of man" (905); "The man is *cause* of alle wo, / Why this world is divided so" (965–66; emphasis mine). But just as mankind is *cause* of its own problems, conversely, for Gower, only individuals themselves can, through right reading of their own lives and those about them, repair the disjunctions. People make choices, and those choices frame and define them as people. Seldom are choices simple, and seldom do they provide liberating effects, simply because individual choice is perpetually constrained by will and desire complicated by the choices of others as all attempt to find an advantageous virtue in necessity. These Aristotelian/Boethian concerns about will and causation open a multitude of channels for analysis of all exempla in the *Confessio*.

In *The Poetics* Aristotle asserts that character discloses choice. Gower would agree. Moreover, he would insist that meaningful human choices are by no means restricted to men. Gower is fascinated by female agency as well as masculine and provides more stories exploring women as actants who determine the outcome of their narratives than any other fourteenth-century English author. Stories like the "Tale of Florent" (*CA* 1.1407–861), the "Tale of Three Questions" (1.3067–402), the "Tale of Constance" (2.587–1598), the "Tale of Ulysses and Penelope" (4.147–233), the "Tale of Rosiphelee" (4.1245–446), the "Tale of Jason and Medea" (5.3247–4222), and the "Tale of Apollonius" (8.271–2008), to name a few, celebrate women's intelligence as they read their way through difficult circumstances that require knowledge of the laws of human behavior and the ability to assess probabilities within circumstances. They can make and understand legal covenants, utilize the arts, and exercise the subtlest of social skills. Above all, they are literate and read well. Others stories, like the "Tale of Mundus and Paulina" (1.761–1059), the "Tale of Pyramus and Thisbe" (3.1331–494), and the "Tale of Iphis and Araxarathen" (4.3515–684), study women trying to make their way through marginal situations where, although the cards are stacked against them, they attempt to work out compromises that sometimes succeed and sometimes don't. Then again, stories like the "Tale of Albinus and Rosemond" (1.2459–661), the "Tale of Canace and Machaire" (3.143–336), the "Rape of Lucrece" (7.4754–5123), and the "Tale of Virginia" (7.5131–307) explore the victimization of women who, nonetheless, maintain through hard choices a precious dignity of character despite the cruelty of their situations.

Gower's humanism is notably practical, a mode of thought that maps the paths of behavior of men and women here on earth, rather than in the life to come. Like Boethius's Lady Philosophy, Gower differentiates between theory and practice (see book 7), but, with Gower, the focus is usually on *practique*: there is a practical side to every component of his poem. It is fascinating to see how close to the surface Gower works in telling his "simple" narratives. Their complexity lies in us: as Daniel and Nebuchadnezzar make clear, we read for meaning, but what that meaning will be may be virtually impossible to understand fully (see Peck, "John Gower and the Book of Daniel"). By constructing his plot around the discourse between Genius and Amans, Gower perpetually confronts us with overt pedagogical issues. The voicing is theirs, not his, and the situations are local, dependent on what went before. Those situations are contextualized by a frame that precedes and continues beyond the divisive world of Venus, Genius, and Amans, but within the diegesis of their understanding the situations remain perturbingly real.

Inside the frame Genius works within categories of syllogistic logic, where terms like *point* and *in special* identify the placement of the minor premise out of which causation may henceforth determine a conclusion. Students often find Genius to be inconsistent or even contradictory in his propositions. Those contradictions disappear when read in terms of the categories within which Genius approaches an issue. It is fascinating to see, for example, how precise the loathly lady is in the "Tale of Florent" as she establishes riddles that only when addressed correctly will lead to the liberation of herself as well as Florent from the snares of evil intention that entrap them. Any hope for a happy resolution is contingent on mutual trust and keeping straight categories within their covenants, choices that define their character, or, rather, *give* them character.

Most issues raised by Genius are exemplified twice—once in terms of the mores of society and a second time in response to the personal demands of the lover, who, like his namesake (Amans) in Guillaume de Lorris and Jean de Meun's *Le roman de la Rose* or Alanus de Insulis's *De planctu naturae*, puts Genius to the test of addressing the myopia of the lover's will. This instilling of feelings of *fin amour* in Amans's brain, as Amans dotes on his lady and can think of little else, is less a matter of convention than an effort to explore the lover's psyche as he stages his fantasy according to the sentiments of love posed by real-life behavior in courtly society at the end of the fourteenth century (Peck, "Phenomenology"). Witness the extravagant fashions of Richard II's court, delight in masquerades and other courtly games, cults of the flower and the leaf, and

the burgeoning of vernacular romance literature. In creating Amans as a literary persona, Gower assumes the favorite guise of another humanist, Petrarch,
who, even more than Boccaccio, provided literary models for love poems in the
Italian Renaissance, and, by extension, the English Renaissance a century later.
Gower works within the same framework of thought in his presentation of individual choice, definition, and consequence.

3. Science and Gower's Reading of Reading through Medieval **Figura** of the Human Brain

Gower's treatment of the myopic components of Amans's desirous preoccu-
pation is "pragmatically" conceived in terms of brain and mind's-eye functions
that are essentially the same in Chaucer, Langland, Shakespeare, and romance
writers. Edwin Clarke and Kenneth Dewhurst discuss this continuity of brain
models from Galen and Augustine to Robert Fludd in their *Illustrated History
of Brain Function*. Like Renaissance humanists, Gower recognizes the senses,
the brain, and the heart as primary mechanisms in shaping human perspectives
and cognition, and he perpetually focuses on the *practique* of brain reception
through the exchanges between Genius, Amans, and the exempla of the *Confessio*. Students enjoy exploring the subtleties of Gower's discussion of sight and
hearing in his initial exempla of book 1 and how the optics of ethics function
within the purview of eyes, ears, heart, and the three-lobed brains of the personae in his narratives.

A brain diagram (see fig.) printed in the 1493 edition of Albertus Magnus's
thirteenth-century treatise *Philosophia pauperum* ("Philosophy of the Poor"),
along with others from Clarke and Dewhurst (who reproduce some sixty-six
illustrations of the brain, eyes, and other senses from manuscripts and early
print editions on anatomy, philosophy, and psychology), is useful when teaching Gower's reading theory and bookish therapeutic. Albertus used subdivided
circles to define the lobes in his essay. His near contemporary Bartholomaeus
Anglicus also drew on similar diagrams for his discussion of the brain; John
Trevisa's translation of Bartholomaeus, a work Gower draws on repeatedly in
the *Confessio*, spells out the functions of each part of the brain. All follow the
three-cell brain structure described in Galen and adapted by Augustine.

Such diagrams help students understand how imagination, thought, and memory work in the shaping and reading of plot structures. The outside world is
intuited through the senses, mainly through the eyes and ears. The first brain
cell, consisting of two parts, *sensus communis* (sensual intuition) and *imaginatio*
(the primary imagination), collects data received as images. The second cell
also has two parts: *imaginatif* (a secondary imagination) reads the images from
the first cell according to the disposition of the individual's previous experience;
estimativa (also called *ratio* or *intellectus*) is the thought processor that makes
intellectual assessments of the new experience. Its medial position is influenced

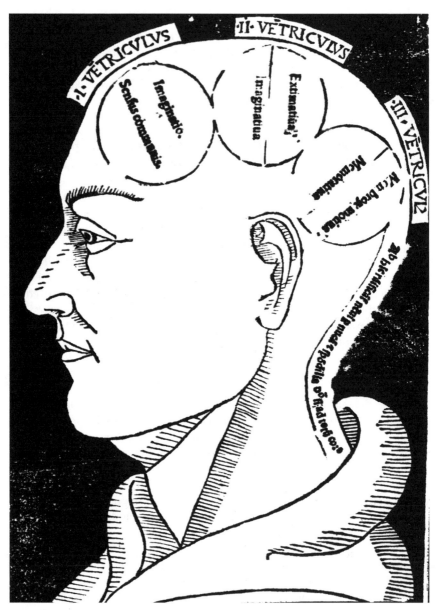

Diagram of the brain from Albertus Magnus's *Philosophia pauperum*, 1493 (Clarke and Dewhurst 26).

by input of biases from the third brain cell, which likewise has two components that operate perpetually, namely, *memoria* (the treasury and storehouse of all experience going back to even the fetal life of an individual) and *motiva* (the motivating energy akin to will and intention), which precipitates action. These mental operations lurk in the image-processing background of virtually every tale of *Confessio* as it is told (imagined) by Genius, read (reimagined) by Amans (and us), and enacted by the *dramatis personae* within the story itself and on the stage of the reader's brain. As is evident in his assessment of Genius's stories, unbiased responses to what Amans intuits are virtually impossible. He views Thought to be a "lusti" cook that supplies his fantasy with delicacies aplenty (6.743–950). These delicate indulgences of thought in the second brain lobe sustain the prejudicial make-believe that leads ultimately to the dark conclusion of the poem, as Amans, though he has heard much and often responded intelligently, falls back into the confusion of his original biases and appears to have learned little. With the departure of Venus and Genius, Amans disappears as well, and the persona becomes once again "John Gower," now an old man who struggles in a cultural desert not too different from Petrarch's view from Mount Ventoux, as he condemns the world for its vanity.

Gower's "Tale of Narcissus" demonstrates precisely how the bias of desire affects perception. In his version of the story (1.2275–358) Narcissus outrides all others and comes alone to a well, where he stops to staunch his thirst. As he "caste his lok" into the well "He sih the like of his visage, / And wende [thought / imagined] ther were an ymage / Of such a nimphe as tho was faie [of fairy]" (1.2313–17), whereupon he is overwhelmed with love as if he had seen a beautiful woman. What he is looking at, of course, is the mistress of his *imaginatif*, as *memoria* and *membron motive* convert his self-image into what he loves most — "faie" ("magic") indeed. It is as if what he sees has been predetermined by his "sotie" ("besotted fantasy"; 2320). The tale provides a good introduction into the problems of objective analysis as Gower understands them as well as recognition of the limitations of any kind of instruction that is contingent on the fictions and metaphors our thought processes require. These are contingencies that teachers of literature perpetually must deal with as they themselves read for class and prepare to teach what Aristotle said in his *Poetics* cannot be taught — namely, metaphor. Metaphor, like all exempla, can only be experienced as it performs its contradictions and incongruities individually within each observer's brain.

4. Gower's Social Humanism

Gower's social message is as complex as his personal one. Gower frequently speaks of the voice of the people — the vox populi — that cannot lie. His tale of Lycurgus, giver of Athenian law, celebrates the need for contracts and agreements by which we choose to live. We understand those agreements through our study of the laws of the land (*lex positive*) and the laws of God and nature (*lex divina*). Both are mirrored in our individual selves, where everyone is a king with a kingdom to justify; if he or she "misreule that kingdom" (*CA* 8.2114–15), they misrule themselves—a basic principle at the heart of every humanistic utopia. Gower, who first wrote the *Confessio* "for King Richardes sake" (prologue 24), changed the designation in 1392 to "a bok for Englelondes sake," thereby emphasizing the social nature of his utopic vision. The lens of his social vision perpetually crosses between the political and the individual. Gower knows, as does his Genius, that there is no guarantee of exact correlation between what he thinks and writes and what others choose to receive, a situation comically illustrated frequently in the exchanges between Genius and Amans. One reason for this complexity is that the distinction between Gower the writer and Genius the protagonist sometimes blurs, especially when the poet is dealing with political issues; and when that blurring occurs, the boundary between Amans and us as readers also clouds over. Instead of Genius talking with Amans we discover that Gower is talking with us. This shift in voicing reflects well the way the receptors of the brain work, especially when categories overlap, as in books 7 and 8, where governance is Gower's concern.

For early humanists the diversity of language on earth is always a troubling but enriching subject. Gower admires and imitates the complexity of voicing in diverse languages and modes of speech and prides himself on his linguistic skills. He toys with grammatical cruces, pressing languages to their limit through inventive uses of conjunctive adverbial constructions, borrows French idioms to complicate his ideas, or stretches morphology through *rime riche*, where homophones take the brain in multiple directions simultaneously. Gower's classically oriented, multilinguistic sensibility is more akin to that of Petrarch than Boccaccio or Ben Jonson than William Shakespeare (though Shakespeare admired and drew on Gower even as much as he did Chaucer). In teaching Gower, I always find it fascinating to reflect on the subtlety of his language itself. That he writes the poem in the vernacular is tribute to the freshness and immediacy of his mental games.

5. Finding the Right Ending for a Humanist Text

Formal matters are always important to the humanist *mentalité*. We have seen the importance of the prologue as the beginning of the *Confessio*, but it is equally important to explore how Gower chooses to end his poem. Gower's tying up the threads of his great English work is intricate, and it is consciously indebted to and intertwined with Chaucer's work, particularly *Troilus and Criseyde*, with its dedication to "moral Gower" (5.1856–59). In both *Troilus* and *Confessio*, the conclusion is accomplished through shifts in voicing to disengage the reader from the diegesis of the retelling of the plot. Both poems create an altered perspective from which to assess the whole of the work. In book 8, Gower moves beyond the confessional platea he had introduced in book 1 by having Amans, apparently unable to learn from Genius's exempla, rehearse in a new verse form (rhyme royal instead of couplets) a dramatic processional of lovers who pass before his inner eye, even as they had processed before Rosiphelee in her tale in book 4. But here the effect and occasion are entirely different. Rosiphelee was young; John Gower is now an old man; the young Rosiphelee was at last ready to begin life; the old "Gower" is ready to give it all up. Confronting him with the empty futility of his wishful thinking, Venus gives "Gower" a mirror in which he sees his withered face. She then disappears amidst the stars, leaving him alone. The two allegorical figures of his former thought processes, Amans and Genius, have likewise disappeared, leaving him bereft (see Peck, "John Gower: Reader").

   The situation is akin to what students of medieval literature will have encountered in many fourteenth-century poems that conclude with a homeward journey. Gower's decisions toward closure place his poem within the context of his literary circle—Geoffrey Chaucer, William Langland, Ralph Strode, John Clanvowe, Thomas Hoccleve, Thomas Usk, and others. But at the same time Gower is set apart from that circle through specific humanistic decisions. At the conclusion of the F prologue to Chaucer's *Legend of Good Women*, the poet is sent back to his books for examples of women true in love about whom he must write. Gower picks up on the device for his conclusion when he has his Venus (rather than Cupid or Alceste) send old John Gower back to his books, not to write further, but to study moral virtue "which of long time thou hast write" (8.2925–27). It is not clear whether his "books" here refer to his library or to the several books that he has himself written—the passage can be read in two ways. If the sense of books is his library, then the passage seems to be an adaptation derived from Chaucer's F prologue to the *Legend*; if it refers to his own writings, then the passage is more akin to Chaucer's Retraction at the end of the *Canterbury Tales*: Gower must put aside his books on worldly affairs, like *Confessio* and his French ballades, to concentrate rather on his more openly ethical writings such as the *Mirour de l'omme* and the *Vox clamantis*. Either way the directive redefines the purposes of the protagonist, extracting him from his fiction so that he can make a more definitive concluding pronouncement.

   At the end, in the Lancastrian recension Gower returns to the voice of his prologue as he takes leave of Venus and "Homward a softe pas y wente, / Wher that with al myn hol entente / Uppon the poynt that y am schryve [confessed] / I thenke bidde [pray] whil y live" (8.2967–70), then prays again for the welfare of England and the three estates (as he had done in his prologue), and finally says farewell to his book. Gower seems to allude to Chaucer, this time to the epilogue to *Troilus and Criseyde*, but again, with a difference. The anaphoristic "such love" (8.3162–72) ties the prayer's vision to the charity of God's grace. This amendment of the soul passage echoes the "swich fin" sequence of Chaucer's epilogue (*TC* 5.1828–32), but Amans does not ascend, like Chaucer's Troilus, to an eighth sphere to see "with ful avisement"; rather, Gower stands with feet firmly on English soil. The "go, litel bok" in Chaucer begins the epilogue in

Troilus (5.1786), but Gower saves it for the very end and gives the passage in Latin, as if the origin of his idea is not Chaucer, but rather the ancients from whom Chaucer borrowed the idea as well. In the context of the humanist tradition, Gower's words echo Ovid's *Tristia* 1.1.1, and his conclusion reveals a deep remorse at the failure of mankind's love story with the world, even as his prayer reiterates his utopic love for his homeland.

Bodily and Spiritual Healing through Conversation and Storytelling: Genius as Physician and Confessor in the *Confessio Amantis*

James M. Palmer

> [I]t spedeth þat a leche kunne talke of gode taleȝ and of
> honest that make þe pacientes to laugh, as wele of the
> biblee as of other tragedieȝ. (8.10–12)

> It behooves a physician to know how to tell delightful
> and instructive tales that make patients laugh, including
> [stories from] the Bible as well as tragedies.[1]
> —John Arderne

John Gower's *Confessio Amantis* brings together ecclesiastical treatises on confession, courtly love poems, and contemporary medical understanding of lovesickness. Exploring how love as a sickness serves as a nexus wherein love literature, medicine, and confession come together is important, since this knowledge helps students see how the healing of Amans's soul through exempla can effect the bodily healing needed to cure his physical illness. Instructors can help students understand Genius's dual roles in the *Confessio* by using medical texts in the classroom. Both a priest and a physician heal in part through narrative; indeed, the type of confession taking place in the poem is recommended in both medieval medical and ecclesiastical treatises. For students to understand the larger framework of the poem, they must realize that the two kinds of healing, like Genius's roles, cannot be seen as mutually exclusive. By emphasizing that both the priest and physician ultimately rely on narrative (stories), instructors can help students come to realize that the poem is about Christian order as well as about courtly love.

Students will readily note for themselves that the lovesick Amans conceptualizes his ordeal as a sickness that needs a physician's cure. He thinks he may "live or dye" (1.127) because of his debilitating "maladie" (1.128), and he has addressed Venus as a physician who has "loves cure" (1.132). Amans even begs Venus, "yif me som part of thi grace" (1.135), as if "grace" is the medicine or "love's cure" that he previously mentions. On the one hand, "grace" here stresses the medical tradition of lovesickness, since some thirty lines later Venus addresses Amans in the manner of a physician:

> Tell thi maladie
> What is thi Sor of which thou pleignest [complain]?
> Ne hyd it noght, for if thou feignest,
> I can do the no medicine. (1.164–67)

Venus appears to understand the term as a demand for some part of her healing. On the other hand, the term can be ambiguous: it can also mean the grace that is the means of Christian salvation. This intentional ambiguity begins the tying together of the medical and penitential traditions.

The two traditions need not be widely separated by modern readers of Gower's text if given the correct tools. The Old English homily "Hic dicendum est de quadragesima" cautions the priest's brothers and sisters against holding back sins during confession, since this is displeasing to "godalmihti." Refraining from giving a full confession, the homily explains, is like asking a physician to heal a wound while the cause of the wound is left in it:

> Ne þe preost þe ne mei scrife bute þu wulle heo alforleten. Hu mei þe leche the lechnien þa hwile þet iren sticat in þine wunde. Nefre.

> The priest may not shrive thee, unless thou wilt entirely forsake thy sins. How may the physician heal thee whilst the iron sticketh in thy wound? Never.   (*Old English Homilies* 23, 22)

The homily's analogy between priest and physician strengthens the view that the term *grace* is ambiguous and that Genius can play dual roles. An exploration of the characteristics of both professions can also strengthen this view.

The characteristics of a confessor as set forth in John Myrc's largely contemporary *Instructions for Parish Priests*, a manual intended to help the confessor perform shrift, are similar to those of a physician. The confessor is to be knowledgeable of sin and of the sinner, be objective, maintain privacy, and prescribe proper penance after hearing the sinner's confession. John Arderne's medical treatise of the fourteenth century affirms that, like the priest, the physician is to practice charity, be studious, and be careful of the company he keeps (4.26–27). He is to be courteous, chaste, friendly, free of jealousy toward other leeches (4.4–5.16), and free from boasting "in his seyingis or in his dedes" (4.9–10). Arderne's manual can be used to draw attention to the connection between a physician and God, too, and one can show by extension that Gower's poem can be about love or lovesickness being cured by a physician, as well as about the curative process in Christian order. The surgeon or leech, Arderne notes, is to "sette god always afore evermore in all his werkis, and evermore calle mekely with hert and mouth his help" (4.4–6).

Using a surgical text like Arderne's illustrates that the physician was subject to the same moral stipulations as those set forth for priests in Myrc's penitential manual, and the most important qualities for a practitioner in the arts of healing tie the two professions together. In his *Cyrurgie* ("Surgery"), Guy de Chauliac offers a concise list for a physican: "The condisciouns of his kepers or of men þat beeþ aboute þe seke man beeþ foure: first, þat þai be pesible [peaceable] or meke, gracious, trewe and discrete" (13). Similarly, for Arderne, the leech must be knowledgeable, find out about the sickness by asking the patient questions, be objective, make a diagnosis only after "he haþ seen and assaied" the problem (5.34–35), and prescribe a proper cure if one is available. Like the confessor, the physician must maintain privacy. Arderne exhorts the physician, in fact, to "Discover never the lech vnwarly the counselleȝ of his pacienteȝ, als wele of men as of wymmen" ("Never carelessly reveal the advice given to patients, whether male or female"; 8.14–15). Practitioners of both professions were exhorted to find out about the sinner and patient in similar ways and to the same level of detail. Like the physician, the priest was to adjust the cure (penance) to the "disease." Thus the confessor was to gather a great deal of knowledge about the sin and of the confessing sinner in order to "prescribe" the proper penance.

To examine the cohesion of these traditions and of Genius's dual roles, we can first affirm for students that Genius adheres to recommendations for privacy in the professional practice of physician and priest alike as expressed in both Arderne and Myrc. Amans points this out in book 2:

> And over that to mi matiere [matter]
> Of schrifte [confession], why we sitten hiere [here]
> In privete betwen ous tweie [two],
> Now axeth what ther is, I preie.   (2.3515–18)

The confession itself and Genius's role in conducting it are another means of looking at the cohesion. And students can benefit from recognizing that "confession" may refer both to the doctor-patient consultation taking place and to the sacramental confession of sins, since they are one in the same in this case. Amans first calls on Venus for help, but she tells Amans to confess to her priest, Genius. While Venus no doubt has the power to cure him from the very beginning, she chooses the confession technique to begin his healing. And here she resembles a responsible and observant (medieval) physician, who, noticing that Amans "may die," recommends confession and extreme unction as (spiritual) medicine. The cure prescribed by Venus, who helps justify Gower's poetic endeavor and captures readers' attention, then, is the telling of stories or exempla through the convention of confession to invoke "remembrance" and to reconnect his reason and his passions (1.221–29).

Commencing the shrift, Genius instructs Amans:

> Benedicite
> . . . .
> What thou er this for loves sake
> Hast felt, let nothing be forsake,
> Tell pleinlich [plainly] as it is befalle.   (1.205–11)

This command for Amans to begin his confession is actually a means of getting the lover to tell him about his lovesickness, and it mirrors the order that a priest gives a sinner in Myrc's manual:

> Telle me boldely & make no scof [be serious].
> Telle me þy synne, I þe praye,
> And spare þow not by no waye.   (790–92)

Like the priest, the physician asks his patient to give an account of his affliction, so he can know the circumstances of an illness and make an accurate diagnosis. In fact, when Venus has asked Amans earlier in the poem to "tell thi maladie," she is acting as a physician and is asking her patient to begin a story. I use the word *storytelling* to emphasize that this is what takes place between a doctor and a patient on a daily basis. And it is exactly what happens between the confessor and the sinner in the poem. Kathryn Montgomery Hunter rightly observes that "[m]edicine is fundamentally narrative . . . and its daily practice is filled with stories. Most important are the opening stories patients tell their physician. These [are] . . . stories of a malady that gain them admission and good standing in the world of the ill" (5). Patients' stories within medicine are essentially autobiographical accounts that chronicle the events of illness and sketch out a commonsense etiology. Amans begins his confession with a story about his illness:

> I am destourbed
> In al myn herte, and so contourbed,
> That I ne may my wittes gete,
> So schal I moche thing foryete:
> Bot if thou wolt my schrifte oppose
> Fro point to point, thanne I suppose,
> Ther schal nothing be left behinde.
> Bot now my wittes ben so blinde,
> That I ne can miselven teche.   (1.221–29)

The patient's account of his malady is far from being the only narrative that takes place between a doctor and patient, however. The physician's own discourse about illness is also a story. Genius's tales can be seen as a physician's story about illness, because Genius is trying to find out all of Amans's sins, which are the symptoms of disease. Genius is to "oppose / Fro point to point" what Amans says, so that all the details of Amans's story are known. Amans can admit to the sins within Genius's tales or deny that they have relevance to his lovesickness. Ultimately, Genius's tales are to heal Amans's soul and his body. Viewed from this perspective, the exchange between Amans and Genius takes on a new clinical importance that students may overlook.

It is important to note for students that the interchange using stories mirrors other advice Arderne gives to physicians in order to enhance their healing abilities. Arderne recommends that leeches know biblical verses and stories of comfort (7.4–29), and he goes on to claim that, "[I]t spedeth þat a leche kunne talke of gode taleȝ and of honest that make þe pacientes to laugh, as wele of the biblee as of other tragedieȝ" (8.10–12). These tales of comfort should "make or induce a liȝt hert to þe pacient or þe sike man" (8.13–14).

While this is advice given in a strictly medical context, it should not go unnoticed that tales Arderne recommends are similar to those told to sinners, as seen in penitential manuals. Arderne recommends stories "of the biblee," and stories related to the Bible are certainly present in Gower's poem. "[T]ragedieȝ" may refer to tales like that of "Narcissus" or "Pyramus and Thisbe," for example. Regardless of their specific content, the tales told by a confessor and physician were meant to achieve an inextricably related goal: heal body and soul.

Some exploration of the interchange using stories as a means of healing both the body and the soul is also needed. Gower accepts a medical cure, though one that is less materialist in nature than others available to him. That is to say, a treatment based on the pleasure of stories and on knowledge derived from storytelling aims at healing the *materia* of the body in only limited ways. The early medieval physician and philosopher Stephanus explains, for example, that "pleasure makes the humor flow, and especially the sanguine humor" (91). Good stories certainly make a patient feel better, it was thought, but Gower utilizes storytelling to encourage rational deliberation. Gower's aim is to encourage the character Amans to see that his own choices have led to the destruction of his body and soul. Gower intends a psychological healing that encourages Amans definitively to reject being determined by love, since the conceptualization of love as a medical malady renders Amans passive, at least from Amans's perspective, and determined by the beloved to whom he is indebted for a cure. Any flowing of the "the humor" is a bonus and a result of rational deliberation and the submission of the will to reason. Nevertheless, it is noteworthy that Arderne encourages physicians to enhance their healing abilities by knowing stories of comfort that induce a light heart in the patient.

Healing through the use of conversation and storytelling, therefore, serves Gower in a number of ways. Through tales, Gower makes more explicit for the reader the connection among love, self, society, and cosmos: to govern oneself properly was to set society in proper functioning order. A lovesick Amans was equivalent to a sick England, but a healthy Amans meant a well-ordered society. As others have noted, Gower has confidence in the supremacy of human reason to promote perfection in the individual and in society. A psychological cure involving moral exempla affirms the importance of the belief in free will, namely by dismantling the conceptualization of the lover as passive and determined by his feelings. The cure prescribed also allows Gower to have a political program, one that is firmly connected to lovesickness and is a convenient one for the considerations and motivations of plot.

Stories are important, but Gower must bring his narrative to a close. Although Amans is decidedly in better spirits after his "confession," since he admits the folly of his past saying, "Min herte hath so bewhaped with sotie" (8.2219), he calls on Venus for final healing. She too emphasizes the importance of following reason, since it is part of natural law, saying:

> Mi medicine is noght to sieke [seek]
> For thee and for suche olde sieke [sick persons],   (8.2367–68)

Venus is less gentle and understanding at this point, but she will eventually heal his body to complete the healing that Genius has begun through storytelling. Cupid withdraws his fiery dart, and Venus gives Amans medicine:

> [Venus] Tok out mor cold than eny keie [key]
> An oignement, and in such point
> Sche hath my wounded herte enoignt,
> My temples and my Reins [kidneys] also.   (8.2816–19)

The efficacy of ointments and herbals to cure lovesickness is seriously questioned by Ovid, but this quick cure is an effective way to bring closure to the narrative and for the suffering lover. The cure also looks back to Amans's petition for "grace" from Venus and the ambiguities found in his use of that word. The reader, however, by this point understands that God can be conceptualized as the true physician who can give "grace" for the body and soul as a doctor gives medicine to a patient. Gower may claim at the end of his poem that "no phisicien can hele" the malady of love (8.3156), but readers understand that this is not quite true. With wisdom and God, one can indeed "governe his oghne estat" (8.3149).

Amans appears convinced of the supremacy of his reason, and he is healed of his sins and of his lovesickness. While it is tempting to give Venus all the credit for the curing because of the immediate effects of her medicine, the dual role Genius has played cannot be overlooked. Genius's healing has taken place through storytelling, and ultimately students may see that Genius has been a fairly successful physician and priest. Arderne's advice to physicians, that they should have a stock of "gode tale3 and of honest" that can make pacients "to laugh," becomes relevant in judging this success, for the only time Amans smiles in the poem is after he has regained his reason: "I stod amasid [amazed] for a while, / And in my self y gan to smyle" (8.2958).

NOTE

[1] This translation is influenced by the evaluative criteria established by Harry Bailly for judging the storytelling in Chaucer's *Canterbury Tales*.

Teaching Gower and the Law

Andreea Boboc

Teaching John Gower and the law to upper-level undergraduates and graduate students can be extraordinarily rewarding. In this essay, I outline several ways of approaching the *Confessio Amantis* from a legal perspective but also suggest ways in which teachers can draw on some of Gower's other works for comparison. Teachers can combine any of the ideas below or use them separately depending on the nature and level of their course.

I usually begin my course by pointing students to some useful legal resources and making these resources available on reserve for individual research. While doing so, I emphasize the differences between various systems of law. Students research a legal topic, such as medieval law of contract or maritime law or natural law and present it to the class as a preamble to our discussion of a particular tale from the *Confessio*. This approach ensures that students become acquainted with legal resources and connect them with their readings. J. H. Baker's index to *An Introduction to English Legal History* allows immediate access to legal definitions and their historical contexts. Equally valuable for looking up definitions of legal concepts and procedures are G. R. Evans's *Law and Theology in the Middle Ages* and, of course, Frederick Pollock and Frederic W. Maitland's legal classic, *History of the English Law*. Alan Harding's *The Law Courts of Medieval England* and Marjorie K. McIntosh's *Controlling Misbehavior in England, 1370–1600* provide valuable insight into the workings of the medieval secular courts. For comparisons with modern law, *Black's Law Dictionary*, now in its eighth edition, is indispensable. One might add further resources to this list. William Blackstone's *Commentaries on the Laws of England* is useful for graduate research, and the same can be said of the CD-ROM containing *The Parliament Rolls of Medieval England*. For understanding how the Roman tradition shaped the English common law, Reinhard Zimmermann's *Law of Obligations* offers an extensive discussion of contracts and delicts.

Modeling interdisciplinary engagements with law and literature is especially valuable in the beginning of the semester. In addition to clarifying legal definitions, a teacher can select a scholarly essay already written on the topic at hand and discuss it with the class. For instance, Sebastian Sobecki's chapter on Gower's "Tale of Apollonius" from his monograph, *The Sea and Medieval English Literature*, encourages a conversation about maritime law, insularity, and identity.

The Field Is Dead! Long Live the Field!

It is best to introduce students to the interdisciplinary work of law and literature with a brief history of the field. John Alford's "Law and Literature in Medieval England" and Richard F. Green's "Medieval Literature and Law" provide crucial insights into the ways in which the field has evolved. Emily Steiner and Candace

Barrington's edited collection of essays, *The Letter of the Law*, aptly exemplifies interdisciplinary work by drawing on legal and literary habits of thought, which are brought to bear on vernacular literary production.

To make students aware of current trends, however, one needs to place medievalists' conversations within the larger field of law and literature. Julie Stone Peters's article "Law, Literature, and the Vanishing Real: On the Future of an Interdisciplinary Illusion" describes some of the field's interdisciplinary delusions as concretized in the erasure of disciplinary boundaries. However, the article also helps graduate students formulate some of the challenges that medievalists encounter in pursuing interdisciplinary work. As a theoretical exercise, one can have graduate students respond in writing to Peters's article from the perspective of medieval studies, which is faced with a different set of problems. For example, incomplete or sparse criminal records before the sixteenth century make a case for "trial literature" as a necessary complement to the work of legal historians.

From "Vernacular Legality" to "New Legal History"

Fortunately, Peters's article provides a way to move beyond disciplinary illusions and into a disciplinary flexibility and multiplicity that refute standardized attempts at definition. When Peters envisions the replacement of "law and literature" by something like law, culture, and the humanities, she speaks, in fact, of what Anthony Musson calls "the new legal history," "a historiographical and methodological revisionism that has developed apace over the closing decades of the twentieth century" (3) and that draws on the contributions of legal history, social sciences, and other cultural and literary texts.

Medievalists can contribute to "the new legal history" by engaging with what Bruce Holsinger has called "vernacular legality" (157): the strategic manipulation of legal discourse by vernacular writers, who contribute to legal imagination and legal discourse by responding (sometimes correctively) to existent legal practices. Andrew Galloway's article "The Literature of 1388 and the Politics of Pity in Gower's *Confessio Amantis*" not only provides students with a compelling example of vernacular legality by showing how Gower theorizes pity as a unreliable political and legal instrument but also offers an essential overview of the sociopolitical conditions under which Gower operated.

Before I turn to the joys of interdisciplinarity, a caveat appears necessary. Although this kind of work typically expands one's analytic vocabulary, English majors often complain that their creativity is stymied by the precision of legal terminology. Teachers should insist, however, that legal terms be used denotatively, that is, according to their legal definition, and not connotatively. One example: in a paper about ordeals, it is inadvisable to allow students to use the word *ordeal* in both its legal and its figurative sense. Instead, teachers must make students aware that the field's broader, interdisciplinary audience imposes some constraints on usage. Otherwise—teachers should explain to students—readers from the field of law or legal history might become confused by a writer's switching between the writing conventions of English and those of the law. As with any kind of interdisciplinary work, it is essential that the terms and tools imported from another discipline are properly introduced and defined before students use them. To make students aware of the challenges one encounters in importing theories and methods from another discipline, I have them read Jonathan Rose's essay "English Legal History and Interdisciplinary Legal Studies." We then discuss possible theoretical directions for expanding the interface among literature, law, history, and social sciences.

Gower's Legal Language: Nominalism versus Phenomenology

Since Gower's legal training is a matter of speculation, a more profitable approach to teaching Gower and the law focuses not on biographical details but on legal vocabulary, which is present in his work either nominally or phenomenologically. Nominally, Gower uses legal terms such as *plaidour, client, tort, tresoun,* and so on, while, phenomenologically, he describes the characteristics or functions of a legal phenomenon without actually giving a legal name for it. For legal terms, Russell A. Peck's glosses and notes, particularly to volume three of the *Confessio Amantis*, give advanced undergraduates plenty of legal terms to connect with a tale or group of tales. Also, the *Online Gower Bibliography*, updated weekly, provides students with ideas about research done on a particular topic. Graduate students should consult, however, the *Concordance to John Gower's* Confessio Amantis for a comprehensive look into the usage of a particular legal term, such as *tresoun*.

One question to ask students is why Gower relies at times on phenomenology to describe legal offenses instead of simply naming them. Students can approach this question linguistically or culturally. A quick look at the *Oxford English Dictionary* shows that the word *seduction*, for instance, did not enter the English language until the sixteenth century and had to be defined in relation to other crimes, such as perjury, in three of the tales in book 5 of the *Confessio Amantis*. The cultural approach leads to profitable forays into late medieval levels of legal literacy and knowledge. Recent research into medieval law supports this kind of cultural work (see, for instance, Musson and the collection of legal documents translated and edited by Musson and Powell). For Gower, language (legal or otherwise) is often a question of strategic multilingualism in the context of the new legal developments of his age.

The Trilingual England of John Gower

The legal bilingualism of the *Confessio* generates fruitful discussions about why Gower chooses at times Latin and at times vernacular English to discuss legal procedures and offenses. Such conversations are edifying in the light of the Statute of Pleading from 1362, which stipulated that

> all Pleas which shall be pleaded in [any] Courts whatsoever, before any of his Justices whatsoever, or in his other Places, or before any of His other Ministers whatsoever, or in the Courts and Places of any other Lords whatsoever within the Realm, shall be pleaded, shewed, defended, answered, debated, and judged in the English Tongue, and that they be entered and inrolled in Latin.   (36 Edward III ch. 15)

One may ask the following question of students: If vernacular English is associated with legal orality and Latin with the written record, how might Gower's bilingualism inform questions of legal, cultural, and political authority?

Questions of authority become even more intriguing given Gower's use of Anglo-Norman in the *Mirour de l'omme*, with its significant legal content, especially where lawyers in training are concerned (lines 24373–493). Gower's linguistic choices give us insight into the legal knowledge of his audience, which saw Anglo-Norman decline as a language of prestige and reincarnate as law French, a dialect that becomes the language of legal pleading and the language of record for the *Statutes of the Realm*, the *Rotuli parliamentorum*, and other documents before the gradual Englishing of the legal and literary culture after the 1370s. (For an overview of the linguistic complexity of legal England, see Steiner and Barrington's introduction to *The Letter of Law*, esp. 8–11.)

Teachers can use the body of scholarship on Gower's audiences and multilingualism to discuss the relation between language and truth, especially in the light of the Ricardian crisis described by Richard F. Green in *A Crisis of Truth*. William Rothwell has analyzed "the trilingual England of Geoffrey Chaucer," which, of course, was Gower's England as well. How, one may ask students, is truth or "truthiness" (to quote the modern political satirist Stephen Colbert) conceptualized in Latin versus French versus English? Or, how do Chaucer's and Gower's conceptions or representations of truth differ in the English vernacular, given that the two authors share a legal and literary culture? Posing the latter question might prove particularly useful while teaching the British survey to 1800 if one compares Chaucer's Wife of Bath's Tale and Gower's "Tale of Florent." Students always wonder why the knights keep their *trouthe* even at the expense of their own lives. An understanding of courtly values and Zimmermann's book *The Law of Obligations* are here of great help.

Gower's Hard Cases: Medea

Another fruitful pedagogical entrée is to ask students whether homicide is ever justified. I often encounter students who strongly favor the death penalty for particularly heinous crimes. "Surely," they argue, "no reasonable person can do something like this [insert atrocious crime] and expect to be pardoned." Ah, but I say, invoking Derrida,

> how does one reconcile the act of justice that must always concern singularity, individuals, groups, irreplaceable existences, the other or myself as other, in a unique situation, with rule, norm, value, or the imperative of justice that necessarily have a general form, even if this generality prescribes a singular application in each case?   ("Force" 245)

I explain to them that the "reasonable person" is one such norm, and a legal fiction at that, open to legal negotiation and interpretation. Clearly, what seems reasonable to some might appear unconvincing to others. While lawmakers try to quantify and evaluate conduct according to a "reasonable" standard, literature invests its energies in exploring the irrational and pathological, especially where crimes are concerned.

As a murderer, Gower's Medea fits right into this category, though students hardly ever find her irrational. I teach "The Tale of Jason and Medea" as part of a course on medieval women. On my syllabus I group women's writing and the writings about women according to women's sphere of activity and influence (the court, the church, the household, the guild), but I also have a section on "deviant" women, which includes lepers, hags, fairies, witches, and felons. In this section, I include Henryson's *Testament*, Chaucer's Wife of Bath's Tale, and Gower's "Tale of Jason and Medea." In our class conversations, we contrast the roles that writers imagine for women (as judges, jury, witnesses, defendants, etc.) with the historical realities that limited women's legal agency, especially as married women (*femes covert*).

While students appreciate the legal intricacies in Henryson's *Testament* and Chaucer's Wife of Bath's Tale, they are usually enraged by Medea's infanticide and Gower's sympathetic depiction of her. Students (some of whom are children of divorced parents themselves) almost never find that Medea's romantic plight justifies her infanticide. Although I encourage them to read Medea in conjunction with Barbara Hanawalt's research on medieval responses to motherly infanticide, in "The Female Felon in Fourteenth-Century England," students rarely find the insanity defense persuasive. They often suggest that everything points toward revenge: Medea's weaving of a poisonous garment for Creusa culminates in her infanticide to destroy Jason psychologically and politically by depriving him of sons and heirs—"Lo, this schal be thi forfeiture" (*CA* 5.4214).[1] They often argue that Medea's desire for vengeance is ample evidence of her *mens rea*, or criminal intent. Even the narrator, they point out, thinks that revenge is in order, and they cite Genius's commentary right after Jason leaves Medea for Creusa: "Bot that was after sone aboght" ("But that was soon paid for"; 4199). They also wonder about Gower's choice of words: Medea slays "his [Jason's] sone," though the sons are, of course, hers as well. Finally, students refuse to believe that someone as reasonable and cautious as Medea—here they note her scrupulosity regarding contracts—could persuade a medieval jury with an insanity plea. This is why, they conclude, Medea must escape to the court of Pallas Athena: in a criminal trial, the jury would have found her guilty of murder. Common sense would tell one that.

I love arguments from common sense, a fiction not unlike that of the "reasonable person." As a standard of judgment, which is how students sometimes invoke it, "common sense" has long been relegated by Clifford Geertz in his essay "Common Sense as a Cultural System" to a kind of residual logic not belonging to any discipline (73–93). As a cultural system, however, common sense teaches us how our responses to motherly infanticide might be different from or similar to the ones of medieval people involved in the practice of justice. Sara M. Butler has recently revised historians' arguments, according to which English mothers often escaped justice when committing infanticide (insanity pleas often got them off the hook, or they were merely assigned penances by the church). Butler's work, which looks at 131 instances of child murder drawn from royal and ecclesiastical courts from the thirteenth to the sixteenth century, provides a more comfortable perspective on Medea's guilt, at least one that is more attuned to modern sensibilities and that undermines the notion of the Middle Ages as a dark time of indifference toward infanticide. An enjoyable exercise for undergraduates is studying some historical cases of infanticide (which one can easily draw from Kellum; Hanawalt, *Ties*; S. Butler; or Helmholz) and convicting Medea in absentia (perhaps also for contempt of court, since she refuses to appear before the judges).

For orchestrating a mock trial, Steven Lubet and Jill Trumbull-Harris's book *Mock Trials* provides excellent background for preparing, presenting, and winning a case. To try Medea before a medieval jury, information can be gathered from Thomas A. Green, *Verdict according to Conscience* and James Masschaele's *Jury, State, and Society in Medieval England*. Medea's guilt is not, however, the only distressing aspect of her tale. Female students typically find Gower's sympathy for Medea patronizing; they view any defense Gower mounts on her behalf as a ploy for reinforcing the disenfranchised legal position of medieval women as *femes covert*, particularly since the women seem unable to control their emotions. In this context, Medea's association with Pallas Athena appears to them as an assault on female reason rather than an act of justice, since Pallas, the wise goddess, condones infanticide as well. This monolithic view, which equates Medea with her crime, has been recently demolished by Russell A. Peck in his TEAMS edition of the *Confessio* and by Natalie Grinnell in "Medea's Humanity and John Gower's Romance." Both emphasize Medea's humanity and the poignancy of her situation: despite her magical powers, Medea cannot preserve her marriage.

Yet even after delving into the complexities of those arguments, students express disgust at Medea's deed. Fortunately, disgust has been theorized in relation to the law and to justice by Martha Nussbaum in two eminently readable books, *Hiding from Humanity* and *Upheavals of Thought*, as well as by William

Ian Miller in *The Anatomy of Disgust*. Teachers can draw on these materials to inquire how such feelings might bias an audience against Medea at the expense of a fair verdict or to discuss whether justice is ever possible in the presence of disgust (especially where outcasts are involved). To pose the same questions from the perspective of a medieval audience, Alexandra Cuffel's *Gendering Disgust in Medieval Religious Polemic* provides a good cultural anchor.

If, however, one teaches Medea not in a class on medieval women but in a course on medieval nature and natural law, one might use the momentum provided by her story to discuss homicide as a negation or, paradoxically, an affirmation of natural law (the latter when acting in self-defense or when defending one's country at war). The "Tale of Orestes" introduces multiple legal issues worth debating with both a graduate and an undergraduate audience. Vengeance is involved, but so are considerations about the slaying of traitors who are also one's kin. Peter Nicholson's treatment of Gower and natural law in *Love and Ethics* (406–10) provides a useful starting point for class discussion and research.

"Falling into Theory": Gower's Kings and Agamben's "State of Exception"[2]

A significant share of research on Gower is dedicated to his contributions to the education of kings or the genre of the *Fürstenspiegel*. In my graduate seminar on the medieval legal imagination, I take a different route. Instead of talking about the prince's education, I draw on Giorgio Agamben's biopolitical theory of sovereignty to investigate the dangers posed by kings to their subjects whenever they reduce subjects to "bare life," that is, disenfranchised entities over which sovereignty can exercise its power of life and death. Kings behave this way because of a lack of counsel, poor judgment, treasonous outsiders or insiders, and so on. In *Homo Sacer*, Agamben argues that the sovereign power challenges the moral and legal order because sovereignty belongs to the law but, at the same time, paradoxically constitutes itself outside it. I link Agamben's theory of sovereignty to the constitutional crisis of 1386, during which the Appellants sought to bring Richard II *sub jure*, that is, under the control of the Parliament. Nevertheless, he managed to obtain judicial opinions that he was *supra jure* in August of the following year.

Several tales in the *Confessio* deplore the situation of the subjects reduced to bare life when kings place themselves *supra leges* and behave imprudently or tyrannically. The three tales listed under the heading "perjury" in book 5 of the *Confessio Amantis* are good examples, but one can draw here on Gower's other works: the *Mirour*, *Vox clamantis*, and even some of the minor Latin works. "O Deus immense" reminds the audience, "If one is with the king in error or honor / It is made known by the cry of the people's mouth" (*Minor Latin Works*, lines 55–56), and the *Mirour de l'omme* points out that "the king's sickness hurts those who are not responsible for the sin; for often the people suffer because the king's obviously outrageous sins are offensive to God" (line 22837). Yoshiko Kobayashi, in "*Principis Umbra*: Kingship, Justice, and Pity in John Gower's Poetry," and Conrad van Dijk, in "Giving Each His Due: Gower, Langland, and the Question of Equity," investigate further examples of kings who place themselves above the law. This angle, from which Gower appears invested not only in the education of the king but also in the well-being of the king's subjects, encourages students to think of him as a social critic and not merely a court poet.

With its trilingual layers of meaning, Gower's opus remains a goldmine for legal and sociopolitical discourses and a fertile ground for teaching and research. Gower's legal puzzles, with their ethical and moral ambiguities, invite creative solutions to age-old questions: What counts as truth or evidence or a fair punishment? How do emotions influence the practice of justice? What are the legal duties of a leader? When does law oppose justice? As students ponder these questions for themselves, perhaps they come to understand how Gower's legal and ethical questions apply to their own lives.

NOTES

[1] Citations to the *Confessio* are to Peck's edition.
[2] "Falling into theory" is Richter's phrase; for "state of exception," see Agamben.

Teaching Gower Aloud

Joyce Coleman

John Gower's best hope for his *Confessio Amantis* was that it, like the books of antiquity, would "Beleve [Be left] to the worldes eere / In tyme comende [coming] after this" (prologue, lines 10–11). Still, in teaching Gower as in teaching other works of the period, we tend to emphasize the mind's eye over the world's ear. Of course, many important issues can be handled only by close textual reading. But this essay proposes that another, and sometimes the best, way to open up a medieval text and its meanings to students is through their own performance—specifically, in the present context, by having them read aloud from the *Confessio*.

After a quick overview of the theory and practice of medieval public reading (or "aurality"), I shall review several exercises that could be used in class. I shall close with an outline of a possible final project based on performance and suggestions for taping the results.

Medieval Aurality

It's a familiar idea that much medieval literature, both vernacular and Latin, was created for performance, whether strictly oral (improvised or performed from memory) or aural (read aloud or "prelected" from a book to an audience). To "prelect" means to read aloud to one or more listeners, and the "prelector" is the person doing that reading. These terms help distinguish public reading as a social event from private, individual reading—whether the private reader is reading aloud or silently (Coleman, *Public Reading* 35–37). As his "worldes eere" comment implies, Gower similarly envisioned an aural context for his work and that of the "olde wyse" he drew on and emulated. Thus, in performing Gower aurally, students will be aligning themselves with the most pervasive reception format of the period they are studying. The experience of hearing a text becomes both a means of understanding medieval literature and a tool for the analysis of literary reception.

While public reading obviously benefited the nonliterate and the book-deprived, medieval writers portrayed it not as a second-best option to "real" (private) reading but as an emotionally and intellectually engaging focus of human interaction. An issue important then and perhaps especially relevant to today's students, whose commitment to multiple and simultaneous forms of input has often been remarked, is the multisensory nature of aural reading. In his treatise on the composition and performance of Latin poetry, Geoffrey of Vinsauf counsels that "the final labor [of poetry is] to see that a voice managed discreetly may enter the ears of the hearer and feed his hearing, being seasoned with matched spices of facial expression and gesture" (36). In a public reading, you hear the prelector and the comments of the other audience members. You see the prelector's person, expressions, gestures, and movements, and you see the place where you are and the people around you. You smell the smells of the place and people, and you feel the touch of the chair you're sitting on as well as the proximity of the other participants. Every sense but taste is involved—and that would be there as well, if you were drinking or eating during the event. This synaesthetic experience may draw students into the material in a way that silent, private reading does less well for many in their generation. At the same time, they can be alerted to think about such effects and to comment on them after the performance has concluded.

Performance has pedagogical benefit on the intellectual level as well. Students who perform a text have to make decisions about interpretation, not to answer an abstract essay question but as the basis of their own embodiment of the material. As representatives of the text's strengths to the audience of other students, especially when the exercise includes a teaching component, the performers invest more in it, and the listening students get more out of it.

What we know of medieval prelection suggests that the readers were valued for their intelligent presentation of the text and for their ability to "point" it well—that is, to place the emphases meaningfully (Coleman, *Public Reading* 121–22). They may have followed some of the guidelines for performance included in the "delivery" (*pronuntiatio*) section of most rhetorics. Prelection could also have an erotic dimension, giving young female readers the opportunity to invite the gaze of men and men the opportunity to gaze openly at the women. In France and the duchy of Burgundy, reading events seem to have been relatively formal, but in England, at least with secular material, the atmosphere seems to have been very open. In particular, and contrary to modern ideas of proper audience behavior, the auditors seem to have felt free to intervene at all points, a dynamic familiar from the oral storytelling modeled in the *Canterbury Tales*

(Coleman, *Public Reading* 65–68, 83–88, 141–44). Almost always, in the surviving records, the prelector was of lower social status than at least the chief member of the audience. Not surprisingly, then, the audience participated in the choice of text to be read and felt free to speak up when a point caught their attention, possibly leading to side or general conversation before, possibly, returning to the text.

I always describe this situation to my class when I introduce a performance exercise, but I have never persuaded students to emulate it. The idea that audiences should sit passively during performances, then applaud at their end, seems too ingrained. Also, the material and its native context are so foreign to modern students that they don't imagine intervening in it, even though many of them may have shared Amans's experience of unrequited love. Even if the students won't act on the concept of interactive reading, however, it is good to recall that as the original context.

One important resource for both instructors and students involved in performance is the Web site *Performing Medieval Narrative Today* (http://wilde.its .nyu.edu/mednar), codirected by Evelyn Birge Vitz and Marilyn Lawrence. Vitz is a pioneer in the pedagogic use of performance, and the results show in many short videos available on this site. Most of these, and of the many other clips she and Lawrence have assembled (involving literature in many languages, including Old and Middle English), have students presenting memorized texts. Many of the principles would apply in a reading-aloud exercise as well, however. I have shown some of the "MedNar" videos to a class, both to acclimatize students to the idea of performance and to give them an overview of how it works. Another good resource for "aural Gower" is the downloadable audio-texts available on the Web site of the John Gower Society (www.johngower .org/audio/). Brian Gastle's readings, including selections from the prologue and the complete tales of "Acteon" and "Florent," offer guidance in pronunciation, intonation, and performance dynamics.

Obviously all examples and details given here are heuristic, to use or adapt as necessary. It may help to cover a few practical issues at the start:

> Where performance fits in: The role of performance in a class devoted to more or less traditional literary study can range from a spontaneous burst (e.g., going around the class with each student reading a few lines of a tale) to a short or extra-credit assignment to a team project worth a significant proportion of the final grade. How much background research and in-class effort to ask of the students depends on the level of the class and on how much weight this exercise carries. Any exercise that requires advance preparation by students would probably include a discussion after the performance.
>
> Pronunciation issues: It is up to the individual instructor to decide how important correct pronunciation of Middle English is for these exercises. Most teachers begin the semester in a course on medieval English

literature by teaching the students about the differences between Middle and Modern English and coaching them in pronunciation. My choice with performance exercises, however, is to go easy on the linguistic side, beyond reminding students about pronunciation features that can affect meter and rhyme. I'd rather have students concentrating on connecting with the text and with their audience—a connection that can be hard to establish if the performers are preoccupied with pronunciation.

Class Exercises

The exercises outlined below focus on the more dialogic parts of the *Confessio*: the confessional frame and the tales themselves. While the prologue and book 7 would equally have been read aloud, they are probably better studied more traditionally. Even if no final project on performance is planned, the ideas in exercise 4 might be of value in one of the shorter exercises as well.

Exercise 1: Performance and the Confessional Frame

This exercise derives from a conference session called "Gower Aloud," which took place at the 2008 International Medieval Congress in Kalamazoo. Alison Baker, Mica Gould, Alexander Kaufman, and James Palmer paired off to prelect two sections from book 4 of the *Confessio Amantis*, where Genius is examining Amans on the subject of sloth. If assigned these (or similar) passages for a class, both students and instructor would probably prepare by reading them silently. The instructor would read dynamically, looking for emphases and nuances to discuss. The odds are, however, that not all the students would read as closely. For most people, in fact, reading silently to oneself produces a sort of mumble in the brain. Medieval literature, read silently by those new to Middle English, may be a mumble interspersed with incomprehension and pauses to check the meanings of words. Add the unfamiliarity of most students with confession rituals and courtly love allegory, and, realistically, some may find such passages fairly meaningless.

It was anything but meaningless to hear the readers at Kalamazoo voice the roles of Genius and Amans. Suddenly, the inherent absurdity of the enterprise came vividly into focus. To hear, in an edited version of 4.2701–926, a "priest" advise constant wakefulness in the pursuit of sex, with the deluded lover multiplying his assurances that he was engaged in a busy-ness that a real priest would consider the epitome of sloth, utterly invigorated the narrative framework. Instead of a mumble, we saw ideas and cultural images in play. That the readers read with skill and a knowledge of Middle English augmented the effect but did not create it. The polyvalent humor was latent in the text; what brought it out was strictly the act of performance.

The reading further highlighted aspects of the text likely to engage a college-age audience and at the same time important for an understanding of the work's context. Most modern students could certainly find echoes of their own romantic frustrations in Amans's hapless protests, or at least laugh or grimace sympathetically, thinking of their friends' experiences. Discussion could attach an analysis of this reaction to the scholarly controversy over Gower's original or "real" audience for the first or so-called Ricardian recension of the *Confessio*. Anne Middleton defined this audience for many medievalists when she wrote, "The king is not [Gower's] main imagined audience, but an occasion for gathering and formulating what is on the common mind" (107). More recently, I have argued that whatever other levels the work includes, many textual and contextual details suggest that Richard II really did commission it and that the young king was indeed its intended initial recipient (Coleman, "Bok"). As audience of the text themselves, students can debate its appeal to the different audiences proposed by scholars, relating their conclusions to previous study, perhaps, of the more overtly homiletic or didactic parts of the text (i.e., the prologue and book 7). If the point of mixing "lust" and "lore" (prologue 19) in the narrative was to guide Richard into a more mature view of his role as ruler both of himself and of England, would the passage performed have had that effect, and how? How would Gower's "Lancastrian" edits have changed the context around the confessional frame? Performance brings into view the many layers at which Gower's narration works, from affective (creating pity) and ironic (creating distance) to critical (creating understanding).

I've used the text on sloth as an example, but of course other sections could be chosen to suit any focus or interest. In some cases, editing might be called for, to allow more emphasis to fall on the dialogue between Genius and Amans.

Other discussion topics for an exercise like this could include:

> For the performers: How did it feel to rehearse and perform the scene? How did they experience and understand the text differently than if they had read it privately?
>
> For the audience: How did it feel to watch and listen to a performance? Would the way they experienced and understood the text have been different if they had read it privately?
>
> How does the performed scene contribute to Gower's frame scheme of a lover's confession? Did Amans make a successful confession, by the terms of the frame scheme? What, if anything, does Amans take from the interaction?
>
> How does this passage work, for those who know that the *Confessio* ends with Amans exposed as a *senex amans* ("aged lover")?
>
> What other levels of meaning does the performance bring out, beyond the basic one of Amans assuring Genius that he is an assiduous lover?
>
> What moral lessons might the audience, if not Amans, take from the passage?

Exercise 2: Performing a Tale

The performance of a tale in Middle English is probably the most familiar format for students of the literature. Many people who will be teaching Gower may have been asked to read aloud all or part of a Canterbury tale. Students might perform solo or as a dramatic group—from two people sharing all the roles to a reader for every speaking role in the text, including Genius as narrator. Students could be left to find their own tale, perhaps within guidelines provided (e.g., setting a minimum and maximum length for the tale or designating preferred topics). Alternatively, students could choose between selected tales to fit the framework of a course (e.g., tales exploring sexuality or tales also found in Chaucer's *Legend of Good Women*). (For a comparative chart of tales told in the *Confessio* and in Chaucer's *Legend of Good Women*, along with the tales listed in The Man of Law's Prologue, see Coleman, "Bok" 121–22n56.) The reading of the tale should normally include the links on either side, that is, Genius's segue into the story and any comments on it afterward.

And what about Gower's Latin glosses to the tale? Since the role of the glosses, in relation to the text, adds an interesting complexity to the tales themselves and has been the subject of much recent critical discussion, students might be asked to include the most substantive glosses, read in Latin (if desired) and then in English translation. If the assigned text of the *Confessio* does not give the glosses or doesn't translate them, they are available through the online text of Russell Peck's TEAMS edition (where Andrew Galloway has provided translations in the footnotes).

Another feature that would enhance the experience is to have a team member assigned to read aloud the tale's source before (or after) the Gower reading. Such a reading (if preceding the Gower) could be followed by a brief discussion of how Ovid, the Bible, or other source presented the story. After both versions have been prelected, in whatever order, discussion could include a comparison of the two tales. This sort of comparison is common, of course, in classes not involving performance, but what the performance adds is a visceral experience of the shift in emphases and in overall impact. The instructor can offer a contemporary comparative angle by choosing one of the seven *Confessio* tales (or eight, if you count Alcestis) also related in Chaucer's *Legend of Good Women*. If the length of the texts allows, the exercise could feature a reading of versions of the same tale from Ovid, Chaucer, and Gower.

Following the performance(s), discussion topics could include:

> For the performers: How did it feel to rehearse and perform the scene? How did they experience and understand the text differently than if they had read it privately?
> For the audience: How did it feel to watch and listen to a performance? How would the way they experienced and understood the text have been different if they had read it privately?

How does the tale fit into its narrative context? For example, "The Tale of Tereus" is supposed to illustrate Ravine, as a form of avarice. Does this seem a good fit?

If the source text is included: How did Gower adapt his source? What effect do those changes have?

If a Chaucerian analogue is included: How do the two medieval authors differ in their interpretation of Ovid's original? What different effects do those changes make? How does each adaptation serve its narrative context? How does each one "play" in performance?

How do the students suppose that a medieval audience would have reacted to this tale?

What about the mismatch that many scholars perceive between Gower's Ovidian love stories and the Christian morals appended to them? Do the glosses successfully contain or redirect the often transgressive sexuality of Ovid's stories?

What do you think Gower meant the prelector to do with the glosses? Read them aloud? Or take silent note of them and use them to guide an interpretation of the story? Alternatively, does the existence of the glosses discount the idea of prelection, since the "hypertext" they create is perhaps best handled in a private reading?

How would the text work differently if Gower had written the glosses in English? Why didn't he?

Exercise 3: Graduate-Level Exploration of the Interaction of English and Latin Elements

A particular puzzle of the *Confessio* is its combination of entertaining, accessible English tales with moral glosses in relatively simple Latin and introductory verses in very difficult Latin. (The discussion here derives from Coleman, "Lay Readers.") Most scholars have analyzed these multiple registers strictly in terms of Gower's own authorial influences and processes. But how did Gower expect Richard II—or the "common sphere" readership envisioned by Middleton and other scholars—to handle the Latin elements? Given what we know about middle- and upper-class lay latinity, most of these people could not have understood the Latin verses, which have challenged the best modern translators. The Latin of the prose glosses, on the other hand, can be understood by anyone with some basic training in the language, including students who have had a semester or two of Latin. One possible explanation is that a household clerk would read the book aloud, adapting the bilingual text as instructed by his audience: translating the Latin verses or glosses as he went, perhaps even expanding on the moralizing glosses, or else ignoring the Latin and reading only the entertaining English.

Ironically, then, the Latin, which is supposed to "stabilize" a text, destabilizes this one. To an unusual extent for an aural work, the *Confessio* was an "emergent" text, one that could come out differently every time it was performed, depending on given audiences, circumstances, and prelectors (Bauman, *Verbal Art*; Coleman, *Public Reading* 28–30). Members of a graduate class might try to recreate such a performance. It would take some acting skills and some chutzpah, but it might make for a wonderful, memorable learning experience. "Audience" members would have to take on roles—whether historical ones based on Richard's or Henry's households or fictionalized households of their devising. The prelector's role could be taken by the instructor or by a particularly articulate (and, ideally, Latinate) student. The group could run the "experiment" several times, trying out different scenarios: heavily Latinate, with the Latin verses given full value and the tale read and then moralized on; an attempt by the prelector to present such a reading variously reshaped by audience protests; the text read with all the Latin anglicized; or only the English text read. As with the previous exercises, these experiments could lead to discussion of the experience of prelecting and being prelected to, of what such performance tells us about literary reception in a multilingual culture, and of Gower's complex authorial strategies.

Exercise 4: A Performance-Based Final Class Project

At its most ambitious, performance can become the focus of final class projects, in which students are asked to select, teach, and perform a text from Gower or a source. Just after midterms, the instructor should hand out a detailed project sheet. It may take a week or so for all the students to decide on their performance teammates, texts, and dates. The instructor would compile this information and provide it to the class as an addendum to the syllabus, since the texts chosen for performance will be the day's assigned reading for all those not on the performance team.

The optimal team size seems to be three: large enough to promote intellectual exchange but small enough that the members can find times to meet. If the goal is to perform and explore a *Confessio* tale in an upper-division class, the project sheet could outline three roles, which the team members would assign among themselves: for example, one source researcher-presenter and two Gower researcher-presenters. If Chaucerian analogues are part of the assignment, one student each could be expected to research and present the source text, Chaucer's version, and Gower's version. If a team picked "The Tale of Tereus," for example, the source person would be responsible for researching Ovid and the *Metamorphoses*, for familiarizing himself or herself with the tale, and for thinking about how Ovid's version relates to Gower's. If there are going to be two Gower people, they would determine between themselves how best to split up the task of reading critical discussions of the tale and its role in the *Confessio*, including commentary on its glosses and on the role of the glosses generally. The Gower (and Chaucer) people would also familiarize themselves with the tale, divide up parts, and rehearse them, informed by discussions with their teammates.

To encourage those students whose research might consist of surfing the Internet for miscellaneous factoids, I require each student to read at least one scholarly article dealing with his or her particular text or with an issue relevant to it. The students are expected to include a report on that article in their presentation. The teams should also write a prep-paper assignment for distribution in the session preceding the one in which they will perform. This prep paper would normally pose discussion questions for members of the prospective audience to consider as they read the text in preparation for their colleagues' performance.

Finally, the assignment invites the teams to engage creatively with their texts, by imagining a performance context for their Gower selection. This entails deciding who the audience and the prelector are, where the reading occurs, the time of year and day, the mood, the interactions, and so on. The team may even, if it likes, design a set for the event, as though for a theatrical performance, and block out positions and movements for the prelectors.

Each team has a class period in which to present its project. The source researcher-presenter would begin with a teaching component, relating what she or he had discovered about Ovid and the tale. Then she or he would read it aloud. The Chaucer person, if there is one, and then the Gower person(s) would then teach their tale(s) and context(s), based on their research. Each teaching component would include engaging the class on the prep-paper discussion points. The team would then jointly introduce the Gower reading by describing the setting it has devised, drawing the class into the imaginative reality it has created by assigning the class an identity in its role as audience (e.g., Richard and his court; the Wife of Bath and her friends). The (Chaucer and) Gower prelector(s) would then do their reading.

After all the performances are over, the team as a whole would act as an expert panel, responding to comments and questions from the class and posing questions to elicit the audience's reactions. Depending on what analogue texts were included, the topics would include a comparison of Ovid's, Chaucer's, and Gower's handling of the material.

To keep students on track, I include a schedule in the project sheet, requiring various elements in writing from students at set times. These elements could include a statement of roles chosen and work divisions, bibliographies, a draft of the teaching notes or prep paper, and/or a draft of the final paper.

The last component of such a project is for the students to write their research as a final class paper, presenting their research on the source, the analogue, or Gower along with an assessment of their project and of their individual role in it. Teams can have the option of writing their papers individually or as a group. If they choose the group option, the paper has to be longer than an individually written one, and all the authors share the paper grade equally. In practice, students almost always write individual papers.

Taping the Exercise

In spring 2005, my graduate class on medieval authorship and I devoted a unit of the course to scripting and creating a short, two-part film. The first half dramatized the prelection scene in *Troilus*, where a maiden is reading the *Siege of Thebes* aloud to Criseyde and her other maidens as Pandarus enters. The second half imagined a reading of that scene to four medieval couples (i.e., the students) as well as to "Gower" and "Strode" (played by two colleagues). This was a full-dress event, filmed in costume on "location" (with Spanish colonial passing as more or less medieval), and it took lots of time and some money. The result can be viewed on *YouTube* and on New York University's *Performing Medieval Narrative Today* site.

The experiment went well—not because a masterpiece of film was produced but because the students became very engaged. They had to think about the text in a much more vivid way than the silent mumble invoked above. I have never seen students work harder to get medieval pronunciation right than this crew, who knew their performance was going to be recorded for posterity. The screenplay for part 2, which included scripted interruptions from the listeners (pastiched from other Chaucer texts), engaged its writers in the imagining of medieval reality. The degree of the students' involvement is reflected in the fact that over the course of research and rehearsals, and with no prompting from me, they sorted themselves into couples and created personalities and backstories for their roles, up to and including one student deciding he was the early humanist Humphrey, Duke of Gloucester. Everyone worked hard, had a good time, and, I believe, learned a lot. Even the "mistakes" were educational; the screenwriters' original assumption that interruptions would be aggressive—disruptive of the prelection and annoying to the prelector—promoted a discussion of the more communal nature of medieval performance.

Invariably, when I have used performance exercises in a class, students report that the experience brought the literature alive to them in a unique and very meaningful way. Engaging both senses and mind, performance is a powerful pedagogical tool that works particularly well as a means of exploring the pleasures and complexities of Gower's lover's confession.

Hearing Gower's Rhetoric

Georgiana Donavin

Teaching is a local art. While many of us strive for a consistent pedagogical philosophy, we also work hard to adapt it to specific institutional programs, demographics, and requirements. I have taught for eighteen years now in a small liberal arts college with an unusually well-endowed poetry series. As a result of several opportunities a year to hear internationally acclaimed poets read from their work, my undergraduates are particularly attuned to and interested in the poet's "voice." "Voice . . . signifies the equivalent in imaginative literature to Aristotle's 'ethos' in a speech of persuasive rhetoric, and suggests also the traditional rhetorician's concern with . . . the physical voice in an oration" (Abrams 218). Having plied this interest in voice while teaching the *Confessio Amantis* in several medieval literature surveys, I am offering some advice on accessing John Gower's voice in this poem through the rhetorical tradition.

Because Gower makes voice and persuasion explicit issues in the *Confessio Amantis*, students understand immediately why I want to place emphasis on the narrator's ethos and the history of rhetoric in our classroom. In my experience with teaching literatures from the past, I have found that students tend to take more interest when the issues discussed arise organically from their first encounter with the assigned text. After reading the prologues and the beginning of book 1, after adjusting to the break between the exhortative narrator of the prologues and the lovesick Amans of the frame, students recognize that the persona, sincerity, and identity of the *Confessio Amantis*'s speaker are all at issue. Whether students trained in Middle English share the pleasure of reading lines aloud or their professor provides a dramatic reading—both of which methods my classes practice—everyone can hear the sharp contrasts among the prologue's preacher, who threatens that "helle is full of such discord" as exists in English society (prologue, line 1046); the defeated old man, who admits in the opening of book 1, "I may noght strecche up to the hevene / Min hand, ne setten al in evene / This world . . ." (1–3); and Amans, who enters the confessional frame with boisterous weeping and wailing over his unrequited love (115). Locating the narrator's position is even further complicated by Genius's narration of the tales and Gower's Latin marginalia, which reveals that the author is only pretending to be a lover, donning the passions of those whom love rules (59).

From the multivocal, bilingual opening of the *Confessio,* it becomes clear that a theory of medieval composition is required to help us "hear" the poem amid apparent narrative cacophony. This theory derives from the rhetorical tradition. In the *Confessio Amantis* Gower defines the art of rhetoric in book 7, a treatise on the liberal arts and mirror for princes. Although James J. Murphy initially judged the *Confessio*'s treatment of rhetoric inept, more recent scholarship has explicated the context for Gower's section on rhetoric and praised the poet's subtlety in the rhetorical arts (Schmitz, "Rhetoric"; Copeland 179–220; Watt 38–62; Mitchell 50–55; Donavin, "Rhetorical Gower"). In response to Amans's request to hear Aristotle's lectures to Alexander, Genius, although uncomfortable in the scholarly mantle, provides a discourse on *theorique*, including theology, physics, and mathematics; *rethorique*, including grammar and logic; and *practique*, including ethics, economics, and policy. Gower adapts these Aristotelian categories of knowledge from his source, Brunetto Latini's *Trésor*, and makes rhetoric the master of the speech arts, over grammar and logic (Donavin, "Rhetorical Gower" 164–65). Genius claims that the art of *rethorique* is "the science / Appropred [Dedicated] to the reverence / Of wordes that ben resonable" (7.1523–25) and teaches the author "[h]ou that he schal hise wordes sette, /. . . / And in what wise he schal pronounce / His tale plein without frounce [ambiguity]" (7.1591–94). According to Genius, the purpose of rhetoric is to teach the logical and verbal skills that convey rational thought and "mai the pleine trouthe enforme" (7.1638). While students may be surprised by the disjuncture between the narrative multivalency and book 7's ideal of a "plain truth," their close reading of the prologue and the opening to book 1 has given them motivation either to sort out this seeming inconsistency or to discover the teachings of rhetoric that enable the communication of truth through a variety of voices.

Gower invokes both Aristotelian and Ciceronian rhetoric in book 7 as methods for delivering the truth. Since Gower's knowledge of Aristotle was sometimes mediated by the Ciceronian textbooks that were ubiquitous throughout the Middle Ages, since understanding Gower's Aristotelianism requires reading Medieval Latin glosses and tables, and since the basic principles of Ciceronian rhetoric are embedded in many of today's composition pedagogies (and therefore students already have a glimmering), I concentrate on the *Confessio*'s Ciceronian references in the undergraduate classroom. In the *Confessio*'s section on rhetoric, Gower raises up Cicero's speeches against Catiline as exemplars of honest persuasion; Cicero's *De inventione* as well as the pseudo-Ciceronian *Rhetorica ad Herennium* would have been readily available to Gower and others desirous to learn such skills for verbal probity. Suzanne Reynolds notes that from the twelfth century, the latter two texts were the "core" of the curriculum providing instruction in all five offices of rhetoric: invention, arrangement, style, memory, and delivery (26–27). As a boy, Gower would have been introduced to these texts after learning basic Latin grammar in Donatus and translating authors such a Statius, Horace, and Ovid to prove his Latin comprehension and gain knowledge of the classics. Many scholars have accepted John H. Fisher's conclusion that Gower must have had some legal training (54–58), and in this case the poet would have been instructed in the *ars dictaminis* in order to construct legal documents and in the procedures and fine points of debate. If a lawyer, Gower may have identified with Cicero professionally and desired to imitate what the poet heard as the plain-speaking vehemence of the Roman senator's voice. If students understand that Cicero and other classical authors were Gower's models for composition, similar to the way that essays in anthologies for writing are models today, and that medieval rhetorical teachings in invention, arrangement, and style correspond somewhat roughly to current composition pedagogy in research and brainstorming, organization, and syntax, they can begin to compare their own means of discovering a writer's voice and Gower's traditional rhetorical tools.

Reading the *Confessio Amantis* through a comprehensive Ciceronian rhetoric, I begin with invention, as "the devising of matter, true or plausible, that would make the case convincing" (*Rhetorica* 7). Whatever one interprets the "case" made by the poem to be—whether an encomium for or a rejection of married love, whether a discourse on rulership or other medieval topics—students understand that the office of invention helped Gower find different approaches to develop it. For the *Confessio*, invention may be treated in two categories: the power of suggestion in Richard II's commission of the poem and the formation of content through resources. On the latter, Rita Copeland has traced Gower's adaptation of sources to the medieval *accessus* tradition, literary commentary taught in both grammar and rhetoric courses that provided information about the author and an interpretation of the text (179–220). Many scholars—including some in this volume—have explicated Gower's appropriation of sources, and even before the publication of *John Gower's Literary Transformations in the* Confessio Amantis, in 1982, Peter Beidler was encouraging students to ascertain Gower's meaning through the differences between his tales and their source narratives. I will add only that to encourage more appreciation for the "invention" in Gower's rhetorical revisions through comparisons with the students' own rhetorical strategies, I assign a radical rewriting of one of the *Confessio*'s tales. A popular option is "The Tale of Pyramus and Thisbe" from book 3 because of its grounding in Ovid's *Metamorphoses* and reworking in Shakespeare's *A Midsummer Night's Dream*. Students can see a continuum from Ovid to Gower to Shakespeare at the same time that they relate to the subject of forbidden love and enjoy the humor of the bard's mechanicals. I ask my undergraduates to situate their rewriting of the Pyramus and Thisbe story in some identifiable contemporary context: many choose to interpret the wall through divisions like class or race. Through their compositions, students acquire an appreciation for the ingenuity of Gower's play with source stories and understand rhetorical revision as an opportunity to insert one's own voice into an authorized tale.

The initial spark for the *Confessio*'s invention, Richard's commission, is described in the first version of the prologue, which Peter Nicholson has dubbed "the poet at his best," despite the fact that G. C. Macaulay's edition of the poem and much ensuing scholarship privileges Gower's revision of the prologue with a dedication to Henry of Lancaster ("Dedications" 175). Dhira B. Mahoney declares the first-recension prologue "more personal and more charming than the Lancastrian one . . ." (24). In a scene from the prologue to the first recension, King Richard and the poet Gower are traveling on the Thames in separate boats; Richard invites Gower to join the royal entourage and there enjoins the poet to write a poem to the court's taste. Concurring with Nicholson and Mahoney about the beauty and primacy of the unrevised first recension, Joyce Coleman argues that "the very conception of a long vernacular poem focusing primarily on romantic love—a subject not featured in Gower's two earlier major works . . . [was] adapted to a young king" and that "Gower seems to have embraced the commission as, among other things, an opportunity to offer moral and political guidance to the king . . ." ("Bok" 107). Students may be asked to read several tales about rulers as examined in Russell A. Peck's *Kingship and Common Profit in Gower's* Confessio Amantis in order to discuss Gower's response to Richard. They may be asked to compare Richard's commission with a paper assignment, in which the challenge is to insert one's own point of view into a predetermined subject matter (notwithstanding the obvious contrast that professors are not regents!). Gower's respectful solution to his sovereign's request for new material is the creation of Amans, through whom the poet finds a new voice.

After impressing on the students that Gower's work with sources required both ingenuity and restraint and after concentrating on the scene of poetic invention in the first prologue, I find that the discussion leads naturally to the rhetorical office of arrangement, through which all the tales are structured with imaginative control and the audience's expectations for order are answered. Particularly important to the arrangement of the *Confessio* is the context for each tale provided by the confessional frame, which is itself modeled on confessional manuals. For instance, "The Tale of Pyramus and Thisbe" occurs in book 3 on wrath and accordingly condemns Pyramus's "folhaste" ("rashness") in turning his passions on himself and committing suicide (3.1447). The students' revisions of the *Confessio*'s tales, it is important to point out, were unbounded by any frame and free to explore a variety of issues. Analysis of ways in which the *Confessio*'s structural frame influences the tales' signification could extend almost indefinitely, but in order to raise a new topic on understanding the poet's voice through the rhetorical tradition, I turn to the first part of rhetorical arrangement, the introduction, whose purpose, according to the *Rhetorica ad Herennium*, is to render the "hearer receptive, well-disposed, and attentive" (13).

Ciceronian rhetoric places great stress on the introduction as the part of the discourse in which the audience's receptivity must be "won" (*Rhetorica* 21). Important strategies for capturing the benevolence of the audience include descriptions of the speaker's position, exposure of common enemies, and references to current events (*Rhetorica* 15). These strategies explain why the *Confessio*'s prologue dwells on the narrator's situation, moral and ethical conflicts, and the current state of England. When the narrator of the *Confessio*'s prologue in both versions presents himself as a John the Baptist figure crying in the wilderness of sins perpetrated by all the estates, he accomplishes the Ciceronian goals for an introduction and sets out to bind the speaker and the audience in resolving common problems. In the first version of the prologue, which is influenced by Ciceronian rhetoric and conventions for book dedications, the speaker's obedient and enthusiastic response to Richard's commission conveys a "a transparent, trustworthy persona" who engages the reader and sets expectations for honesty in addressing the failings of the estates (Mahoney 25). When, under duress of weighty sins and demands to satisfy a court appointment to compose in a new vein, the narrator fragments into a variety of speakers, students understand and sympathize with the tone of exhaustion that begins book 1 and the ensuing eruptions of Amans's sobbing voice.

While invention and arrangement are important rhetorical strategies for conceiving and organizing the *Confessio Amantis* (and for determining poetic voice), Gower actually concentrates most on the office of style—and the superiority of plain speech—in book 7's section on *rethorique*. To teach Amans the principles of persuasive speaking, Genius uses examples from the Catilinian orations as models of both good and bad style. In an imitable style, Cillenus's argument for the execution of Catiline and his conspirators conveys "trouthe" and "comun profit" (*CA* 7.1608–09). Agreeing with Cillenus (D. Junius Silanus), Cicero and Cato deliver "a tale plein withoute frounce" (7.1594), that is, a discourse grounded in the facts and unobscured by appealing, but empty, language. In contrast, Julius Caesar's response on the unconstitutionality of subjecting the conspirators—Roman citizens—to capital punishment is a shameful display of tropes and figures adorning falsehood. According to Genius, Caesar "[c]oloureth" his words (7.1624–25), while Cillenus, Cicero, and Cato had "spieken plein after the lawe" (7.1623); history reveals the superiority of Cillenus's, Cicero's and Cato's rhetoric, since the Catilinian conspirators were conquered or executed. The case for straightforward language without gratuitous flourishes is also made in the *Confessio*'s first-recension epilogue, with its dedication to Richard II, in which the narrator eschews more ornate examples of Cicero's rhetoric and promises not to "peinte and pike [embellish and polish], / [a]s Tullius som tyme wrot" (8.3117–19).

To discuss the plain style in more detail, students bring to class at least two papers, one that they consider straightforward communication and another they consider more ornate or "poetic." While my undergraduates are sometimes quite articulate about the constitutive differences among types of styles, many discover that they do not have a vocabulary—grammatical or rhetorical—for describing syntax and diction in depth. I find it helpful to teach a few of the figures of thought and speech from the *Rhetorica ad Herennium*'s book 4 and to lead students in exercises by which they create their own figurative sentences on Gower's models. From these exercises, the class can begin to generalize about the components of the poem's style. Most students conclude, with the overwhelming majority of scholars, that in all the *Confessio*'s narrative voices—the preacher and obedient subject of the prologue, the compromising author of book 1's beginning, Amans, Genius—the plain style allows each to convey a worthy point of view honestly and urgently.

Since Gower foregrounds narrative voice by speaking directly to the reader in both versions of the *Confessio*'s prologue and since that voice shatters into a variety of speakers who utter their lines in a variety of tones and languages, students are eager to sort out some reasons for these vacillations in narrative voice. Review of the *Rethorique* section in the *Confessio*'s book 7 and of some basic principles of Ciceronian orations promote the understanding that invention, arrangement, and style are rhetorical offices that solicit, confine, and characterize the poet's voice. In one of Gower's subtle responses to the rhetorical tradition, the many speakers in the beginning of the poem actually rise out of the expectation that the Ciceronian introduction please the hearers and render them attentive. The narrator of the prologue addresses issues, current events, and concerns that he shares with the audience but discovers the need for a new persona—Amans—to satisfy at least one reader—Richard—and the king's request for a poem to the court's taste. As students practice the rhetorical principles applied in the *Confessio Amantis*, they learn a new appreciation for Gower's craft and hear his compelling voice.

Gower before Chaucer: Narrative and Ethics in "The Tale of Tereus"

Leonard Koff

My title suggests that perhaps this essay reflects a purely ahistorical approach to teaching John Gower, an out-of-context approach, so unfashionable these days. And yet I want to argue that entering Gower's text through formalist literary criticism is the best way to situate him in his own time and to hear him in his own voice. Indeed I hope this essay provides those who teach Gower, as well as other late medieval English literature, with a window on the connection that should be drawn between the formal elements of Gower's English work, the *Confessio Amantis*, and the purpose he articulates in it. The theme of social discord, treated in all prologues to the *Confessio*, concludes with a wish for some singer like Arion, who brought harmony between Lords and Commons, to appear to the English nation:

> As if ther were such on [a person] now
> Which cowthe harpe [who could harp] as he tho dede
> He myhte availe in many a stede [place]
> To make pes wher now is hate.   (prologue, lines 1072–75)

For Gower, musical harmony is the sound—the expression—of social peace achieved, and because Gower imagines himself as the new Arion, the form that achieving peace takes in the *Confessio* is the "measured measures" of a storytelling discourse that promises social harmony by asking its readers to participate in the evaluation of values at a certain narrative distance.

I have singled out the *Confessio Amantis* in this essay because its place in English literary history ought first to depend on its literary pleasures—its pleasures of expression that support its exemplary purpose, the pleasures that establish Gower's independence as an author and make possible our considering Gower as more than a mere context for other Middle English writers.

Gower's English style has been likened, correctly, to the style of the English Augustans. Gower writes in octosyllabic couplets that, however, move thought forward at a pace that seems to make couplets go unnoticed. This accounts, I would argue, for the marked musicality of Gower's line. His diction is polished—one wants to say well-bred—a characteristic of a courtly style or of those who would speak to the court that yields a certain grace and directness, a telling limpidity, and a sometimes understatement, a species of wit, that rarely calls attention to itself. And these stylistic features serve Gower's wish to enable readers to evaluate human behavior at unruffled perspectives.

Gower is perhaps the most "used" of Middle English authors for those who would define medieval English literary tradition and rank authors within it. But if we want to talk about Gower's place in literary history, his actual as well as projected connections to English centers and peripheries of political power, or the relation between Gower and his "public purpose," then the soundest way is to establish what is of value about him in his own voice, as if he stood alone. From that first place of focus, students can begin to know something about his connection to late-fourteenth-century English "literary circles," which include Chaucer, to his presence in the Renaissance and beyond, as well as the Lancastrian use of Gower *and* Chaucer to establish a national literary vernacular and to frame power—to legitimate it—using a literature that imagines the community at a perspective that lets its harmonies and disharmonies be heard.

We have not been able, I think, to connect Gower's limitation of conceptual scope ("I may noght strecche up to the hevene / Min hand, ne setten al in evene / This world, which evere is in balance" ["I may not stretch up to the heavens / this hand of mine, nor set in balance / this world, which is ever subject to change"; *CA* 1.1–3]—not a retreat from large subjects but simply an envisioning of them where they play out destructively—with his transforming purpose because we have not quite understood the connection for Gower between form and content. Gower's thought—the articulation of his values in a calm register—seems to not entangle us in ethical and social rectification. Gower's reformist voice has disappeared in the *Confessio*, as has any vehement intervention into the moral or social values of the tales Genius tells. But if Genius is the moral guide to his stories, he is so because he keeps his stories at schematic removes. His speculative capacity in the text is not, admittedly, great. Rather he offers the clarity that the procedures of rectification provide: a summing up before or after stories are told. Moreover, Genius tells stories and positions them in their evaluative schema in the same voice. Gower sounds as if he will not be any immediate help; he only—merely?—categorizes. Indeed Genius avoids the speculation characteristic of Chaucer's narrators, who encourage entanglement in the text. Genius can sound too far from the issues of thought and behavior that he raises.

But this is misreading Gower and the subtle, original connection he makes between content and purpose. Gower's regularity of line—his ongoing, unruffled voice—is, for him, a perfect mode for breaking not the surface of a text but the concepts the text speaks. Indeed Gower, like us, though in different ways, values form that works against itself: for Gower's style lets students hear narratives as projections of clarity and coherence when they may not be. His storytelling creates the intellectual space in which moral and social problems can be brought to readers. Recognizing this—recognizing both the pleasures of Gower as an author and the way he achieves, or hopes to achieve, reform—makes him more accessible to students and more significant in the classroom.

To illustrate the connection I would draw between form and purpose and provide a specific example that would serve teachers and students of Gower, I want to look at the central passage of the tale Macaulay labels the "Tale of Tereus" (I would call it the "Tale of Tereus *and* Progne") from book 5 of the *Confessio*—Tereus's rape of Philomene—a passage that illustrates Gower's least valued literary technique as I have been describing it: his calm voice, particularly in the face of sensational events that should be condemned. The "Tale of Tereus," I would argue, is one of the clearest examples of what (erroneously) looks like a disconnect between story and application.

Unlike its source in Ovid or its analogue in its own day (Chaucer's "Legend of Philomela"), Gower's tale of Tereus and Progne presents itself as a conscious telling that removes a narrator's volatile response to his own work within that work itself. Gower has indeed created there the voice of "a man noght textueel" (ManT 235). Genius seems to have an evaluative blindness that suggests that Gower's eyes are really closed. By contrast, Chaucer's narrator is everywhere and is "all distress," a feature of Chaucer's connection to his text that is satisfying *just because* we see that Chaucer knows, even before he begins the "Legend of Philomela," what its values are and what its uses may be; indeed he draws some surprising applications from the legend: purely prudential ones that miss the mark or that serve other purposes. Chaucer's moral complexity issues from an adequate *and* inadequate narrator and finds expression as literary play. Gower's reflections on his own stories are both fair and serious, and although he has a sense of play and irony, he is not present in his own work in immediately prepossessing ways.

But Gower's conscious and persistent distancing from the horrifying events of the "Tale of Tereus," his refusal to engage in textual conversations about a story being told, his refusal to show himself, as it were, opens the "Tale of Tereus" to ethical, even ontological, analysis as well as psychological speculation in ways that Chaucer's volatile response in his "Legend of Philomela" does not. Teaching students to appreciate Gower's evaluative distance allows them to value the position Gower stakes out for the reform of Amans and his readership (with respect to the distinctions of love) as well as the position Gower takes up for the reform of his nation.

Tereus's sexual assault in Gower comes as a surprise to many students, though it is foreshadowed, and Progne's desires are as much an issue for Gower as Tereus's are.

> "I wole," he seide, "for thi sake
> The weie after thi soster take
> Miself, and bringe hire, if I may."
> And sche with that, there as he lay,
> Began him in hire armes clippe [embrace],
> And kist him with hir softe lippe,
> And seide, "Sire, grant mercy."
> And he sone after was redy,
> And tok his leve forte go;
> In sori [inauspicious] time dede he so.   (5.5587–96)

Gower gives his tale from the start a certain disingenuousness because he knows that we already know, before we begin reading Gower, that Tereus is a rapist. Tereus seems simply obliging when Progne asks him to bring her sister to

Thrace. This is occulting on Gower's part of Tereus's dark sexual nature, his desire for power that we only recognize in Gower after the rape of Philomene. But does Tereus's willingness to bring two sisters together reveal something darker still in his nature? or Progne's? Why indeed does she want her sister with her—suddenly want her? And why does the idea come to Progne while she is in bed with Tereus? We are not told, but we can conjecture. And if we do, we get a window into Progne's sexuality, as much as Tereus's. We can only begin to propose answers, of course, after Tereus's insatiability shows itself. Perhaps, then, Progne's "lusti lif" with Tereus (5572), and his with her, which sounded innocuous enough, is more gnarled than we thought, and this may account for the lead Progne takes in revenging her sister's rape.

When asked to bring Philomene to Progne, Tereus arrives in Athens without delay, without any real sense that he has journeyed there. He is, the text implies, singleminded; the immediacy of his presence in Athens suggests that he should be thought of as a bundle of desires—and hidden desires—whose connection to Philomene must be as uninterrupted as is his amatory response to Progne. His love errand to Philomene seems, and seems not to be, the innocent bidding of a brother-in-law.

But by not letting us know of Tereus's attraction to Philomene before Tereus and she are isolated on the boat returning to Thrace, Gower asks us to come to know Tereus, and indeed Progne, unprepared. Gower's "Tale of Tereus" works against our cultural knowledge; it hides Tereus's history and something of Progne's nature, too. This puts the sudden revelation of Tereus's inner nature in a virtually unexplained context, and it is in this context, where Gower has persistently hidden his sources (sources we know), that we have to struggle with the psychologically and morally inexplicable. Gower sees revelations of behavior as "first" problems of psychology and morality, for both Tereus and Progne. There is even, I would argue, a passing antifeminism in Gower's "Tale of Tereus," an implicit allusion to the Fall in Genesis, where woman leads man into sin. Gower wants us to experience both the psychological terrors and the moral chasms that sudden breaks in behavior open up for us. His conscious distance from his sources and his self-distancing as a storyteller have about them an innocence, a naïveté, that we finally cannot believe, and are not supposed to.

Tereus's sudden change on shipboard, where he and Philomene are alone in a moral crucible, as it were, is diabolical.

> And he with al his hole entente,
> Whan sche was fro hir frendes go,
> Assoteth [became infatuated] of hire love so,
> His yhe myhte he noght withholde,
> That he ne moste on hir beholde;
> And with the sihte he gan desire,
> And sette his oghne herte on fyre;
> And fyr, whan it to tow [straw] aprocheth,

To him anon the strengthe acrocheth [gathers],
Til with his hete it be devoured,
The tow ne mai noght be socoured [rescued].   (5616–26)

Tereus's mania — his self-consuming fire (Tereus is likened to straw on fire) — is revealed not so much as a change of behavior as a revelation of character, indeed a change of nature, an ontological change, and this opens issues of judgment that could not have been revealed had Gower already commented on them, registering the same moral outrage as Gower's audience does because we know the story of the rape of Philomene before we read it. "Assoteth" is Gower's usual description of passion that reason cannot restrain. The issue is not that Gower's audience would have registered no shock at what becomes sexual compulsion in Gower's version of Ovid's story but that Gower registers it coolly. This makes his tale *in its telling* an object of moral and psychosexual speculation as if from afar. Such a perspective lets students rush into moral evaluation because nothing is assumed in Gower's "Tale of Tereus." Gower deconstructs our expectations from the beginning. We should add that Gower ties Tereus's insatiable desire to his having forgotten that he is married (5627–33). Tereus's rape of Philomene is thus as much a compulsion as it is adultery; his love is unrestrained on several counts, and we need to puzzle out the relation between desire and the social institutions meant to manage, to contain, it. This is no small social issue.

Tereus's assault on Philomene takes place in a vacuum, as it were, at a narratively perfect distance. Where are the others on the ship? That no one seems to hear the rape gives to it a certain hermetic nature, airless and demanding; it is morally pressing. The implications that might be drawn from it or that ought to be drawn from it (Gower's indeterminacy may seem outrageous) are not articulated. As a rapist, Tereus is an example of the inexplicable behavior of rapine, the desire to have, to take, to ingest, and if this expression of his being is characterological, it is also ontological. Tereus's moral nature requires that he be a human being to demonstrate his theological distance from grace (5630). Tereus's rape of Philomene is already beyond a God-sustained world, and it is for this reason not entirely tied to Tereus's character. Tereus's rape reflects a lapse in the moral nature of nature itself.

Once raped, Philomene laments her change of state twice, the first time to Tereus directly, threatening to tell even the stone walls that enclose her should she be walled in (5665–68). Tereus's response is to cut out her tongue. When he returns home, bringing Philomene with him (he has her imprisoned), he tells Progne that her sister is dead, and she, in response, seeing him weep, puts on "blake clothes" (5724). But Gower adds, "So was ther guile under the gore" — deceit concealed under a gown (5730). This one line suggests that Progne is mourning for more than her sister's death, for she puts on black clothes "in worschipe of hir sostres mynde" (5726). Does Progne figuratively wear, as Philomene wore, the gown Tereus lifted? Philomene's second outcry, a prayer that is only thought, "[t]hogh sche be mouthe nothing preide" (5739), becomes a universal cry to Jupiter, to Tereus in absentia and, "withinne hir herte" (5740), to her sister. It is in a prison, literal and figurative, that Philomene weaves her story—and her outrage—into a "cloth of selk al whyt" (5770). For her, "wepinge is noght the bote [remedy]" for such "oultrages [outrages]" (5792–93). Philomene's change of state and the range of her emotions are forced on her because unrestrained desire—familial and social discord—has been let loose. This makes it possible for the "Tale of Tereus" to work as an example of moral speculation in the context of theological allusion and not merely as the story of one woman's rape. In this we can see the value of abstraction for ethical engagement. Gower's narrative, which is devoid of decor and a narrator's righteous (and right) response to his own tale, makes the reader the site of complexity. On some level, Gower's "Tale of Tereus" finally becomes not a telling but a showing, a speculum, continuously making room for queries, and complex ones at that.

What, for example, is the relation between rape, a species of rapine for Gower, and eating? As an act of revenge, Tereus is fed his own son. Why indeed serve him this food? Serving it is meant, I think, to violate the integrity of Tereus's family; this is implicitly social revenge, just as the rape of Philomene is a violation, in Progne's mind, of her bond with her sister, an erotic connection that marriage has not transformed,

> Whan he myn oughne soster tok
> And me that am his wif forsook.   (5841–42)

It is also ironic, I think, that Progne becomes the agent for moral punishment. The rape of Philomene is in the end not only about sexuality but about disruptive power, which is, of course, consonant with our modern view of rape. Rape for Gower is a species of rapine, of plunder, of "taking," of having Tereus "take," ingest, be gratified on several levels, a species of social hatred that requires revenge. Tereus is thus made to "eat his own son":

> Himself devoureth ayein kinde,
> As he that was tofore unkinde.   (5905–06)

He is turned into the ravenous being he fundamentally is. In this way Tereus enacts his own nature; this is Progne's revenge, which enlightens us.

Let me conclude by bringing Gower and Chaucer together in a mode of analysis that this essay at first argued against. But in the light of what I hope I have isolated about Gower, placing Gower and Chaucer together in the same classroom will not cause Gower to fall. Indeed he can stand up to the rigors and pleasures of literary inquiry because he offers in his reading of the story of Tereus and Progne a view of human behavior that sees it as both the cause of the derangements of love and the site for understanding love's darker paths. Unlike Gower's "Tale of Tereus," Chaucer's "Legend of Philomela" already assumes answers to questions not yet asked, and this closes off the "Legend" in significant ways. The work opens with an indictment of creation itself before one actually hears the story of Tereus and Philomela, which indicts Tereus. Chaucer's legend calls into question the world's moral logic—God's logic—in creating Tereus. Tereus is described as a disgrace to humankind ("slaunder of man" [2231]), which suggests that Tereus was implicitly free to not do what he did.

Chaucer's legend indicts, too, the moral logic of transformation that *preserves* depraved identity. These questions, which reach to heaven, place the "Legend of Philomela" in a metaphysically disturbing context that recalls the indictment of creation in Dorigen's complaint against the existence of the "rokkes blake" (FranT). The "Legend of Philomela" is thus not initially about redefining or indeed understanding events, except in a sense that assumes we know what Tereus did; why he did what he did is put in a context so large than Tereus as a site of psychosexual and moral complexity disappears. For Chaucer, he is merely a deranged being.

Chaucer thus interposes himself between a story from another book and his own readers in ways that Gower does not. Chaucer stands between his story and his readers, who, I think, take their cue from him. Chaucer is a guide in his own text. He leads with judgments both before he begins the "Legend" and in the course of telling it. He registers dismay at Tereus's very existence in a world that should not accommodate Tereus's existence; he reveals disgust at Tereus's behavior, pity at Philomela's violation. This makes the "Legend of Philomela" less open for the kind of pure moral and psychosexual speculation than Gower's "Tale of Tereus." Philomela's rape takes place in a cave, not on a ship—the cave a hidden place that does not sustain the illusion that Tereus is fetching his wife's sister in a husbandly way. Rather, Chaucer's cave is a place in which Philomela quakes "for fere, pale and pitously" (2317), a figurative feminine space that affords her no protection but that gives way, as it were, to a rhetoric of pathos. Gower starkly connects Tereus's entrance into Philomene with her raised gown; she is at risk "under gore."

The actual conclusion of Chaucer's "Legend" is a curious retreat of sorts; it moves from theological indictment to prudential caution, even paranoia. Chaucer suggests that his "Legend of Philomela" is intended for a company of women: that Philomela's rape gives women the opportunity to be aware of, or to beware of, all men, "Ye may be war of men, if that yow liste" (2387). And this suggests, I think, that the "Legend of Philomela," like all the legends of good women, had indeed an occasional setting, a court setting among women. Chaucer's metaphysical opening is finally not consonant with a tale about abuse. His "Legend" is finally alarmist.

In short, Chaucer's "Legend of Philomela" is proleptic in ways that Chaucer usually isn't. The "Legend" points to its meaning, or meanings, even before it speaks: an indictment, on the one hand, a moralized telling (a warning), on the other, less open than Gower's to deep questions, less intellectually complex than Gower's—we don't puzzle out the moral connection between rape and eating, for example — and less shocking than Gower's; its pathos closes down questions. The "Legend of Philomela" is more determinate than Gower's "Tale of Tereus," very much a performance, more personal than Gower's, and its treatment of Philomela more sentimental.

Indeed, we can imagine the "Legend of Philomela" as having been written for a real occasion, for the prologue to the *Legend of Good Women* says that the legends Chaucer is commanded to write are to be given to Queen Anne (F 496), perhaps at an occasion where she presides. We should add that the line, "For I am wery of hym for to telle" (2258), usually taken to argue that Chaucer tired of writing all the legends of good women, means in the context of the "Legend of Philomela" that Chaucer is made weak by the story of the rape of Philomela, even before he tells it. Who wouldn't be? It is a terrible violation. Line 2258 is thus another appearance of Chaucer's moral presence in his own work, figured as a physical effect on his person.

If indeed students are deepened with an appreciation of Gower's gifts for moral and psychological analysis, his conceptual way to moral reform — and I hope this essay has contributed to that — comparing Chaucer and Gower reveals Gower in a very sophisticated, indeed daring light. And if Chaucer's *Legend of Good Women* has not commanded the sympathy of Chaucerians because it does not rise to Chaucer's heights of speculative play in his other works, the reason may be that Chaucer's *Legend* reflects something of the anxiety of influence that Gower's presence, which has yet to be valued by us, may have awakened in his friend. My argument has been, of course, that teaching Gower clearly requires setting his work in the literary circles of his own day, where he may have led rather than followed. To do so, we should read him alone, and only then in the context of others who talked to him and with whom he talked. This is seeing Gower and his literary circles in the history that Gower would transform.

Gower's Triple Tongue (1): Teaching across Gower's Languages

Siân Echard

Gallica lingua prius, Latina secunda, set ortus
Lingua tui pocius Anglica complet opus.

But French, then Latin stirred your tongue,
That, last and best, in English sung.
— "Eneidos Bucolis"[1]

I have never taught an undergraduate course with exclusive focus on John Gower, and the perils of teaching Gower in a survey course or a Chaucer-centric course will be familiar to readers of this volume. Gower is often worked into a course on Chaucer by means of analogues: one reads, say, The Wife of Bath's Tale alongside the "Tale of Florent," or one compares the characterization of Amans with that of Chaucer's dreamers. This kind of comparison has a long history, and it has never been a particularly advantageous one for Gower. The first summary of this reception was John H. Fisher's, in *John Gower: Moral Philosopher and Friend of Chaucer* (1–36), and it was followed by Derek Pearsall's "The Gower Tradition" and by my own introduction to *A Companion to Gower*. Even students without many preconceptions—who do not know that they are meant to find Gower dull or moralistic or contemptibly conservative in his politics—know that Chaucer is famous and Gower is not.

However, Gower—and more particularly, Gower's trilingualism, which is my focus here—*can* in fact frame a survey course, becoming a touchstone and recurrent point of reference. In what follows I suggest how Gower's "triple tongue" allows us to point students toward issues of significance for the reading not only of Gower but also of Middle English literature more generally. And in such a context, Gower becomes central rather than peripheral. I organize these issues under four main headings: Material Culture, Manuscripts, Multilingualism, and Authority. Throughout I call attention to literary history and issues of editing. The sections that follow do not describe the whole of a syllabus; rather, each explains a single class or part of a class. These are modules that can be scattered throughout a syllabus, whether of a half- or full-year course.

Material Culture

We begin at the end, with Gower's tomb. Because I am a book historian and because I have found that old objects interest my students, I often circulate a copy of Henry J. Todd's *Illustrations of the Lives and Writings of Gower and Chaucer*, a book that includes engravings of both Gower's and Chaucer's tombs, but which gives pride of place, despite its title, to Chaucer. I also show three slides. The first shows Chaucer's monument in Westminster Abbey and the second, Gower's tomb in Southwark Cathedral. The third slide, for John Lydgate, shows a blank monument upon which I superimpose William Dunbar's famous lines, in *The Goldyn Targe*, about the three laureate poets of the English Middle Ages (lines 253–70). I highlight the connection that Alexandra Gillespie makes between Lydgate's print history and the lack of a physical monument to the poet, and I point students toward the discussions of Chaucer's tomb in Derek Pearsall's "Chaucer's Tomb: The Politics of Reburial," Joseph Dane's *Who Is Buried in Chaucer's Tomb? Studies in the Reception of Chaucer's Book*, and Thomas Prendergast's *Chaucer's Dead Body*. The contrast between Chaucer and Lydgate, particularly when accompanied by modern criticism linking Chaucer's monument with the monumentality of Chaucer studies, sets the stage for Gower and for his singularity. Lydgate lacks both a monument and a tradition (the recent renewal of interest notwithstanding); Chaucer's monument is of a piece with the desire of later tradition to canonize him (in the secular, literary sense)—but Gower's tomb is clearly the poet's own statement, his summary of his poetic career, his staking of his own posterity.

Archaeological work on Gower's tomb and on Southwark and Saint Mary Overeys (Hines, Cohen, and Roffey; Epstein) allows me to map for students a precise physical location for the tomb, putting it in a highly meaningful context from which we can extrapolate much about Gower's positioning—as a city poet, as a moral poet, and, most important for me, as a trilingual poet determined to carry that reputation beyond the grave. We focus first on the books upon which the effigy's head rests, and their Latinate titles open a discussion of the role of Latin in medieval culture. At this point I introduce "Eneidos Bucolis," and while I offer my own (verse) translation, I also show the class the Latin. I tend, with R. F. Yeager, to believe that this poem is Gower's own (Yeager, "John Gower's Audience" 93), even though G. C. Macaulay suggests that the author might have been Ralph Strode—the same "philosophical Strode" to whom Chaucer directed *Troilus and Criseyde* (4.419). Even if the poem is not Gower's, it indicates clearly how successfully, in his own lifetime or immediately afterward, Gower had built his reputation on his mastery of three tongues. I point out to students that the prose *Quia unusquisque* that appears in many Gower manuscripts moves, as "Eneidos Bucolis" also does, through the three languages—while the colophon lacks the overtly triumphalist assertion that English is the "last and best" of Gower's tongues, colophon and poem share the insistence that Gower's unique poetic contribution is to be found at least in part in his mastery of three languages. We move back, then, to the tomb, to discuss the French text and figures, and these I then connect to the *Mirour de l'omme*. The tomb figures offer an opportunity to introduce the *Mirour* and to discuss its possible audience. Students can explore the connections between French and court culture (underlined by the collar worn by the effigy) and the role of poetry and patronage in the period.

The tomb performs one final service, and that is to point from the remains in stone to the remains in parchment of the Latin indulgence. Folio 129r of Glasgow University Library MS Hunter 59 features a painting of a tomb, along with the text of the indulgence and the epitaph that also appear on the tomb. The more famous image in this manuscript is the full-page illustration of an archer shooting at the globe of the world (a figure that appears as well in British Library MS Cotton Tiberius A.iv and in Huntington Library MS HM 150), sometimes referred to as an author portrait. This is a manuscript of the *Vox clamantis* and the *Cronica tripertita*, along with some of the poet's other Latin and French pieces. I use my own translation of the epitaph, a translation that, I freely admit, occasionally bends sense in favor of rhyme:

> Armigeri scutum nichil ammodo fert sibi tutum
> Reddidit immo lutum morti generale tributum
> Spiritus exutum se gaudeat esse solutum
> Est vbi virtutum regnum sine labe statutum.

> Henceforth the shield no shelter yields
> To th'armèd one. Instead the clay
> Grants death his day, the tribute done.
> The naked soul rejoices all
> In its release: in virtue's realm
> It's 'stablishèd, never to cease.   (Echard, "Last Words" 99)

While there might still be some discussion about "Eneidos Bucolis," there is little doubt that the epitaph (along with all the arrangements for the tomb) is Gower's own, and it is useful to connect the stone and ink versions of the piece.

Manuscripts

Once I have introduced Hunter 59, a manuscript focused on Gower's Latin works, the way is now clear for me to introduce and discuss the representation of Gower's multilingualism in manuscript.

The *Mirour* survives in Cambridge University Library Additional MS 3035. The poem was not formally identified until 1895, when Macaulay, in consultation with the librarian of the Cambridge University Library, recognized it in the manuscript acquired by the library in 1891 (1: lxviii). The *Cinkante balades* are preserved in British Library Additional MS 59495 (the Trentham manuscript), and the *Traitié* survives in thirteen manuscripts (Pearsall, "Manuscripts"). The solitary manuscript survival of the *Mirour* and the *Cinkante balades* might suggest that Gower's French was less significant to his own age than his English work, but there are two teaching points to be made here. One has to do with underlining the vagaries of manuscript transmission: I point to the occasional mismatch between manuscript survivals and our estimation of medieval poetry more generally (one copy of *Sir Gawain and the Green Knight*, an acknowledged masterpiece, against 115 copies of *The Prick of Conscience*, for example). Another has to do with Gower's own repeated insistence on the significance of his French work. I take this opportunity to underline the number and generally high quality of surviving Gower manuscripts, and I tell the class that while Gower's reputation today tends to rest on the English *Confessio Amantis*, the manuscripts that survive often combine more than one language, whether in the Latin framing of the *Confessio* or in the common pattern of manuscripts with more than one work. I then turn to the Trentham manuscript, a collection of pieces in Latin, French, and English.

Like Gower's tomb, this manuscript is a physical object from which various lessons about Gower's oeuvre and its survival can be spun—lessons that extend beyond Gower. I show my students images not only of the manuscript but also of the eighteenth-century transcription made for the aristocratic Gower family and of the early-nineteenth-century Roxburghe Club printing of Gower's *Cinkante balades*, done from this manuscript by another noble Gower (Echard, *Printing* 97–125). The facsimile frontispiece to this latter printing reproduces various provenance signatures found in the manuscript, linking it to Thomas, third Baron Fairfax and, it was thought, to Henry VII. This reproduction of the signatures underlines the role of aristocratic owners and collectors in the survival of many medieval texts—the Gowers believed themselves to be the descendants of John Gower, owned several manuscripts of his work, and had a vested interest in preserving them; the same nineteenth-century Lord Gower who owned the Stafford manuscript of Gower's *Confessio* also owned what is now the Huntington Ellesmere-Stafford copy of *The Canterbury Tales*. Depending on the syllabus and on student interests, it is then possible to spend some time discussing ownership and readership of medieval vernacular manuscripts more generally, and the comparison of Gower with Chaucer here does not, for once, immediately disadvantage Gower. Whether the Trentham manuscript was an actual presentation copy for Henry IV's coronation or an exemplar for such a copy, it is clear that Gower chose to stake his poetic reputation on his multilingual abilities.

Multilingualism

Any Middle English course I teach invariably needs to include an overview of the state of English in the later Middle Ages. The Trentham collection points to a simple fact that students often find surprising: that is, that English was not the only, or even always the most significant, of the languages in medieval Britain, even toward the end of the fourteenth century. My touchstone here is the opening Latin verse of the *Confessio Amantis*, in which the poet promises to sing in Hengest's tongue, with the help of Carmenta, the goddess who invented the Latin language. Gower's Latin framing of his great English poem points in part to different kinds of audiences, and we discuss the role of Latin in clerical and scholarly culture more generally. I show my students images of pages from *Confessio* manuscripts, alongside images from glossed scholarly texts and glossed Bibles, to give them a general sense of what the treatment of languages on the page might signal to a medieval reader in terms of authority. At the same time, I am careful not to leave the impression of Latin as a monolith; as tempting as is Mikhail Bakhtin's notion of the "word of the fathers" (342), the idea of a hierarchy of languages tends sometimes to blur the playful and even subversive qualities of much medieval Latin (particularly Latin political satire, a genre that is important if one is to understand fully Gower's own political positioning). We then talk about reading practice in a manuscript culture. My examples here are the later *Confessio* manuscripts—the majority—in which the Latin glosses move into the text column, often in red ink. Joyce Coleman's thoughts about the value of these Latin headings to prelectors are useful here ("Lay Readers") as are the (very occasional) manuscript notes that suggest social reading contexts, like the tendency to number the questions in the "Tale of the Three Questions" (Pearsall, "Manuscripts" 95–97). The famous passage from *Troilus and Criseyde* in which Criseyde and her ladies are seen reading from a romance helps clarify for students that a medieval reader's experience of a text, no matter what its language, was often very different from what they are accustomed to. The Latin framing of Gower's *Confessio Amantis*, then, can be mapped over the poet's knowledge and expectation of manuscript culture: Gower might well have expected a range of reading practices, and he might have produced a text to address a range of possible audiences.

We discuss other manifestations of England's linguistic complexity in the period, such as the macaronic passages in *Piers Plowman*, the dialectal jokes in Chaucer's Reeve's Tale, the French of Chaucer's Prioress, and the complicated situation of the law courts, in which pleadings could occur in one language and be recorded in another. A simple explanation for Gower's trilinguality, then, might seem to be that it offered a kind of insurance—that English was not yet the obvious victor, that it lacked the snob appeal of French or Latin. Certainly it is clear that royal and noble readers were still consuming French romances during Gower's period, and to the *litteratus* still meant to be able to read and write in Latin. Gower himself opens the Henrician version of the *Confessio* by apparently suggesting the lowly status of English:

> And for that fewe men endite [write]
> In oure englissh, I thenke [plan to] make
> A bok for Engelondes sake,
> The yer sextenthe of kyng Richard.   (prologue, lines 22–25)

Perhaps the point here is that English is not yet serving as a national (nation-building, nation-asserting) language, and sometimes these lines will lead to a class discussion about the links between language and nationalism. Students can address the arguments of Thorlac Turville-Petre's *England the Nation*, Derek Pearsall's "The Idea of Englishness in the Fifteenth Century," and Andrew Galloway's "Latin England" under this heading. But in any case, whether nationalism is at issue or not, it was not strictly true to suggest that "fewe men" were writing poetry—or even courtly poetry—in English in the 1390s (the sixteenth year of Richard's reign, according to Gower), and it was in fact even later that Gower made that particular claim, since the Ricardian version of the prologue is actually less linguistically specific than the Henrician revision, stressing instead the novelty of "som newe thing" and the Horatian combination of teaching and delight [line 51* [p. 4]). Similarly, the simplicity claimed by the speaker of the Ricardian version has become the assertion that the author is "a burel clerk" (52) in the Henrician; in other words, as we approach a period when English has most definitively won the day, the pose adopted in the prologue to Gower's great English poem becomes apparently *less* confident. It seems, then, that we must search for more complicated answers to the "why" question. Tim William Machan's essay on Gower and medieval multilingualism can be introduced to graduate students and perhaps advanced undergraduates at this point, and then it is time to engage directly with some passages that underline what I think is at issue here, and that is the idea of poetic authority.

Authority

In configuring authority for my students as meaning, in Gower's terms, the right and obligation to speak, I turn to several short passages in his three languages, each of them exemplifying an anxiety that is to be set against the impression created by our discussion of Gower's material and manuscript remains. In stone and parchment, Gower seems to root his reputation in his linguistic mastery, but once we leave "Eneidos Bucolis" behind, his actual representation of language and its functioning is considerably more fraught. In the *Mirour*, Falssemblant, one of the daughters of Envy, is described as having two tongues (3517–20). These physical tongues are not, of course, specifically assigned to any one language, but the point about dangerous tongues is clear and persistent: the poet's first (Latin) plea in the *Confessio* is to be protected from wicked tongues. Many of the personified sins in the early part of the *Mirour* are specifically related to deceptive and dangerous speech; a short list includes Hypocrisy, Vainglory, Flattery, Boasting, Detraction, Malebouche, Falsseeming, Perjury, Treachery, Deceit, Fraud, Malengin, and Conspiracy. The *Mirour*, then, presents language as frequently dangerous, part of the fallen world of the flesh so repeatedly (and futilely) addressed by the soul in the opening lines of the poem. The exhortation "He, Char" ("Ah, flesh") precedes thousands of lines of (French) verse whose didacticism can easily project smug confidence, but we discuss how the poem concludes in prayer, and we look at the suggestion that the best prayer is often silent (10383–86). I then turn the discussion to Gower's discomfort with aure-ate language in the *Vox clamantis*, where poetic tongues themselves are suspect (lines 1065–70).

In the *Vox*, as in the *Mirour*, we find the poetic voice ultimately turning to prayer and to silence, despite the thousands of multilingual lines already writ-ten. What, then, to make of Gower's glorying in his linguistic attainments? If he is indeed the author of the "Eneidos Bucolis," are we to conclude that finally, in the *Confessio*, Gower arrived at a place from which he found the authority to speak? Was English, the last of his three tongues, the language in which he decided to stake that claim?

In the *Confessio Amantis*, Gower offers the story of the Tower of Babel as the emblem for the division that corrupts the world:

> Wherof divided anon ryht
> Was the langage in such entente,
> Ther wiste [knew] non what other mente,
> So that thei myhten noght procede.   (prologue 1022–25)

I draw students' attention to the fact that the English in these lines is less spe-cific than the Latin marginalia, with their reference to Hebrew as a first, origi-nary language:

> Qualiter in edificacione turris Babel, quam in dei contemptum Nembrot erexit, lingua prius hebraica in varias linguas celica vindicta dividebatur.

> How in the building of the tower of Babel, which Nimrod raised in con-tempt of God, language, once Hebrew, was divided by heavenly vengeance into various tongues.   (lines 1018–26 [p. 252])[2]

The English presents the consequences of Nimrod's pride as a fatal failure of communication, while the Latin underlines the corruption of a pristine linguis-tic singularity, but in both cases, it is suggested that the *reason* the flesh will never hear the soul is that it can no longer do so or will to do so. The prologue's pessimism concludes with the wistful appeal for a new Arion, and it is of course tempting, and probably right, to suggest that Gower is trying on the harpist's role for himself. My concern here, however, is to argue that the role is not quite as comfortable as we might have been led by the tomb to think. Macaulay was singularly *not* intrigued, as I am (and as Machan is), by Gower's languages, writing instead that

> Gower, in fact, was a man of stereotyped convictions, whose thoughts on human society and on the divine government of the world tended con-stantly to repeat themselves in but slightly varying forms. What he had said in one language he was apt to repeat in another.   (1: xxxvi)

To me, however, this repetition speaks to a searching, one that preoccupied Gower throughout his poetic life. In framing Gower's trilingualism as part of a quest for poetic authority, I can then broaden the focus to the larger context of the survey class and discuss how medieval writers might have viewed their opportunities, responsibilities, and limitations as creative artists.

At this point, I return once more to the pairing of Gower's tomb and his Latin verse—in this case, the poem "Quicquid homo scribat":

> Quicquid homo scribat, finem natura ministrat,
> Que velut vmbra fugit, nec fugiendo redit;
> Illa michi finem posuit, quo scribere quicquam
> Vlterius nequio, sum quia cecus ego.
> Posse meum transit, quamuis michi velle remansit;
> Amplius vt scribat hoc michi posse negat.   (*Complete Works* 4: 365)

> Whatever man may write, it's Nature writes the end;
> Who like a shadow flees, nor fleeing, comes again.
> She's dealt my end to me; I'm blind; and nevermore
> And nowhere will I write—for though my will remains,
> My power's gone, and all I long for, she denies.   (Echard, "Gower's" 149)

In these Latin lines Gower falls silent, ceding to the inevitable death of the flesh. But the tomb and its trilingual claims remain to posterity, and certainly that tomb remained an object of conversation for antiquarians through the early modern period.

I make use of *Early English Books Online* to show my class that only the *Confessio Amantis* was published in the first age of print (although in their sixteenth-century printings both William Caxton and Thomas Berthelette did preserve much of Gower's Latin framing). I circulate the second volume of Thomas Warton's *History*, which prints four of the *balades*, while mentioning the fact that most of Gower's work had to wait until the nineteenth century to see print, and even then first appeared in what we might think of as amateur rather than professional contexts. This point allows an opening to talk about the recovery of Middle English more generally, and I have found David Matthews's *The Making of Middle English* helpful here. Because this discussion occurs in the context of a survey course, I can then return to my opening slides (or online images) from the tomb discussion and point to the differing reception histories of Chaucer, Gower, and Lydgate. I spend time on the later nineteenth century and on the transition from amateur to professional editing; depending on time and interest, I might underline current editorial issues (the struggle between Ellesmere and Hengwrt, for example, fits nicely here, not least because the students will remember that *other*, Gowerian, Ellesmere manuscript). To draw attention to the crucial role of editors in creating and preserving literary reputations, I point to the difference between the available texts for other authors on the syllabus (Chaucer, the *Gawain* poet, Malory) and for Gower. I do tell my students how much easier it is to teach Gower now, thanks to the ever-growing number of TEAMS volumes; at the same time, I let them know that Macaulay's remains the only complete edition of Gower's works. I then show them the effects on reading of some apparently simple decisions made by Macaulay: the below-the-line printing of the Ricardian version of the *Confessio*, certainly, but, even more important, the division of Gower's works into French, English, and Latin volumes. The tomb has shown us that Gower to some extent thought of his work this way as well, but the manuscript record suggests a far more active multilingualism. A combination of materials, languages, and literary history, then, can give students a more complicated—and perhaps more complete—sense of both Gower and his age.

NOTES

[1] The quotation is from "Eneidos Bucolis," lines 11–12, printed in Gower, *Complete Works*. The translation is my own.

[2] Citations to the Latin marginalia are to Macaulay's edition, and translations are my own.

Gower's Triple Tongue (2):
Teaching the *Balades*

R. F. Yeager

John Gower's *Cinkante balades* and *Traitié pour essampler les amantz marietz* are unique and important in several ways. The *Cinkante balades* in particular presents a side of the poet that is very different from the "moral Gower" — narrow and preachy — that students and many of their teachers reflexively have come to accept. Gower's *balades* are among the most ambitious projects undertaken in Anglo-French by an English poet at the end of the fourteenth century. They are also the sole examples known of sequentially linked poems written by an Englishman, in English or French, before Philip Sidney's sonnet sequence *Astrophil and Stella*. Doubtless, had Gower elected to compose his *balades* in English instead of in French, our sense of the development of letters in England would be different altogether — a point that itself suggests a viable instructive avenue. Notable for teachers and students alike, however, is the fact that Gower did choose French — strong indication that in the London he inhabited he felt he had an audience for his work. Gower's *balades* thus furnish a solid keystone for fruitful discussions of late medieval multilingualism and an across-the-channel aesthetic and intellectual influence and exchange. In the classroom they have other advantages too. All are thoroughly well crafted (hence they offer accessible examples of then-popular *formes fixes* verse for discussions of style), and many of them — especially in the *Cinkante balades* — can be amusing, even moving, in their depiction of affairs of the heart. Nor, at between twenty-one and twenty-seven lines each, should their short length be overlooked. In surveys, when so much must be compressed into so little time, brevity accompanied by rich possibilities for discussion is always desirable. And fortunately now both the *Traitié* and the *Cinkante balades* are available from the TEAMS Middle English Texts Series, in an inexpensive, facing-page translation, with an introduction and textual and explanatory notes.

 With many possible directions to take a class using the *balades*, selecting just a few to highlight perhaps best suits the present compact space. Basic to any choice might be a recognition of how the *Cinkante balades* and the *Traitié* differ. The former (actually numbering fifty-four) is a true sequence, in that, like Petrarch's *Rime*, Sidney's *Astrophil and Stella*, or Spenser's *Amoretti*, the individual poems collectively follow the course of an affair between two lovers — in Gower's case, unnamed. The eighteen *balades* of the *Traitié*, however, are technically not a sequence — though they are most often so called, for convenience, one supposes. They are topically, not narratively, connected: all are concerned to establish the nature and role of sanctified marriage, most particularly by warding off adultery. The *Traitié* poems have much in common with the

Confessio Amantis, sharing *in parvo* many of the same exempla found there in longer form (e.g., Hercules and Deineira, David and Bathsheba, Lancelot and Guinevere, Tristram and Isolde, Tereus and Progne), as well as Latin prose commentaries in the margins. Indeed, it seems apparent that Gower intended the *Confessio* and the *Traitié* to be seen as companionate works, connected through their parallel narratives and Latin commentaries—an observation underscored by the many surviving manuscripts in which the *Traitié balades*, codalike, follow the *Confessio*. (Indeed, no manuscripts are known where the *Traitié balades* stand alone.)

Thus the unique natures of the *balade* collections themselves suggest clear teaching opportunities. Side-by-side reading of shorter versions of the same narratives from the *Traitié* and longer from the *Confessio* (and the Latin prose commentaries attendant in each, which emphasize different aspects) can bring Gower's abilities as a storyteller into sharp focus—a unit with potential for subsequent comparison with Chaucer's narratives and with (for example) *Pearl* or *Sir Gawain and the Green Knight*. Comparing the *Traitié* and the *Confessio* versions facilitates discussion of variant audiences, as well: what sort of reader—of what occupation, what level of education, from what economic circumstances— did Gower envision for these narratives in French and English? Also found in the TEAMS edition of the *balades* is a translation made by one otherwise anonymous "Quixley" of the *Traitié* poems into fifteenth-century Yorkshire dialect (plus a nineteenth *balade* Quixley apparently composed himself). While Quixley was more an energetic than an accurate translator, his work provides a rare glimpse of a late medieval reader engaged with a contemporary writer. Quixley's versions too can furnish a class with interesting comparative opportunities. Who might Quixley have been? For whom was he translating? Why did he feel he needed to do so? Does his hailing from Yorkshire instead of London have any bearing on his translation project? (This last question could easily lead into a class discussion on the differences between London and the rest of England in the early fifteenth century.)

The *Cinkante balades* opens up other topics, especially the close literary interrelationship of England and France. The *balade* form itself is borrowed from the French, and Gower had as much influence as anyone, Chaucer included, on its becoming the most popular of the so-called *formes fixes*—essentially the *balade*, the virelay, the rondeau, and the carol—in England. Obviously in class readings that include medieval lyric or a near-contemporary writer of *balades* like Charles d'Orléans (who was imprisoned in England for twenty-four years and died in 1465), the *Cinkante balades* represents an accessible, attractive inclusion. Again too, the difference between the *balades* of the *Traitié* and of the *Cinkante balades* offers a teachable opportunity. Those of the former, all without a concluding four-line envoy, seem modeled primarily on the practice of the late-fourteenth-century French master Guillaume de Machaut; those of the latter, with envoys, more after the slightly younger poet Eustache Deschamps.

Also, certain of the *balades* of the *Cinkante balades* have lines discoverable in troubadour lyrics of an earlier era—an observation valuable as a lead-in to discussion not only of interconnections that took place in Languedoc between music and poetry (a subject accessible all the more directly through Machaut) but also of what was meant by "originality" in the Middle Ages. Juxtaposition with *balades* of Christine de Pisan (a contemporary about whom Gower probably knew and whose work in translation is readily available) can further a consideration of influence and encourage awareness of an important woman of letters and her work too.

Although the *balades* of the *Traitié,* with their uncompromising moralizing and occasionally knotty theological arguments, can strike some students as austere, the lovers of the *Cinkante balades* usually prompt an opposite response. Gower brings a man and a woman to life through their interchange of poems, he to her for most of them and she responding in 41–43 that he has been unfaithful and unworthy of her love. In 44 she either takes him back or—the more likely possibility—looks toward a second lover, who praises her in 45. When she accepts him in 46, he rejoices in 47. The remaining four *balades* are in the poet's voice, addressing and honoring love. The course of the sequence, traceable by seasonal references (Christmas and the New Year, Saint Valentine's Day, etc.), spans roughly two years. In the process Gower's fictive lover passes through all the phases of "courtly love"—sighing, moaning, begging the lady to soften her heart—and provides thereby excellent entrée into that ubiquitous, and therefore essential, discourse. Connections can easily be made with Machaut (his *Voirdit,* built also around a poetic correspondence between a man and a woman, is an evident precursor), with Petrarch's persona, with Elizabethan sonneteers, and even with the epistolary novel of Richardson and others. The lady, moreover, is by no means a pushover—rather, she defends her right to decent treatment acerbically and vigorously; she thus presents a discussable model of an eloquent, thoughtful woman, which opens the door to a variety of contrasts and comparisons.

The *balades* are useful too as beginning points for political discussion. One approach is to call attention to the envoy of *balade* 51 of *Cinkante balades*, in which Gower in his own voice praises "gentile Engleterre" blessed by the "noble Roi Henris" come to the throne to rule in "peas, honour, joie et prosperité" (*Complete Works* 1: 378). The sentiments flow from Gower's affection for his country and also from close associations with the Lancastrian house that extend into the early 1380s and continue through Richard II's deposition and Henry's usurpation in 1399–1400. Although it is less clear when the *Traitié* poems were completed, the *Cinkante balades* would appear to have been written with the future Henry IV in mind, in or around 1390, while he was still Earl of Derby and jousting in France with French peers during a truce in the Hundred Years' War. The sole copy extant of the *Cinkante balades* is contained in British Library MS Additional 59495, a carefully chosen and copied selection of Gower's work in all three languages that, as its heraldic devices show, was prepared for a Lancastrian family member. Because of such multiple links to events of great political importance and to the Lancastrians, the *Cinkante balades* especially lends itself to teaching about premiere events and figures shaping the decades on both sides of the century.

Learning Gower by Editing Gower

Erick Kelemen

At the end of *Confessio Amantis*, John Gower writes, "Explicit iste liber, qui transeat obsecro liber / Ut sine livore vigeat lectoris in ore"—which, in Andrew Galloway's translation, runs, "Here ends this book, and may it, I implore, travel free / so that without a bruise it may thrive in the reader's ear" (1: p. 227).[1] Joyce Coleman, the author of *Public Reading and the Reading Public*, might tell us whether Gower wants his *Confessio* to thrive in the reader's ear ("aure") or mouth ("ore"), but it is the other pun, on "book" and "free" ("liber"), that makes this antepenultimate distich an ideal beginning for thinking about how to use textual questions to teach Gower's works. The book offers words freedom to travel, but Gower is anxious about the bruises ("livore") his text might sustain in transmission, the variations that come with living too freely, as it were, "lectoris in ore." And so he falls back on the vain hope to protect his words after publication by sending yet more words after them. The trope will be foreign to most students, who have mass-culture beliefs about their books, objects that appear unbidden and as though from nowhere on bookstore shelves. But they can understand that their textbooks have a history, one they believe might begin with a reader who marred its pages with highlighters before selling it back. Students expect that the textbook contains *the* answers, that it is not simply credible but correct. Having students investigate the documents editors consult and the choices their texts' editors make when faced with textual variation begins to expose that history to students and to challenge the notion of the infallible text. I aim not to make my students sophisticated textual editors but to instill in them textual skepticism. And assignments drawn from textual criticism do more than that.

It is no wonder that, as undergraduates and graduate students come to learn of textual criticism and its theories, something about it sits uneasily with them. Though the traditional understanding of textual criticism is that it aims to bring stability, studying textual criticism is itself profoundly destabilizing to mass-culture notions of textuality. Each time I help a class learn to decode textual notes, I have at least one student for whom the implications are an epistemological crisis, driven by the discovery that no text comes to students unmediated. Contemporary culture holds that in a book a reader can find communion with a great author's mind. Studying textual criticism endangers that idea of communion. Textual criticism challenges students with the history of the text before it arrived in the books that they buy, a history often not simple or clear or certain. Other hands have been involved in bringing that text to them, hands that may have been diligent and honest but that have one way or another effected changes. In discussions students often seem comfortable with the idea that a wiki, like *Wikipedia*, can be a multiply authored, constantly shifting text whose content and changes to it are discussed in its "back pages," but when the same idea is applied to their canonical authors, something profound shifts in their minds. The crises students experience are nevertheless ultimately productive, opening new possibilities for them as readers and thinkers.

Russell A. Peck's TEAMS edition of Gower's *Confessio* is gentle but unrelenting in bringing students to these moments of productive crisis. The *Confessio's* revision history is preserved in more than one manuscript recension, and Peck, instead of privileging one over another, prints some of the variations in parallel-text format. Parallel-text editions foreground what John Bryant calls a "fluid text," a work in which textual difference and textual history are very much a part of its literary interest. We may be tempted to have students focus on the narratives of the *Confessio* or on their dialogue frames, but spending any time with the prologue or the colophons practically requires students to attend to the minutiae of Gower's revisions — in short, to do as editors do: read closely by collating. Collation of this sort can lead very easily to a discussion of the collations laid out in table form in the textual notes, and it is well worth the fifteen minutes it might take to guide students through decoding these tables. They will find it easier if taught how to think with some basic terminology: *lemma* and *stemma, witness, reading,* and *emendation.* I usually provide a handout with a mocked-up text and textual note, anatomized and then translated into English sentences. It may seem impenetrable to students at first, but with just a few minutes' practice, they can begin to reconstruct important features of witnesses by reading the textual notes.

To get them started, I point students toward notes that record large omissions, like prologue, lines 147–320: "Omitted in S (missing leaf)" (303). I ask them first to reconstruct the text in that manuscript and next to decide how, if there were no obvious physical disruption to tell us differently, an editor can still be sure it is an accidental omission and not a revision. After all, I tell them, Peck points out in his introduction that, though it is missing many leaves, manuscript S, or the so-called Stafford Manuscript (Huntington Lib. MS Ellesmere 26), preserves a "very high quality text" (37). It's an easy question to answer, once students have tried to read what remains, but it may in fact change the way students read. Even when they finally become familiar enough with Middle English to have some comfort reading Gower, students will assume that the fault lies with them when they cannot make sense of the text. To suggest that a passage might be nonsensical and might need emendation changes their relation to the Middle English text. As with all easy questions, it can lead to other questions that are not so easy to answer.

The Stafford manuscript also omits two lines early in the prologue, "Men se the world on every side / In sondry wyse so diversed" (29–30). How does the omission affect meaning? How do we explain their omission? And in book 1, lines 2343–58 are omitted not only by Stafford but also by Bodleian Library MS Bodley 294 and Cambridge University, St. John's College MS B.12. Asking students to interpret this omission takes us back to the introduction to discover that

Stafford and Bodley 294 are second recension and that St. John's B.12, a first recension, is very like the one that Gower used to revise for the second recension. Perhaps it isn't much of a textual problem for the more advanced textual scholar (and we are only dealing with a handful of the available manuscripts), but it may take students some time to map out the stemma and to discover that the omission, which occurs in one first-recension manuscript (St. John's B.12) but not the other (Bodleian Library MS Bodley 902), appears in both second-recension manuscripts (Stafford and Bodley 294) but not in the third-recension manuscript (Bodleian Library MS Fairfax 3). At some point, students will discover that the introduction lists a manuscript (Cambridge University, Sidney Sussex College, MS 63) as being consulted to compose the volume but that it is not collated with the notes, while the notes collate two manuscripts, Oxford University, Corpus Christi College MS 67 and Cambridge University, Trinity College MS R.3.2, that are not described in the introduction, so that we do not know (without doing our own collations or consulting Macaulay's edition) to which recensions they belong. For some, still wrapped up in mass-culture expectations, this inconsistency in the edition will simply rankle. For those who already feel somewhat empowered by textual criticism, it provides challenges and further avenues for investigation. Figuring out where Corpus Christi 67 and Trinity R.3.2 should be classified is a puzzle that students now have the tools to try to solve. These sorts of questions are good for out-of-class and library assignments.

Not all will feel so empowered. It shouldn't take long before some students begin to question the approach. Why should they care, after all, if in book 1 at lines 393–94, Stafford and Bodley 294 write the rhyme words as *constellacioun* and *nacioun*, while St. John's B.12 writes *constellacioun* but *nacion* and Macaulay amends to *constellacion* and *nacion*? It's a fair question, one that I try to turn back on the class to see if they can come up with ways in which such data might be useful — and they usually can, especially since at least one student will be far enough along in thinking about textual criticism to see, for instance, that dialect can matter in trying to reconstruct an authorial text. My goal is to generate literary discussions out of textual questions, so I ask them to scan the variants to find places that perhaps matter for their concerns. The point is not to find places where we might disagree with Peck but to begin to reconstruct his thinking. If the text we have is mediated by Peck (and others), reconstructing the textual history in this way can begin to lay bare that mediation. It can help students see, in short, how and why the text has already been interpreted for them.

It is one thing to "unedit," a term used by the early modern scholars Randall McLeod and Leah Marcus, meaning to read against the grain of an edition, to critique it (if implicitly) by attending to its apparatus and its documentary sources. It is quite another thing to try to edit for oneself, and doing so even on a small scale is a remarkably instructive activity. While exposing a textbook's mediations is productively disruptive, editing even a portion of a single document is more likely to bring students to a kind of rapprochement with the intractable nature of the literary text. In the process of editing, students begin to understand that, although the text is always already mediated, mediation is not a hindrance but the condition of its freedom to travel; and perhaps mediation is itself the point. The structure of the *Confessio* emphasizes Gower's role as mediator, putting the tales of lovers in the mouth not of Amans but of his confessor. While unediting might produce frustration with the editor and his or her choices or with the information-poor textual displays of the textual notes, editing produces another view of the editor and the process that brings the textbooks to students. What's more, students come to realize that, to edit well, one will need to understand the text and the work very, very well. It is important to reiterate here that the goal of the assignment is not to produce budding editors but to produce readers who are aware of the ways in which their texts are mediated and what that mediation means.

As for assigning editing of Gower's texts, the spirit may be willing, but the resources are weak. Unlike Chaucer, Gower has no facsimiles of whole manuscripts in print, though there are a handful of single-page samples from *Confessio* manuscripts viewable at library Web sites, such as the Bodleian's Image Library or the University of Glasgow's online exhibition catalog "The World of Chaucer," produced for an exhibit held at the Hunterian Museum in the summer of 2004. Also, *Early English Books Online (EEBO)* hosts digitized images of fifteenth- and sixteenth-century printed editions of the *Confessio Amantis*. And there are microfilm series both of manuscripts (Cambridge Literary Manuscripts) and of early printed books (on which *EEBO* is based). More and more resources will become available in time, but for now the choices are rather limited.

Students will feel a bit at sea with an editing assignment, anxious about format and goals, not to mention how their work will be evaluated—so it is best to be very clear about any rubric when first setting out. It will also help to have some discussion about editorial theory and methods, a topic large enough to occupy weeks on its own but that I think can be covered sufficiently for undergraduates in a rough sketch. I recommend placing on reserve Vincent McCarren and Douglas Moffat's collection *A Guide to Editing Middle English* and pointing students to the third chapter, "A Bibliographical Essay on Editing Methods and Authorial and Scribal Intention." I usually distribute a one-page cheat sheet of the essay with other assignment prompts and use it to lead a brief discussion about editorial theory and practice. I allow students to decide what sort of edition they wish to produce. Most ultimately choose a diplomatic edition of a single witness, but many confess that they intended to produce an eclectic edition but chickened out, worried that they would somehow make matters worse if they made too many interventions.

An editing assignment (which can range from a few lines to multiple passages or leaves) will begin with transcribing the selection as completely and as accurately as possible. Students will want help reading the gothic script or the black-letter typeface, but it does not take long and it is worth the class time to work on this as a group, since learning to read again, letter by letter, pays a kind of dividend by requiring very slow, close attention to the text. Giving students even simple charts of letter forms and common abbreviations will help — my own textbook *Textual Editing and Criticism: An Introduction* contains a basic chart (developed with the assistance of Brian Gastle) of letter forms derived from multiple hands. But the best thing is to jump right in (69–72). Oscillating between reading a facsimile alone and reading it alongside the textbook makes for the quickest learning, especially since students will begin to notice places where the textbook and the manuscript seem not to agree, and these places come either where the letter forms or abbreviations are unfamiliar or where the manuscript is variant. Either way will lead to a valuable discussion and reduce any desire to rely more on the authority of the textbook than on their own discernments.

After transcribing comes collation. If students can transcribe only one document, they can still collate it with their textbooks. Even if the text is very clean, the process of collation cannot be underestimated as a means to bring students closer to the text. It can be a dull process, yes, but they will usually see the text differently after doing so, even if they catch no errors or variants. Having students record at first all variations in some sort of table I think is best, though I stress to them that they may choose how much of their collations to present in the final product. The point is to see the recording of notes as a part of communicating an understanding of Gower's work. Students will discover that their interpretation of the text resides as much in what they are silent about as in what they report.

Third comes the editing proper. Students must decide not only for what readership and what purposes they are preparing their edition but also what sort of edition they will produce. It is here that they must decide about any substantive emendations they wish to make as well as whether they wish to regularize spelling, how they wish to punctuate, and so on. Before they begin, it will perhaps seem a slight activity, mere assembly, and they are usually surprised by the enormity of the task and by the remarkable discipline it requires. Though on the assignment sheet I list the creation of textual and explanatory notes as separate steps, I find it important to stress to students early that the two cannot be divorced entirely from each other. This often comes home to them as they work on content notes, since producing glosses for hard words or phrases makes them realize that their interpretations of those phrases will often alter the way they choose to punctuate and may make them rethink their emendations.

Finally, students write an introduction. Here they can apply the skills they are developing in traditional essays on literature, offering historical background, brief biographies of the author — all those things we expect in an introduction but suspect that students never read. I feel it is essential that the introduction also contain discussion of the text and how the editor has arrived at it, explaining in a broad outline the editor's goals, the evidence with which he or she had to work, the rules adopted for the edition, and the choices made. This step can be the most difficult, since students often discover that they have not been consistent, that they have been illogical, and that their work is therefore difficult to justify. Every step of the way in such an assignment, they discover and rediscover how editing is what they would have initially called subjective but what I would ask them to call interpretive. And, in the end, they almost always report that they know the text they have edited better than any other work they have encountered.

As I hope is evident from my presentation, editing is best thought of as a kind of academic writing that can be a useful exercise for undergraduates and graduates alike. It is a flexible and scalable assignment, in that it can be easily altered to be more or less complex, more or less lengthy. Unlike many kinds of writing about literature, it allows students to work in large and small teams to produce a single document. In fact, group editing assignments bring some students to productive crises more quickly, frustrated as they tend to become in disagreements about editorial policy. Disagreements over how to handle the quirks of a particular text (one of the most common disagreements is whether to modernize punctuation or follow the manuscript) can bring students to greater theoretical engagement not only with editorial practice but also with Gower's text, since their arguments are inevitably rooted in specific examples in the text they are editing. Student editions will of course fall very much further from the publishable standard than the student essay will from a typical journal article, but we should not be afraid to embrace this deficiency. Students will have written many essays, but it is unlikely they will ever have edited critically. I emphasize for my students that the point is not the product so much as the process. These editions will be lacking, but by the end the students will know it, and, what is more, they will know *why*. No modern confessor could ask for more.

NOTE

[1] Citations to the textual notes and text, as well as the Latin marginalia, of the *Confessio* are to Peck's 2002–06 edition; page numbers are given.

THEORETICAL APPROACHES

Teaching Gower's Liminal Literature and Critical Theory

J. Allan Mitchell

John Gower's *Confessio Amantis* excites serious students of literature to ask tough theoretical and methodological questions, partly because the work is not easily assimilated to the typical repertoire of concepts and practices that belong to academic criticism. So teaching Gower in a theory-savvy way is a unique opportunity to promote self-awareness (especially among advanced undergraduates or graduate students), a chance to expose and take stock of the first principles and primary functions of literature. Since Gower requires students to speculate about premodern sensibilities and reading habits, a salutary effect of teaching his work is to show up institutionalized features of our "episteme" and "habitus" that may be concealed or barely conscious in the classroom.

Introducing students to the *Confessio Amantis* through Michel Foucault's concept of the "epistemological field" is a particularly useful way to frame the difference and difficulty of Gower. Students should start by considering definitions of *archaeology* and *episteme*: in Foucault's account *archaeology* is "an inquiry whose aim is to rediscover on what basis knowledge and theory become possible; within what space of order knowledge was constituted . . ." (*Order of Things* xxiii), and *episteme* is "the total set of relations that unite, at a given period, the discursive practices that give rise to epistemological figures, sciences, and possibly formalized systems" (*Archaeology* 191). With these conceptual tools, students can start excavating a premodern order of things. The lush *ordinatio* ("arrangement") of the manuscript page, the varied discourse (amatory, dogmatic, and scientific), and the diverse representational strategies (literal and allegorical) all command attention. How can all the matter hang together? What attitudes must one bring to such a compendious poem? What readership is posited or produced by it? With the right set of questions, students can begin to pursue historical understanding not by reading off a set of meanings from the past but by unearthing a foreign field that past texts inhabit.

At the same time, students should reflect on their own positions and dispositions. Pairing a Foucauldian approach to medieval knowledge with Pierre Bourdieu's sociological accounts of the modern "logic of the literary field," teachers can introduce a reflexive element into the classroom. How judgments of literary taste are formed is suggested by way of *doxa*, "an adherence to relations of order which . . . are accepted as self-evident" (*Distinctions* 471), and *habitus*, the "system of dispositions" social agents develop in a given cultural field (*Outline* 82; see also 78–87, 164–71), concepts with ancient and medieval pedigree, as Bruce Holsinger has discussed in *The Premodern Condition* (94–102). The terms have added resonance given Gower's evident orthodoxy and interest in habituation: "Usage is the seconde kinde" (*CA* 6.664). What has become second nature for us? How far are we from inhabiting the historical and literary field of the text? What is familiar and foreign about it? Given the peculiar forms of life presupposed and produced by the poem, the *Confessio Amantis* can function as an incidence of interruption into the contemporary epistemic fields both of the "literary" and of the "theoretical."

Literariness and Academic Habits

The point can be quickly demonstrated and opened up for discussion. For moderns a hallmark of literariness has long been its avowed resistance to system or method, reacting against totalizing forms of cognition; the poetic stands charismatically apart from the instrumental and informational—even the theoretical. In *The Singularity of Literature* Derek Attridge updates the notion for students by arguing that literary texts somehow move and have their being *causa sui*, forming a special category of aesthetic experience—a notion traceable in French-inspired theory down through New Criticism all the way to German and English Romanticism. Among the cherished axioms of post-Romantic literary theory and practice (notwithstanding almost *any* differences) are claims that great literary works cannot be paraphrased, translated, or indexed without breach of decorum. The Kantian definition of art as "purposive without purpose" and the New Critical "heresy of paraphrase" are well-known instances of the attitude, but the bias persists in the way literary critics characteristically abhor "reductive" readings. As Bourdieu observes, literariness has long been characterized by its ineffability and pure autonomy; impure and reductive texts tend to fall on the side of "low" culture in the market of symbolic goods (*Rules*

141–73; *Field* 112–41). As this suggests, literariness can be seen as a solution to the problem of technocratic modernity, a contemporary cultural malaise. Didactic and scientific writings have been treated to such mandarin contempt among academics, moreover, because such texts appropriate the means of interpretation that professional critics guard for themselves in the academy. In any event, the dispute here is not really with medieval literature. The quarrel is with modern forms of bureaucracy and corporatism where instrumentality reigns and with a popular culture where texts are consumable.

Gower's *Confessio Amantis* does all the merely functional things that are supposedly subliterary while inhabiting a specialized cultural field of the late fourteenth century. Students reading the poem for the first time may be fascinated or frustrated by the evidence. At least they will register the different profile of the work arising from such aspects as taxonomical divisions, dogged polemic, moral didacticism, and a scientific curriculum that propel the text outside the realm of fiction and fantasy. Current theoretical approaches are further complicated by the fact that the work contains much *theorique* (e.g., rhetorical, astrological, humoral theory), all the while demanding *practique*. The alterity of Gower's work can make our work seem anachronistic.

Teachers can explain that in interrogating scholarly practices we are trying not to circumvent or suppress current assumptions but to elucidate them. Gower's poem puts in especially high relief the routines, rationalities, and temporalities of the classroom. If the academic habitus tends to objectify, Gower rouses and riles subjects; if scholarship tends to privilege studious, unhurried reflexivity and leisurely critique, Gower's writing insists on its urgency and utility. Ordinarily the literature classroom is no place for mere efficiency and utility—instead we cultivate the "neutralizing disposition" of the scholastic point of view, a disinterested perspective entailing "the bracketing of all theses of existence and all practical intentions" (Bourdieu, *Practical Reason* 128). A literary education is of course useful, credentializing and professionalizing students—but do we often remark on the irony that literariness seeks sanctuary from instrumental goals while serving them (Aers, *Literary Theory* 5; Menand 52–54, 105)? Gower exposes the contradiction.

Gower belongs to an alternative literary experience. One of the first points to make with students ready to undertake a measure of self-critique is that their university probably expects less of them than does Gower. His texts are rallying points, jeremiads, cris de coeur. A lot of his writing leans hard into the world of its readers. Students can consider the manuscript image (available at www.johngower.org and in many editions) of the poet as archer along with the verse caption beginning, "Ad mundum mitto mea iacula . . . ("I send my darts at the world . . .").[1] It is no less applicable to *Confessio Amantis* than to *Vox clamantis* or *Mirour de l'omme*. Gower's lesson: "Naturam superat doctrina" ("Teaching conquers Nature").[2] His poetry is not like the usual subjects of our discipline. Readers are to become practitioners who accept the poet's discipline.

Time for Theory

Letting Gower speak from the past can be unsettling because his writing insists on an exigent temporality, a point to explore in relation to the prologue to the *Confessio Amantis*. There the poet's plaintive, even insurgent, voice articulates a vision of the monster of time foreboding imminent disaster arising from calamitous "divisioun" and "confusioun" (prologue, lines 851–52). Gower's apocalyptic tone positions readers at an impasse: How to theorize in these confused times? What leisure remains for scholarship (Greek *skhole* means leisure time) given the desperate situation? Students can think about how critical theory tends to stand aloof from situations such as Gower's, "detemporalizing" them (Bourdieu, *Outline* 8–9). Should we not conclude that Gower inhabits a radically different time, an earlier episteme? Yet Gower's sense of time pressing also invites consideration of an analogous problem with which intellectuals always wrestle: witness Bourdieu's attempt to reinsert time into critical analysis and Derrida's pleading "for lack of time and space, to insist even more on what commands us today, without delay, to do everything we can so as to avoid the neutralizing anesthesia of a new theoreticism" (Derrida, *Specters* 32). Gower's olden-time eschatology stimulates self-reflection that is now timely. But more than this, Gower's satire indicates something out of sync in his own critical moment. He positioned himself at odds with his corrupting times; he also corrupts and temporizes in *Confessio Amantis*.

Indeed students soon discover that Gower's capacity for moral seriousness is only outdone by his sardonic humor — making him as mordant as he is a moral poet. His temperament bears comparison with Julia Kristeva's "laughter of the apocalypse," a humor amused by scenes of defilement, perversity, and folly and associated with oracles and prophets (Kristeva 204), including those after whom Gower fashions himself, namely Saint John in *Vox clamantis* and Daniel construing the monster of time. Moving from *contemptus mundi* ("contempt for the world") of the prologue to *fol amour* ("mad" or "foolish love") beginning in book 1, Gower's satire turns inward in much the same, now self-deprecating, spirit.[3] Gower is amusingly estranged from himself *in persona aliorum* ("in the person of others"; 1.60 [Latin marginalia]). A melancholic lover (3.33–133), he manifests the temporal division and disequilibrium about which he complains in the prologue. Students can explore the way, correspondingly, he scandalizes his own authorities — for example, exposing Venus's incest five books in and describing Aristotle as a *senex amans* in the eighth. And of course the fiction ends in a deflating *remedia amoris*, when Amans comes to his senses as "John Gower," as if to render everything coming before comically impertinent. Both prophetic iconoclast and droll provocateur, Gower employs even as he impugns romantic idealism, inflated rhetoric, and overwrought theory. Gower points up our belatedness to anxious theorizing about representation and rationality, as if anticipating by six centuries the latter-day skepticism about truth, identity, and value.

But belatedness has its advantages. Students can come to see theory as an *enabling anachronism* because the meanings of any historical text are not all available to itself. Some of the most important meanings exist as conditions of possibility and modes of perception to be elucidated later; they are known only when the slips, subterfuges, barely conscious know-how, systemic deficiencies, or unconscious desires become evident. A simpler way to put this is to remind students that, just as the writer is not always the best judge of his or her work, so a specific historical consciousness does not know everything that is historical about itself. Texts may lack self-presence. Gower's work is not coincident with history since the poet sought not merely to describe the world but to change it. Yet his poem is not even coincident with itself. I propose that while we may not share Gower's precise commitments (e.g., his views of a paternalistic aristocracy or eschatology), he knew so much about idolatry, temporality, contingency, and refractory desire that the poem appears to produce an imminent ethico-political critique of its most conservative judgments. A practical point to discuss with students is that doubts and prejudices are indispensable to engaging the historical past dialectically. I simply wish students to appreciate Derrida's description of the "archive as an irreducible experience of the future" (*Archive Fever* 68). The *Confessio Amantis* continues to engage us because the poem is itself so untimely.

Teachable Moments

A similar conception of the timeliness of old books is evinced in Gower's prologue, lines 1–11. A common way of studying Gower is to trace the dialectic of tales against sources, uncovering their exemplarity in his historical moment, "In oure tyme among ous hiere" (prologue 5). But exemplarity has become a problem in its own right. As the prologue, lines 12–21, shows, Gower's didactic impulse is complicated because Gower deliberately mixes modes and motivations. The question throughout is how to theorize the "middel weie." How do we understand the relations that obtain not just between "lust" and "lore" but also and analogously between disjointed imperatives of narratives and normative morality, the mimetic and paratextual, the imaginative and scientific, and the polite and polemical?

On the one hand, Gower's text seems deliberately narrowing, taxonomical, regulatory, and teleological, as if conforming to what Genius says, "an end proveth everything" (6.2383); it has marks of what Susan Suleiman would call an "authoritarian fiction." On the other, the *Confessio Amantis* seems pluralizing, proliferative, interrogative, and contingent, something less digestible and programmatic than a *roman à thèse*. Gower's didacticism, a topic worth exploring in greater detail if only to complicate complacent opinion, demonstrates just how teachable the *Confessio Amantis* is using a variety of theoretical perspectives. Students can explore the mimetic and didactic strategies by examining any number of exemplary cases.

Presented with the "Tale of the King and His Steward's Wife" in book 5, for instance, students witness a hermeneutic process unfolding. They can be asked to describe the implicit theory of interpretation. Genius's narrow moral application shows that the text lacks self-identity. Arguably a double infidelity takes place: a case of adultery and exploitation is occluded by a moral text that adulterates and exploits. Other examples of incongruous moralization are not far to seek: comparisons can be made to the selective or ad hoc applications of "Acteon" (1.333–84), "Canace and Machaire" (3.143–360), "Aeneas and Dido" (4.77–142), and "Apollonius of Tyre" (8.271–2008). How can we account for so much latitude? Is moralization a corruption or a correction? The "Tale of the King and His Steward's Wife" also belongs to a subset of moral tales that deviate from conventional morality: for example, "Phebus and Cornide" (3.783–817), "Pygmalion and His Statue" (4.371–445), and "Vulcan and Venus" (5.635–725). Equipped with reception theory, students could be asked to identify an "implied" or "fictional reader" distinct from an "ideal" or "informed reader."[4] Genius's interpretive license may consequently seem ironic. In contrast, and something more interesting to contemplate, extravagant rhetorical invention is inherent to medieval moralizations. How much is attributable to an obsolete *habitus*, some lost rhetorical mode of moral manipulation? At the same time students can profitably consider whether reading for the moral is ever avoidable: "Could we ever narrativize without moralizing?" (Hayden White 25). The monitory exemplum, a form of rhetoric that explicitly seeks a form of life, has special narrative qualities, and there are several theoretical accounts of exemplarity to choose from. Giorgio Agamben speaks of the example as an empty space of singularity (*Coming Community* 9–11). There are Derrida's scattered remarks on the example as prosthesis, as opening up a testamentary dimension, or as the condition of writing.[5] Speech-act theory clarifies the rhetorical pressure of the exemplum: we come to understand how "locutionary" utterance becomes "perlocutionary act," aiming as it does to achieve something by saying something (Austin 101).

All of these interpretive problems arise in the text before one even considers the margins. Attending to the Latin annotations, for example, appended to the "Tale of Pope Boniface" in book 2, we can enlarge the scope of the inquiry. Here and elsewhere Gower's compressed descriptions raise questions about the adequacy of paraphrase and translation and may call to mind the "orthodoxy of paraphrase" (J. B. Allen 211). Questions about ventriloquism are still relevant but now rebound more directly on authorial or scribal intentions: ironies we perceive cannot be referred to a feckless moralizing Genius since they bear not on unreliable fictional or implicit readers but on a higher authority, if only as Foucault puts it in "What Is an Author?" an "author function." In this case, Latin paraphrase takes the synoptic perspective of divine providence, daring to describe how God ordained events to turn out the way they do, which is nowhere so evident in the English narrative. God's absence is more conspicuous in this tale of all-too-human intrigue and the impersonation of divinity. What level of meaning takes precedence here: narrative or normative, immanent or transcendent, eventful or doctrinal, lay or clerical? What room is there for dogmatic judgments in literary art anyway? Teachers can sharpen the point heuristically by referring to Roland Barthes's definition of *doxa*—much less sophisticated than Bourdieu's—as vulgar opinion and violent prejudice (47). Janet Coleman calls Gower's poem "an encyclopedia of current prejudices and ideas" (129), but how much is Gower on the side of consensus and convention, and how much does he cut across them? In this tale about the overthrow of a hypocritical pope the *doxa* remains ambiguous at best, and we may think Gower comes close to an expression of heterodoxy (despite the orthodoxy of paraphrase). Bourdieu's more subtle identification of *doxa* in the literary field may then indicate that we have not yet escaped the old problems created by medieval exegesis and scholarly commentary.

One can extend discussion of the *mise en page* by showing classes high-definition images of medieval manuscripts—for example, Plimpton MS 265 (available online at the *Digital Scriptorium*) or Pierpont Morgan MS M.126 (online at *Corsair*)—so that students can consider other elements of the apparatus, including running titles, verse headings, rubrication, illustrations, and colophons designed to organize content. Here again we run up against the problem of literariness and historicity. The apparatus has been described as performing an "indexing" function in the text, facilitating cross-referencing and nonlinear reading (Echard, "With Carmen's Help" 11); it has also been considered "auto-exegesis" (Copeland 185). One can refer to Gérard Genette's theory of the paratext or Derrida's notion of parergon to ask further questions about the specific functionality and framing of the apparatus. Does literary narrative ever exist apart from functional purposes that frame them? All these formalizing and regulating devices of the work need to be contextualized historically, too, by exploring how medieval moralization was a conscious form of *reduction*—recollection, restoration, or application (Mitchell 17–19). Students will benefit by interrogating the various definitions (medieval and modern) of "to reduce." With all this information students will be in a good position to see how even such a carefully arranged text can remain expansive and unstable, stimulating continual reassessment and redefinition of terms.

Minority Literature

Over a broad sweep one begins to see how Gower works by employing substitution, repetition, juxtaposition, and copiousness—so that readers are always, as it were, situated in the *middle* and unlikely to settle the meaning by turning to the *ending*. Besides restating what Gower says ("See, Gower is going the middel weie"), teachers can call on broad-gauge theoretical concepts with which he had no acquaintance to help characterize the mediating process. Different aspects of the work will be illuminated depending on the theory of difference brought to bear—for example, intertextuality, bricolage, dialogism, or hybridity.

The multiplex nature of the work and the circumstantial, improvisatory reader-response provoked by it need theorizing generally. Adopting terms of Gilles Deleuze and Félix Guattari, I prefer to speak of "nomad" reading that traverses the open space between points in the text ("The life of the nomad is the inter-mezzo"), deterritorializing the striated space of the state (*Thousand Plateaus* 380–87). At least students can be asked to debate whether the text is not more "nomadic" than "sedentary" (i.e., occupying territory organized by the state), in the light of the dual dedications to Richard II and Henry of Lancaster. Allied concepts such as the machinic assemblage enable students to consider the work as a system of processes, oscillating signals, and asignifying ruptures. How is the *Confessio Amantis* a literary machine geared toward producing effects, flows, pressures, intensities, vibrations, or lines of flight? How does it construct—not just represent—a reality or experience?

The play of differences has its limits. Gower is not a poet who nothing af-firms, and this again returns us to the question of what sort of literary object we encounter in the *Confessio Amantis*. In its reformist mode the work prompts action, finds fault, pledges allegiance, observes social distinctions, and so on; and it is full of wise counsel (prologue 67). At its most theoretical, the work makes truth claims and codifies knowledge. Students may review what Walter Benjamin says of how early storytellers were typically oriented toward practical prudence: story existed before the rise of the news media—ephemeral information without consequence—and the novel, or rich description of human life without counsel (Benjamin 86–87). Again Deleuze and Guattari offer novel ways of attending to the difference of this earlier form of storytelling, their concept of "minor literature" indicating what is at stake in the politically interested, purposive, "collective enunciation" (*Kafka* 17)—or, in this case, Gower's "common vois" (prologue 124).[6] While some of the minoritarian status of the *Confessio Amantis* may derive from its precocious vernacularity (English being relatively new on the scene for polite letters) and bilingualism (causing diglossic friction), from this theoretical perspective the point is that a minor work discovers variations within the major languages it employs. Gower's radically eclectic and encyclopedic poem—fraught as it is with multiplicity, potentiality, becoming—qualifies as minor in this specific sense. Gower's work stands apart from corrupting routines and rationalizations of its own time—and ours. It does not merely inhabit a different field of cultural and literary production; it can produce a new cultural field and redefine what literature can do.

NOTES

[1] For the image and text with translation, see, for example, Yeager's edition of Gower's *Minor Latin Works* 10–11.

[2] This quotation is from line 3 of the Latin headnote to book 7. The translation is from Echard and Fanger 72–73.

[3] For the significance of this move it may be useful to compare Gower's discussion of *fol amour* in the *Mirour*, lines 925–36.

[4] For terminology see Iser; Fish; and Strohm, "Chaucer's Audience(s)."

[5] See, e.g., *Truth* (79), *Specters* (34), and *On the Name* (17–18, 144n14).

[6] See also Deleuze and Guattari's *Thousand Plateaus* 100–07 for a general discussion of the concept.

Gender, Sexuality, and Family Ties in the *Confessio Amantis*

María Bullón-Fernández

While one could certainly teach an undergraduate course devoted to John Gower's *Confessio Amantis*, most of us do not teach such courses. Instead, we usually incorporate Gower's work into courses focused on broad topics. In this essay I discuss teaching Gower in two such courses: one titled Medieval Sexualities (a senior-level English course) and the second called Family Ties in Medieval Literature (a junior-level course for a broad range of humanities majors).

Medieval Sexualities

Medieval Sexualities emphasizes theory, as is expected of 400-level courses in my department at Seattle University. It has two chief aims: to explore medieval notions of gender and sexuality as imagined in a variety of medieval literary texts and to introduce students to feminist and queer theory through the study of key theorists. While our department's 200- and 300-level courses often incorporate feminist approaches, they rarely have students read and engage directly with theoretical texts. Medieval Sexualities therefore functions as an in-depth intro-duction to feminist and queer theory and assumes that students have some basic prior knowledge of medieval literature.

The course is divided into three units: sex and gender, heterosexual desires, and homosexual desires. The unit on sex and gender, the shortest, explores the relation between sex and gender and questions the very terms and their impli-cations, including essentialism and constructivism. When discussing essentialist and constructivist theories, I find that current students, at least those at our university, are often quick to subscribe to constructivism, but their constructiv-ist ideas are usually far from sophisticated. When I challenge them by pushing constructivist ideas about gender to limits that may feel uncomfortable to them, some realize that they are not simply or purely constructivists. At the same time those who do confirm their constructivism realize that they need to find more complex ways to argue for their viewpoint. Although it is now more than twenty years old, Toril Moi's *Sexual/Textual Politics* is still very useful to introduce de-bates about sex and gender in early feminist theories, especially as they relate to literary criticism. Moi's historical look at the development of these theories also provides us with a solid base that helps students understand queer the-ory later in the course. After reading selections from Moi's book, we move on to the first chapter in Judith Butler's *Gender Trouble*, where Butler ques-tions the relation between sex and gender and also proposes a constructiv-ist view not just of gender but of sex itself. We also read the section called

"Bodily Inscriptions, Performative Subversions" in the third chapter of Butler's book (128–41).

Alongside these theoretical texts, during this first unit of the course students read medieval texts that present gender as naturally related to sex as well as others that interrogate the perceived naturalness of such a relationship. We read several tales in Gower's *Confessio Amantis* that allow us to look at these issues from complex perspectives. The "Tale of the False Bachelor" (2.2501–802), with its emphasis on knightly acts as constitutive of masculine identity, points to masculinity's dependence on performativity. Also, the sections in the *Confessio Amantis* on "Lachesce" and "Pusillanimity" (both at the beginning of book 4), including the stories "Eneas and Dido," "Ulysses and Penelope," and "Pygmalion," enrich the discussions on gender and performance. In these stories the men are blamed for not being active or "performative enough"; when they finally do act, as in the cases of Ulysses and Pygmalion, Genius praises them. We end this unit with the "Tale of Florent" (1.1407–875), which is paired with Chaucer's Wife of Bath's Prologue and Tale. Both raise complex questions about medieval perceptions of women, particularly in the case of the Wife of Bath, with her multiple and contradictory constructions of what women are like and what they desire. The Wife of Bath's "Venerien and Marcien" qualities help us interrogate further the relation between sex and gender.

The course moves into the second unit, on heterosexual desires. This unit is divided in three sections: virginity, sex and marriage, and heterosexual perversions. For a theoretical view, we read Gayle Rubin's "The Traffic in Women: Notes on the 'Political Economy of Sex'" and continue reading Butler's *Gender Trouble*, both of which examine compulsory heterosexuality and its perversions, including incest. For a historical perspective on the topic students also read Ruth Mazo Karras's *Sexuality in Medieval Europe*. The primary texts for this section treat virginity and its centrality to notions of sexuality in the Middle Ages. We read Gower's "Tale of Lucrece" (7.4754) and the "Tale of Virginia" (7.5131–306) along with Chaucer's versions of these stories, the story of Lucrece in the *Legend of Good Women* and that of Virginia in The Physician's Tale. We then move on to the section on sex and marriage and read a chapter in Karras similarly titled "Sex and Marriage" (59–86) along with Chaucer's Clerk's Tale and Gower's "Tale of Rosiphelee" (4.1245–466). Griselda's complete subjection to her husband in The Clerk's Tale provides a contrast to the Wife of Bath's purported desire for "maistrie" in marriage, while Gower's "Tale of Rosiphelee" serves as a cautionary story for women who do not show any interest in love, or, in other words, in marriage and heterosexuality.

The course then turns to heterosexual perversions, concentrating on rape and incest. Gower's "Tale of Tereus" and Chaucer's version of this story, the section on Philomela in the *Legend of Good Women*, are both about rape. I pair these texts with Gower's "Mundus and Paulina" (1.761–1076), which is about deceitful seduction, in order to examine how Gower distinguishes between rape and seduction. Finally, the most notorious heterosexual perversion in Gower's *Confessio Amantis* is incest, and thus a significant portion of this section focuses on it. We read the tales "Canace and Machaire" (3.143–336) and the longer "Tale of Apollonius" (8.271–2008) as well as Gower's account of the origin of the incest taboo in the first two hundred lines of book 8. We compare Gower's treatment of the issue with Chaucer's Man of Law's apparently condemnatory references to Gower's explicit treatment of incest in his "Tale of Apollonius."

The third unit of this course focuses on homosexual desires. Here we continue to read Butler's *Gender Trouble*, and we do this side by side with selections from Michel Foucault's *History of Sexuality*. I find particularly helpful Carla Freccero's critique in *Queer/Early/Modern*, in the chapter "Undoing the Histories of Homosexuality" (31–50) of the ways in which Foucault's argument that the "homosexual" was invented in the nineteenth century has been misinterpreted; this chapter raises questions about historicizing that are crucial for students of medieval texts. Regarding primary texts, I briefly depart again from the English fourteenth century by having students read Heldris de Cornüälle's *Roman de Silence*. The unusually long and explicit debates in *Silence* about gender in the context of nature and nurture as well as the ways in which the poem explores both cross-dressing and same-sex desire challenge students' preconceptions about medieval writers' ability to address these apparently taboo subjects. This in turn makes students more open to considering what Chaucer and Gower might be suggesting in the texts that we subsequently study in depth. Before turning to Chaucer and Gower, though, we focus on the historical case of John Rykener, a male transvestite prostitute in late medieval London. This case, published by Ruth Mazo Karras and David Lorenzo Boyd (111–14), allows us to examine the complex interplay of gender, sex, and sexual desire in the late medieval imagination. We then read Chaucer's portrait of the Pardoner in The General Prologue as well as The Prologue to The Pardoner's Tale and Carolyn Dinshaw's chapter on the Pardoner, the Wife of Bath, John Rykener, and Foucault in *Getting Medieval: Sexualities and Communities, Pre- and Postmodern*. We also read The Miller's Tale; by this point students can easily perceive the homoerotic aspects of this tale. Two tales of Gower's are apt for this unit, the "Tale of Achilles" (4.1963–2013) and the "Tale of Iphis" (4.451–538). In the former, Achilles is cross-dressed by his mother so that he cannot be recruited for the Trojan War, but he is discovered when he chooses a knight's harness among other gifts presented to him. This cross-dressing story raises fascinating issues about gender when compared with *Silence*. In the "Tale of Iphis," Iphis, a girl, is raised as a boy and becomes attracted to another girl. Cupid intervenes and turns Iphis into a boy so that her love accords with "kinde." Cupid's transformation of Iphis (which one could interpret as unnatural or at the very least supernatural) and Genius's explicit discussion about "nature" and "kinde" in the tale lead the class into complex discussions, especially in the context of the debates between Nature and Nurture in *Silence* and Butler's and Foucault's theories.

While the study of feminist and queer theories gives students specific tools to approach the medieval texts we read, I always encourage students to consider how one might do the opposite, that is, use medieval texts as tools to rethink contemporary theories. Since feminist and queer theorists often fail to take the Middle Ages into account and often give a simplistic view of the period, I ask students to reflect on the ways in which medieval texts may challenge contemporary theories.

Family Ties in Medieval Literature

The second course I describe here, Family Ties in Medieval Literature, is one I have not taught yet but hope to teach in the near future. This course's primary aim is to explore notions of the family and family roles in medieval literary texts as a relatively unusual lens that can yield innovative interpretations. A secondary aim is to enable students to use this lens to interpret literature from other periods. Although, unlike Medieval Sexualities, this 300-level course does not emphasize theoretical readings, it does take an anthropological and historical approach and offers students an opportunity to contemplate the relation between literary and other historical and cultural texts. The course thus starts with Ross C. Murfin's short introduction to new historicism in the Bedford edition of The Wife of Bath's Prologue and Tale as a way of engaging students in thinking about the connections between literature and history. Also, at the beginning of the course, students are introduced to anthropological notions of the family as well as sociohistorical readings about the concept of the family and familial roles in the Middle Ages. Two collections of essays are useful for background on the medieval family: Cathy Jorgensen Itnyre's *Medieval Family Roles* and Carol Neel's *Medieval Families: Perspectives on Marriage, Household, and Children*. Throughout the term students read various essays from these books.

In the first week students explore the definition of *family* in the Middle Ages. From our twenty-first-century perspective we tend to interpret *family* as comprising parents and children. While this nuclear family was also fundamental in the Middle Ages and most of the course centers on it, scholars show that an appropriate term for the medieval family is *medieval household*, a term that includes not only parents and children but also any relatives, friends, or servants who lived in the same house. As part of this initial discussion, students read selections from Howard Bloch's *Etymologies and Genealogies: A Literary Anthropology of the French Middle Ages*. Bloch's book introduces them to the concept of the medieval family from an anthropological point of view, focusing on the importance of kin and lineage for the medieval aristocracy. Because aristocratic families were obviously not the only model, though, we also read at the outset Judith Bennett's "The Tie That Binds: Peasant Marriages and Families in Late Medieval England." Comparing this article with Bloch's study of the French medieval aristocracy and using both to analyze family ties from aristocratic and peasant points of view also provides much-needed background for reading literary texts.

In the first week the aim is to challenge students' preconceptions about what constitutes a family and to approach the medieval notion of the family, as Bloch puts it, by "view[ing] its strangeness with unfamiliar eyes" (11). This act of distancing discourages students from easily mapping their experiences and notions of the family onto the medieval texts we read. The second set of initial readings aims at introducing a model of the family whose influence was pervasive in the Middle Ages: the Holy Family. We read Middle English lyrics about the Virgin Mary as well as excerpts from the *Book of Margery Kempe,* in which Margery reflects on the familial roles of the members of the Holy Family. Our secondary reading in conjunction with these primary texts is Pamela Sheingorn's "Appropriating the Holy Kinship: Gender and Family History," which helps illuminate the roles of the Holy Family in medieval texts and its productive function in constructing notions of the family in the Middle Ages. The interchangeability of roles in the Holy Family (the Virgin is the mother, wife, and daughter of God) helps us ask about the boundaries between familial roles in the Middle Ages.

After the first introductory week the course is divided into four units: husbands and wives, parents and children, siblings, and a final unit called "beyond the biological family." In this course, as in the previous one, the main literary texts are by Gower and Chaucer because both authors' works show a particular interest in familial relationships and because, given the importance of the sociohistorical in this course, focusing on authors from the same century and country allows for greater and deeper historical coherence; but they are not the only literary authors we read.

The unit on husbands and wives starts with excerpts from Gower's *Traitié . . . pour essampler les amantz marietz,* where Gower writes about, among other topics, the purposes of marriage. We then move to two tales from Chaucer's so-called marriage group, The Wife of Bath's Prologue and Tale and The Clerk's Tale. As is well known, the Wife explores the appropriate relationship between husbands and wives and the distribution of power between spouses. The Clerk's Tale seems to disprove the Wife and advocate a wife's complete submission. Of course, The Clerk's Tale only *seems* to do so and includes enough ambiguous moments that its apparent lessons can lead to rich discussions with students. One of Gower's tales for this section is the "Tale of Florent," an analogue to the Wife's tale that discusses power in marriage somewhat differently. The second tale by Gower takes us in a significantly different direction: the "Tale of Ceix and Alceone" (4.2927–3186) ignores issues of power and shows a romantic view of marriage. The contrast between this tale and The Wife of Bath's Tale provides students with a more complex view of marriage in the Middle Ages. Alceone's suicide, moreover, raises the question of sacrifice for love, a question that we contemplate later in texts about familial relationships and that allows us to start considering the depths and boundaries of medieval familial affectivity.

As secondary sources for this unit, we read chapters 4 and 5 (on marriage and the family in the late Middle Ages) in David Herlihy's *Medieval Households*. Chaucer's Clerk's Tale is also particularly relevant to the second unit of the course, on parents and children. Whenever I teach this tale in other courses, Griselda's apparent lack of emotional response to being told that her children will be taken away and killed tends to disturb students. Students' reaction becomes an opportunity to explore the tension between parent-child and husband-wife relationships and the privileging of one over the other by different cultures and time periods. When Griselda is forced to make a choice between her husband and her children, she chooses obedience to her husband. Can we take this as a comment on parent-child relationships in the Middle Ages? Does the tale suggest that it was more acceptable in the Middle Ages than it might be now to sacrifice one's children for the sake of the father? Or does Griselda's attitude suggest something about the tale itself or about the narrator? Finally, how do these realistic questions complicate possible allegorical readings of the tale? This conversation can lead the class to consider more broadly how medieval parents saw their children in the Middle Ages or (to put it more productively) how parents saw their relationship with and their obligations to their children. What were the sacrifices that parents were ready to make for their children? And what were the limits of parental bonds? These questions become particularly challenging when posed in the context of another tale, Gower's version of the story of Jason and Medea (5.3247–4222), in which the mother kills her sons as a reaction to being abandoned by her husband.

To discuss family obligations in The Clerk's Tale in greater depth, we read essays on the ethics of familial ties versus other types of ties. For this purpose *Kindred Matters: Rethinking the Philosophy of the Family*, edited by Diana Titjens Meyers, Kenneth Kipnis, and Cornelius F. Murphy, Jr., is most useful. The section titled "Family Life and Moral Theory" helps us reflect on parental and familial responsibility, moral obligations and familial bonds, and the nature of the emotional attachment among family members. Although all the essays discuss these issues from a contemporary philosophical perspective, their inquiry about the naturalness of family bonds and the historical and cultural construction of the family helps frame discussions about medieval family ties. John Boswell's essay "*Expositio* and *Oblatio*: The Abandonment of Children and the Ancient and Medieval Family" further reinforces the point that the notions of family ties vary depending on cultures and time periods, even as the essay illuminates our medieval texts.

As they keep in mind how The Clerk's Tale examines the limits of the affective bonds between two parents and their children, the students read tales that raise the opposite concern, tales in which the parents, especially fathers in relation to daughters, take their affective bond too far and commit incest. Gower's "Tale of Apollonius" (8.271–2008), which explores the father-daughter bond through various father-daughter pairs, one of which commits incest, as well as Gower's "Tale of Constance" (2.587–612), which suggests a kind of symbolic father-daughter incest toward the end, are excellent examples of such a concern. These two tales are paired with Chaucer's introduction to The Man of Law's Tale and The Man of Law's Tale. In his introduction the Man of Law indicts both incest and Gower specifically for writing about it; but in his own tale, itself an analogue to the "Tale of Constance," he, like Gower, points to a symbolic father-daughter incest at the end. When read together, these tales raise fascinating questions about the boundaries of familial roles. These roles need to be examined, though, in the context of the political and religious implications of the story, since Constance's father is the emperor of Rome and Constance is married off for political and religious reasons before she returns to her father. A similar interplay of the familial and the political appears in the other story we read concerning fathers and daughters, Gower's "Tale of Virginia" and its analogue, Chaucer's Physician's Tale. Both versions complicate the discussion since Virginia's father sacrifices his daughter either to preserve her virginity or to defeat a tyrant, depending on whose version, Chaucer's or Gower's, one focuses on.

The unit on parent-child relationships also considers mothers and sons, and the main primary texts are Chrétien de Troyes's *Perceval* and Gower's "Tale of Achilles." Both *Perceval* and the "Tale of Achilles" warn against the danger of mothers excessively influencing their sons, replacing their fathers, and turning them away from war. In Chrétien's romance, Perceval has to overcome his mother's influence to become the knight that he is meant to be. In Gower's "Tale of Achilles" the mother dresses Achilles as a girl in an attempt to prevent him from going to Troy and dying. In both texts the influence of the mother needs to be undone, and it is undone through the child's "instant" and supposedly instinctive attraction to arms and chivalry. Our discussion of *Perceval* is further deepened by Bloch's argument that the story is clearly haunted by the absence of the father (198–212). While in the father-daughter relationships the danger the tales warn against is explicitly sexual (i.e., the father will love the daughter too much and transgress against the incest taboo), in the stories of mothers and sons, the danger is not so much sexual as gendered: the son will be prevented from "becoming a man" and performing his masculinity. Nevertheless, what both sets of stories have in common is the fear that the parent will not allow the child to separate from him or her. This point is also manifest in Gower's "Tale of Orestes" (3.1885–2195), in which the son, Orestes, kills his mother, Climestre, to avenge his father's murder by his mother and her lover. Although the oedipal echoes are undeniable, one can also argue that this tale, like the others read in this unit, reveals a fear, realized in this tale, that the son's mother will displace the father.

Sibling relationships appear to be a less common focus in medieval literature than spousal or parent-child relationships, and yet there are some fascinating sibling stories that not only illuminate ideas about family ties but also demonstrate how other types of bonds conflict with those between siblings. In this unit the first primary text is Gower's "Canace and Machaire" (3.143–336), a sibling-incest story that, like other incest stories, explores the limits and definition of affectivity and love within the family. The ties between sisters are explored in Gower's "Tereus" and Chaucer's version of it in the *Legend of Good Women*. In both versions the sisters' ties become more important than husband-wife and mother-son ties. When Tereus, the husband of Progne (Procne in Chaucer), rapes Progne's sister, Philomene (Philomela in Chaucer), and cuts out her tongue, Progne avenges her sister by killing her own son, whom she sees primarily as Tereus's son, and feeding him to her husband. When scrutinized through the lens of the conflict between family members, this story reveals the complex interplay of contrasting emotional responses to different familial ties.

The unit on sibling relationships dovetails with the final unit, "beyond the biological family," which focuses on nonbiological familial relationships and has only one primary text as the focus: the Middle English version of the popular story of *Amis and Amiloun*, in which two knights are sworn (not biological) brothers. In the context of the course's focus on family ties and the depths of affectivity between family members, it is particularly significant that at the end of the story the nonbiological relationship between these two sworn brothers takes precedence over the biological family of one of the knights: at the end Amis kills his own children to save Amiloun. Miraculously, the children survive, and the story ends happily for everybody. Nevertheless, that Amis is willing to kill his children to save his sworn brother points to the instability of biological family ties and suggests that family in the Middle Ages was more than a biological concept. In this context, it is useful to return to Margery Kempe's struggles to remain loyal to the divine family, which in a sense she adopts, over her family of origin. The course thus ends by interrogating the extent to which biology plays a role in defining the boundaries of the family in the Middle Ages.

Courses that offer innovative thematic approaches to medieval literature are often more attractive to undergraduate students than courses that focus exclusively on one author, genre, or specific period. At my university, it is unlikely that many students would be drawn to take a course devoted to Gower, partly because they would not know much about him beforehand. However, they are drawn to courses that focus on themes or issues they have an interest in and have questions about. Although their questions often start with their own contemporary perspective, I find that students are similarly curious about how other periods and other cultures have dealt with them. Teaching Gower's *Confessio Amantis* through themes and by comparison with other literary texts, even though it may be a piecemeal approach to the *Confessio*, can be a first step toward encouraging undergraduate students to engage with the whole poem.

Postcolonial/Queer:
Teaching Gower Using Recent Critical Theory

Steven F. Kruger

Bringing critical theory and medieval texts together should be a dialectical process in which we ask, on the one hand, what raising the questions of contemporary theory might enable in our reading of medieval culture and literature and, on the other, what the unique dynamics of medieval texts, histories, and social formations might suggest about the limitations of theory, what we might need to rethink in our theoretical formulations to use these most productively in treating medieval materials. Recent medieval scholarship has engaged such questions in regard to both queer theory (Burger, *Chaucer's Queer Nation*; Burger and Kruger, *Queering the Middle Ages*; Dinshaw, *Getting Medieval*; and Lochrie, *Heterosyncrasies*) and postcolonial work (Cohen, *Postcolonial Middle Ages* and *Cultural Diversity*; Ingham and Warren, *Postcolonial Moves*; and Kabir and Williams, *Postcolonial Approaches to the European Middle Ages*). Gower studies itself raises questions indebted to queer theory (Watt, *Amoral Gower*). But although much critical work has focused on Gower and English nationalism and Gower criticism has been attentive to the poet's engagement with contemporary (late medieval) political questions, there has not yet been extensive work that uses postcolonial theory in reading Gower, even though some recent scholarship raises questions that might be further explored using postcolonial formulations (Williams, "Gower's Monster"; Kruger, "Gower's Mediterranean").

In any class, I try to foreground methodological and theoretical questions, discussing explicitly why it might be productive and important to test theoretical formulations elaborated largely to take into account a certain kind of historical, cultural, or textual material in situations quite distant from that original one. Of course, the way I pose such questions differs depending on the kind of class I am teaching. In the (rare, and probably graduate-level) class devoted largely to Gower's work, I would center the syllabus on a reading of the *Confessio Amantis*, *Vox clamantis*, and sections of the *Mirour de l'omme*, but I would surround the Gower texts with several other kinds of material: historical writings (on, for instance, the rising of 1381, to read alongside the *Vox*), literary analogues and contrasts (for example, parts of Chaucer's *Legend of Good Women*, to compare to the narratives of the *Confessio*), and literary-cultural theory. Queer and postcolonial theory would figure prominently in my version of such a course since, in my view, such theoretical frames engage questions crucial throughout Gower's poetic corpus.

More likely undergraduate and graduate-level classes would of course read Gower in conjunction with other medieval authors and texts. Gower could play an important role in advanced undergraduate or graduate seminars on medieval gender and sexuality or on nation and (post)coloniality. Here, a theoretical line of questioning and texts would structure the course as much as would the selection of medieval materials themselves. In a queer course, we might read important formulations by Michel Foucault (*History of Sexuality*), Judith Butler (*Gender Trouble* and *Bodies That Matter*), Eve Kosofsky Sedgwick (*Between Men* and *Epistemology*), Lee Edelman (*No Future*), Judith Halberstam (*In a Queer Time and Place*), along with the aforementioned queer medievalist work, as we made our way through a series of medieval texts that take up the complexities of gender and sexuality. In a postcolonial course, readings by Benedict Anderson (*Imagined Communities*), Homi Bhabha (*Location of Culture*), Gayatri Spivak (*Spivak Reader*), Dipesh Chakrabarty (*Provincializing Europe*), Robert Young, (*Colonial Desire*), as well as selections from the aforementioned postcolonial medievalist scholarship, would work alongside medieval texts representing national (or protonational) politics, intercultural exchange and conflict, colonial or imperial encounters and dynamics. Gower would fit well among medieval texts emphasizing either gender/sexuality or nation/(post)coloniality.

In all these teaching contexts, I prefer using original theoretical texts (even relatively brief extracts) rather than derivative summaries or explanations of theoretical schools and positions. The grappling with difficult philosophical, psychological, and critical texts strikes me as an important part of the work of introducing theory into the literature classroom. Although I have often been warned by colleagues that Foucault, Butler, Bhabha, or Spivak will prove too difficult for undergraduate students, these writers seem to me no more difficult than Gower or Julian of Norwich—though of course they are difficult in different ways. Often students who struggle with Middle English or with understanding medieval literary and cultural differences show greater facility with abstract, theoretical formulations. Having such texts in play provides them with opportunities to enter into the classroom discussion that they might not otherwise have been afforded.

In what follows, I do not attempt to sketch a unified method for teaching Gower using queer and postcolonial theory; instead, I identify some of the sites in Gower's work and some of the questions active in Gower's writing and thinking where I believe postcolonial and queer theory might be productively introduced, and I propose, briefly but I hope suggestively, ways in which theory and the Gower text might prove mutually enlightening. I organize my discussion around critical terms that play major roles in queer and postcolonial studies, suggesting how Gower's poetry resonates with these keywords and might also lead us to rethink them.

Hybridity

Perhaps the most common way Gower is currently introduced into our teaching is as an example that foregrounds the complex linguistic situation of late medieval England, a situation in which an author might choose to compose works in any of three languages (English, French, and Latin), as Gower does with his three major works—the *Confessio Amantis* (English), *Mirour de l'omme* (French), and *Vox clamantis* (Latin). This attention to Gower's linguistic virtuosity occurs (glancingly) in Chaucer courses, as a way of highlighting Chaucer's decision to write (so far as we know) solely in English. It also occurs, with somewhat fuller reflection on the sociopolitics of language use, in courses on the history of the English language. But rarely do we have the opportunity in the classroom to reflect more fully on what the choice of language might suggest about each of Gower's works. Does the choice reflect different sorts of literary (genre) expectation, attempts to reach different audiences, changes across Gower's career as a writer, a sense that different subjects are broached more appropriately in one language or another, a desire precisely to demonstrate a kind of poetic virtuosity?

Of course there are many critical-theoretical approaches that enable thinking about the politics of language use, but prominent among them is postcolonial theory. Might there be a way of bringing Bhabha's or Young's work on postcolonial hybridity—work that recognizes the complex power dynamics in play when different cultures and languages come together in colonizing situations—to a consideration of Gower's language use, including the ways in which, in his great English work, the *Confessio Amantis*, Latin poetry and glosses are intimately incorporated? Is Gower's negotiation with all three dominant languages of his moment an instance of hybridity, reflecting some sense of the author's multiple identifications in relation to a set of contemporary cultural and linguistic positions? To what extent does the use of an institutional language like Latin and a classed language like French, with its explicit colonial history, resonate with the kinds of language use analyzed in contemporary, postcolonial contexts? What kinds of authority do Latin and French provide Gower that might not be presented by English alone? Posing such questions about Gower would allow us, then, to return to other English authors—Chaucer or Langland, for instance—with a more complex set of questions to ask about their decisions to write primarily in English. It would also enable a comparison of Gower with other authors—notably Langland—who incorporate Latin and French into English texts in a hybridizing manner. And, of course, in a period when French loanwords were rapidly entering English, we might consider Middle English itself as irreducibly hybrid. Can we conceive of Middle English as somehow like the new world Englishes that arose, and continue to develop, in the wake of colonization and decolonization, as some recent work might suggest (Görlach; Dalton-Puffer; Hsy)?

Identity

That Gower frames his work—both the *Confessio Amantis* and the *Vox clamantis*—not only in relation to contemporary events but also "autobiographically," recounting the visions and dreams of a first-person narrator, suggests some of the multiple ways in which his writing constructs a sense of identity, a sense of the subject both as interested and deeply implicated in the historical and (especially in the *Confessio*) as possessing a complex internal life.

Scholars have paid a good deal of attention to Gower's Englishness and his interest in English politics. Students can use postcolonial theory to think about the ways in which English identity is not, in any given moment, a single thing. They might discern different Englishnesses among those standing on different rungs of the social scale and in different positions in relation to political power, and they might see Gower, intensely aware of social division and stratification and of the locations of power, trying to place himself at a certain center of Englishness.

At the same time, of course, Gower as a poet negotiates with a set of traditions that are not simply English but more broadly European. In developing his poetic identity, Gower shows himself the heir to Latin, classical tradition; French dream vision and courtliness; European folktale; and much else. How does his writing in Latin and French, as well as English, acknowledge or claim this European poetic identity? How does Gower's claiming of such an identity compare with Chaucer's Europeanness in bringing French, Latin, and Italian materials into English through translation and adaptation?

The negotiation with French materials is especially complex for any late-fourteenth-century English writer. On the one hand, as suggested above, French language and culture have been incorporated into English through a certain process of hybridization. French language and culture have also been traditionally associated with English (Norman) aristocracy and royalty, though decreasingly so in the late fourteenth century. They belong, too, to an enemy power in the current moment of the Hundred Years' War, though this is complicated since some of England's foreign allies in that same war (Burgundy, Aquitaine) are themselves French. What does it mean, then, to use the French language and French literary models at this particular point in time? Colonial and postcolonial analogues—for instance, the negritude movement, with its use of a colonial language like French to assert resistance to European power—might provide useful points of comparison. So, too, might the very different postcolonial position taken by Ngũgĩ wa Thiong'o in his argument against former colonial subjects' using the languages, and hence the thought systems, of colonialism.

Another kind of politicized identity at play in Gower's work is Christianity, which again moves beyond Englishness to suggest a certain trans-European identity. In Gower's moment, however, the self-identity of such a *Christianitas* would be troubled by movements at home—a growing, native, Lollard heresy—and abroad, with the papal schism. Might there again be postcolonial analogues or useful comparisons to be drawn with postcolonial situations in which dominant ideological schemas are challenged from within and by populations that have been traditionally disempowered? Do Europe's internal conflicts, during the period of colonization, bear any useful resemblance to the religious and political divisions associated with the papal schism? Do indigenous challenges to colonial power bear any relation to Lollard resistances to Christian orthodoxy and the institutional church?

Queer theory might usefully elucidate an additional set of questions about identity. The *Confessio Amantis*—"the confession of the lover"—echoes, from its title onward, Foucault's account in volume 1 of the *History of Sexuality* of how a certain deployment of sexuality that makes the truth of the self its sex and sexuality develops from practices of confession. Of course, Foucault locates this deployment of sexuality in modernity, tracking its establishment particularly to the nineteenth century; we should not, then, expect full-fledged, modern sexualities to emerge in Gower's fourteenth-century writing. Still, what is Gower's "confession of the lover" but a certain kind of *scientia sexualis*, to use Foucault's term? The follow-up to this question, however, must be whether and how this "science" of the sexual self, as developed by Gower, lines up with Foucault's modern *scientia*.

Relatedly, a line of thinking following on Foucault suggests that sexuality defined as an identity—as opposed to a set of juridically permitted or disallowed acts—is a modern (again, nineteenth-century) invention. Much disputed, this claim might be usefully interrogated in the figure of Amans. Is "the lover" an identity in a modern sense—that is, the same sort of identity that Foucault defines when he sees the modern homosexual as a "species" emerging over against that "temporary aberration," the sodomite (43)? To what extent is the lover defined by acts that might be confessed, repudiated, and moved beyond, to what extent by some kind of solidified, internalized psyche or self? Entailed in addressing such questions, too, might be a consideration of the gender identity of Amans. Does the identity of "lover" entail a normative or dominant masculinity, or, contrastingly, does the lover's passion and passivity challenge his masculinity? A whole line of queer-inflected work on masculinities (e.g., the essays in Berger, Wallis, and Watson) might be brought into the classroom to help frame and elucidate such questions.

This line of thinking might lead then to a full consideration of the complex ways in which Amans as a figure is investigated in the long course of the *Confessio Amantis*. A speaking, confessing subject, Amans is also defined vis-à-vis a set of externalized figures—most notably Genius, but also all the figures used exemplarily in the narratives of the *Confessio*, as well as Venus in the poem's closing frame. We might ask students to consider whether these external figures are to be thought of as parts of a complex self, in fact as *internal* functions externalized in the process of the confession and the poem's self-reflection. Or are these figures instead "others" that help define a self relationally, by contrast? Alternatively, we might consider them in less psychologizing fashion, as universal human qualities significant for all human beings and for an Amans conceived of less as an individualized psyche than as an Everyman or Everylover. In taking up such questions, I would want to have in play the complex, psychoanalytically inflected reflections of queer theory on identity formation—for instance, Butler's treatment of the formation of a gendered-sexualized self through a series of melancholic identifications (*Gender Trouble*; *Bodies*; *Psychic Life*) or Diana Fuss's consideration of the interplay of desire and identification. When complex changes in Amans's self are mediated—in the closing frame of the *Confessio*—through a dream vision, we might ask whether there are any parallel models in (post)modern theories of psyche and self for the radical transformation here identified, too, with growing old. It seems to me that contemporary transgender theory (e.g., Prosser's reflections on transsexual identity as an identity of transition in *Second Skins*), despite the differences, would be useful for understanding this kind of transformational, conversionary experience.

Sociality/Sexuality

Questions concerning identity are of course closely linked to questions about social formations, questions, that is, like those Gower consistently takes up as he returns, in each of his major works, to consider the overall structure of society. Reiterating the medieval model of the three estates, Gower also rethinks that model (particularly in the *Vox clamantis* and *Mirour de l'omme*), giving emphatic attention to the emerging mercantile and artisanal classes that do not fit neatly into the traditional, tripartite schema. Students can explore such abstract reflections on social order by addressing Gower's depiction of characters occupying varying social positions elsewhere in his work. Thus, for instance, idealized depictions of the working estate (peasantry) stand in a certain dissonance with Gower's strongly disapproving depiction, in *Vox clamantis*, of the peasants in revolt. The representation here of an animal-like, hardly human mob itself resonates with postcolonial critiques of discourses that ontologize natives as less than human or animalistic (McClintock; Bhabha; Spivak, "Can the Subaltern Speak?"). It also resonates with queer theory's recognition that certain kinds of lives are defined, in Butler's formulation, as "unlivable," not falling within the realm of the properly human (*Undoing Gender*).

By putting characters into action, in the many narratives of the *Confessio*, Gower also places individuals into social worlds, and students can see Gower deeply and repeatedly interested in the dynamics of love, marriage, family, community, and kingship. Here, introducing Sedgwick's treatment of male homosociality (*Between Men*) would provide one model for thinking about how Gower depicts male-male cooperation and conflict. To what extent do love, marriage, and family in the *Confessio* depend on the solidification of male-male bonds? To what extent are male-male bonds challenged or undermined by male-female relations? Are there spaces (e.g., in the Apollonius story) where Gower also considers the possibility and implications of *female* homosociality as an alternative social space? My thinking here has been influenced by Gary Lim's treatment of the Apollonius narrative in his dissertation "Familiar Estrangements." To what extent is the "heterosexuality" in play in Gower's narratives *like* modern heterosexuality? Can we speak of a medieval heteronormativity, and, even if we can, to what extent are male-female relationships of sex, marriage, alliance, and family sexualized differently in the Middle Ages?

Certain aspects of Gower's treatment of sex and sexuality—for instance, his representation of incest (Donavin, *Incest Narratives*; Bullón-Fernández, "Confining"; Scanlon, "Riddle"; Archibald; Nowlin) and of rape (Dinshaw, "Rivalry"; Sylvester)—have received extensive critical attention. Focusing a class on incest, for instance, would enable the reading of Gower's text alongside such critical medievalist work as well as important theoretical formulations and rethinking of the incest taboo (Lévi-Strauss; Rubin; Butler, *Antigone's Claim*). Is the taboo on incest universal, or is it subject to historical change and rearticulation as a certain line of queer thinking (including especially Butler) would suggest? And more narrowly, are Gower's representations of incest themselves historically specific, reflecting a particular kind of thinking about family relations and sex in his own late medieval world?

(Trans)Nationalism

As with so many other entities that contemporary theory defines as having emerged in modernity—homo/heterosexuality, the subject/individual, race—the nation-state has been reclaimed for the Middle Ages by historicist work: while the Middle Ages certainly did not know the nation in its modern form, medieval political structures are in many ways analogous to those we identify with the modern nation and its associated nationalisms, as Kathy Lavezzo's collection *Imagining a Medieval English Nation* has addressed. Given Gower's interest in English politics, as demonstrated in the revisions to the prologue of the *Confessio Amantis* or the treatment of 1381 in the *Vox clamantis*, it makes sense to consider how his England did or did not correspond to the kind of nation defined in contemporary theoretical formulations as emerging in modernity. Does England, for Gower, bear any of the features, for instance, of Anderson's "imagined communities"? Does Anderson's thinking of the modern nation-state and its development work in relation to Gower's nationalism, or does a wholly different sense of nation pertain?

In many of the narratives of the *Confessio Amantis*, Gower depicts national and international interactions, if often in nonmedieval (and particularly classicizing) situations. Nonetheless, we might read such stories as a piecemeal but extended consideration of rule, interstate conflict, and international diplomacy. A segment of a course might usefully bring together three or four narratives that take up questions of international interaction differently—the tales of Constance, Jason and Medea, the false bachelor, and Florent, for instance—and consider these in comparison with one another and in connection with theories of nation and the transnational (including, of course, postcolonial formulations). The four narratives present very different representations of political structures—some more fully institutionalized and governmental, others more kin-based. Some of them ("Constance," "The False Bachelor") also depict religious difference as an intimate feature of international relations. In addition, all four concern themselves with love, marriage, alliance, and family, and hence all could simultaneously be considered in relation to queer theoretical formulations. Here, too, it would be useful to think about how, elsewhere in his work, Gower reflects more abstractly and explicitly on contemporary international relations — the condemnation of crusading activity included in the *Confessio* (3.2490–515, 4.1656–82); the treatment of an international mercantile network of trade in the discussion of "Triche" ("Fraud") in the *Mirour de l'omme* (25237–60) — while also taking into account a sense of England's complex international and (post)colonial relations not just with France but also with Wales, Scotland, Ireland, and Iberia. Interactions with Iberia, including especially fourteenth-century Lancastrian intervention and its aftermath, have not received much critical attention; but see R. F. Yeager's "Gower's Lancastrian Affinity" and María Bullón-Fernández's collection *England and Iberia*, especially Joyce Coleman's essay on Gower ("Philippa").

It is also productive to consider how Gower's political thinking treats ideas of empire, which are explicitly in play in the medieval notions of *translatio imperii* and of an ideal, "global" *Christianitas* and which are repeatedly invoked, for instance, in Gower's representations of Roman imperial politics and narratives. Here, the writings of Michael Hardt and Antonio Negri on empire, Rey Chow on "the age of the world target," Spivak on "planetarity" (in *Death*), and Chandra Talpade Mohanty on decolonization and globalization would all provide challenging theoretical discussions useful for thinking medieval politics but themselves subject to recalibration in their encounter with "globalizing," imperial *medieval* formulations.

Periodization

Questions of periodization have been central to the elaboration of postcolonial and queer theory, given that each has depended to a significant degree on historical accounts of the development of the nation and of (de)colonization, on the one hand, and of modern identitarian sexuality, on the other. Queer and postcolonial work in medieval studies partly serves to call the standard periodizations into question, arguing that medieval situations benefit from queer and postcolonial analysis and that attending to medieval histories might lead to productive reconceptualizations of gender, sexuality, nation, (de)colonization, and empire. Such questions are invigorating to take up particularly in the context of survey courses that bring medieval and (early) modern material together. Here, we might ask to what extent the medieval world and modernity in fact stand separate from each other — generally, and more specifically in relation both to international/(post)colonial relations and to gender/sexuality. Gower himself consistently uses historical material to think about his contemporary world. Do Gower's reflections help us think about our own contemporary situations? And how might Gower and later writers considered in a survey (e.g., Shakespeare or Aphra Behn) take up similar kinds of questions to similar and different ends?

Such issues can, of course, be introduced without the explicit inclusion of theoretical readings—but they can be made much more pointed if considered in relation to challenging theoretical formulations that make us rethink twentieth-/ twenty-first-century and medieval gender and sexuality, on the one hand, and (trans)national power relations and histories, on the other.

This bringing together of contemporary theory and medieval culture is one of the most important kinds of work we can do in the medieval studies classroom. It enables us to foreground with our students the ways in which medieval texts might echo, comment on, and clarify our present situations while also representing experiences and structures radically different from our own; hence it might open up, for the twenty-first-century student, radically new ways of reading. Having taken on such work in medieval studies, students might then be prepared, in a class on critical theory, to recognize some of its historical limitations and partiality. They might also come to recognize that raising the same kinds of questions—about empire or nation or gender or sexuality—in different historical moments and with different kinds of literary-cultural material might necessitate different sorts of investigation and lead to radically different answers.

COMPARATIVE APPROACHES

Gower and *The Canterbury Tales*:
The Enticement to Fraud

Craig E. Bertolet

I situate Gower and Chaucer as poets in and of London wrestling with the problems that commerce and its sporadic regulation caused late-fourteenth-century readers. This approach is a useful way for students to see these two important writers commenting in different ways on buying and selling, an activity that does not appear in English-language literature with the same thoughtful evaluation much before the period of Chaucer and Gower. We do not, for instance, tend to entertain doubt when we purchase a package in an opaque container — say, a bag of frozen peas — that the items inside the container are not the items depicted in impossibly clear color photographs on the package. We do not open the package before we purchase it to be certain it contains peas, that they are indeed frozen, and that the amount corresponds to the weight written on the label. Should we decide to investigate whether these assumptions are well founded before we pay for them, our behavior would be greeted as decidedly odd by our fellow customers and would perhaps upset the owners of the store in ways that a calm explanation will not easily assuage. If we find that the frozen peas are not what they are advertised to be, we can return them and get our money back. The situation was somewhat different in the late fourteenth century. What was different was that advice about buying and selling moved into the literature of the period as a means of warning against the immorality of particular kinds of fraud.

Students need to understand that many people from various parts of England and Western Europe passed through London. They often could not rely on royal or noble sponsors to protect them against litigation even if their trade practices were not dubious, nor could they be assured of legal recourse should they become victims of fraud. Also, a person who could make money and rise in status by purchasing luxury items was counted to be a worthy individual in the city and a person of great respect. Then as now, the enticement to fraud was too great for some people to resist.

Both Chaucer and Gower have different ways of addressing fraud in their works. Gower's account of urban frauds in the *Mirour de l'omme* and *Vox clamantis* provides the argument for how trade (particularly London's) is so corrupted and corrupting that everyone engaged in it cheats and how punishment is nonexistent. Chaucer addresses commercial fraud in conversation among his characters or demonstrations within the stories they tell. My approach to teaching Chaucer and fraud in context with Gower focuses on three events in three Canterbury tales: the Miller's account of Nicholas's lie about a second Nowell's flood, the Reeve's characterization of Symkin as a cheater, and the Cook's conversation with Harry Bailly. Reading the passages from the *Mirour* and the *Vox* together with these tales helps students see all the texts as responding to a suspicion of commerce shared by writers and many ordinary Londoners.

While Chaucer's Friar, Summoner, and Pardoner are also engaged in questionable revenue enhancement, the fraud they commit is not the same as that of traders and merchants because their ultimate goal (salvation) is materially intangible. The Pardoner's relics are fakes, but the faith that good would come of believing in them is not falsifiable. On the other hand, no amount of faith will make the Cook's twice-baked pies a culinary miracle regardless of what the Cook says about them. As Harry Bailly remarks, the Cook's boast of the high quality of his wares can be proved false by material examination. This is the nature of fraud prosecution in London.

Then as now, when a person was accused of fraud in London, he or she would be brought to trial, and his or her allegedly fraudulent good or service examined by witnesses expert in the trade. The medieval guilds would provide the expert witnesses and often bring the charges against the accused with the understanding that the behavior of the errant member brings shame to all the guild's members. In fact, the common formula is that the malefactor committed his or her misdeeds to the deception of the commonalty and the scandal of the entire guild. The burden of proof, though, falls on the guild members to show, on the basis of their authority in the trade, that the good or service (when they examined it) was substandard. Of course, those persons who were not in a guild, such as Chaucer's Canon, may slip through the porous world of late medieval litigation. I distribute to students a few examples from A. H. Thomas's edition of the *Calendar of Select Pleas and Memoranda*, which records summaries of cases tried before the court of the mayor and aldermen, to help illustrate

Gower's particular complaints. One example is that of Walter Kyng, who was accused by his fellow grocers of selling fraudulent spices. In the mayor's court, the grocers showed that Kyng's apprentice had sold a bag of dust, garbage, and rotten cetwall as spice. Kyng was fined for his misdeed (219–20). The testimony of the grocers, as practitioners of the spice trade, proved that Kyng was at least a negligent master, at worst a harmful food seller. But what of the average person buying spices, or any good for that matter, who lacks the expertise to tell fine work from false? Gower argues that buyers are on their own because fraud is rampant.

I pair The Cook's Prologue and Tale with Gower's account of fraud in the *Mirour de l'omme*; The Reeve's Tale with Gower's condensed criticism of fraud in the *Vox clamantis* ("Voice of One Crying");[1] followed by The Miller's Tale and Gower's account of the Whisperer from the *Vox* (216–19). The order can be reversed if the focus is on Chaucer. Since my focus here is on teaching Gower with Chaucer, I describe the first order because it follows Gower's composition history.

The *Mirour* passage focuses on how commerce has been corrupted by merchants and traders. Gower provides specific instances of the various frauds, grouping them in three categories: merchants, artisans, and victuallers. The groupings correspond to clearly delineated functions of commercial agents in the city. The merchants transported goods to and from London. The artisans (who produced durable goods, such as clothing, furniture, and luxury items) and the victuallers (who produced and sold food and drink) were under the authority of their individual guilds. Therefore the fraudulent activity of any artisan or victualler affected the integrity of the entire guild if the crime went unchecked. Gower cites a litany of abusers in this passage. Among others, he complains about drapers who sell their cloth in low light so that a customer cannot tell the difference between cheaper green or more expensive blue cloth (332), goldsmiths who use alloys rather than pure gold (335), brewers who sell bad ale made from inferior grain (343), and bakers who sell bread by false weights (343–44).

Gower concludes that fraud is everywhere and that he "will not except a single one as not attending on Fraud" (346). This account is admittedly an exaggeration and in the mode of the medieval topos of the corruption of the world. However, Gower localizes these abuses to London. Here, the Kyng example cited earlier is particularly useful because the apprentice actually sells the fraudulent product. Moreover, since Kyng was a victualler, he shared the same occupation as Perkyn's master in The Cook's Tale. Gower claims that, even though the perpetrator of a fraud is an apprentice, the master "shall rightly bear the sin before the apprentice; for his estate is higher and he also takes the gain from it" (338).

From this situation, the victualler's dilemma in The Cook's Tale is easy to understand. His negligent apprentice can ruin the entire trade, which is why he uses the metaphor of the rotten apple spoiling the entire bunch to describe Perkyn (4406–07). Perkyn steals money from his master's box to cover his debts

(4389–90). He surrounds himself with a group of riotous young men (4381–82). He pays more attention to what is going on in the street than what is going on in the shop (4377–80). This behavior is not conducive to the success of the business, so his master cuts Perkyn off rather than bear the liability of bringing him into the trade as a bad member. He is mindful of what Gower warns about the master's suffering for the sin of the apprentice, just as Kyng did. The Cook's victualler has indeed suffered much.

Beyond the tale, the conversation that Harry Baily and the Cook have about the Cook's own wares, of which the Cook boasts in his portrait from The General Prologue (379–87), shows the discrepancy between advertising and reality. Gower cites butchers and poulterers as victuallers who will sell bad meat rather than take the financial loss accrued from disposing of it (344–45). Harry makes the same claim for the Cook, who will sell his pies twice hot and twice cold (4346–48). In both cases, the victuallers put their business ahead of concern for the health of their customers. I also share with the students the ordinance of the pasty bakers from *Letter-Book H* (Riley 438), which sets out what can and cannot be baked into a pie sold in London. For instance, goose meat cannot go into a pie, and this meat is exactly what Harry says the Cook uses (4351). Here, both the guild's rules and Harry's allegations show the Cook to be engaging in shady commerce despite dismissing what Harry says about him (4356–63)

Harry argues that the people who come into the Cook's fly-blown shop will fare the worse since they are falsely enticed into purchasing a product, the praises of which are easier to digest than the actual food. In the *Vox* Gower complains that, when Fraud calls people into her shop, "no one can go away uncheated" (214–16). The situation is similar for the Cook's customers. It is also similar for Symkin's customers in The Reeve's Tale, because the Reeve draws the portrait of Symkin as a fraudulent trader who obtains a false prosperity based on cheating. Gower remarks that Fraud "often takes even a sixth part for herself through clever weighing" (214). In fact, The Reeve's Tale begins with a fraudulent transaction. Symkin steals a bushel of flour from the students when they are distracted by their horses running in the fens (4092–94).

In The Reeve's Tale, part of the reason that John and Aleyn get duped is their belief that they can learn how the milling process works merely by watching it once (4036–45). Where the average apprentice might require five to seven years to learn the trade, they figure, on the basis of their superior training as university students, they can learn it quicker. The Reeve's point here is that a trade requires an expertise that needs to be acquired through constant practice. Certainly everyone would know this. However, Gower argues that a person who knows the process can abuse it in ways that no one except perhaps another practitioner of the trade could recognize: "If a smart man enters [Fraud's shop], she is smarter than he; and if a fool goes in, he goes away a bigger fool" (*Vox* 213). This is exactly what happens to John and Aleyn. They learn that they are bigger fools because they realize after the fact that Symkin has cheated them. They have entered his shop where he is the undisputed master of the trade.

Moreover, no other miller is in the area to provide competition for Symkin or evidence that his processes are false. His daughter betrays Symkin not by knowing the process but by producing the tangible result of the fraud.

The other deception working in this tale is that Symkin's family members believe themselves to be better than they really are. This kind of misrepresentation of social status annoys Gower. He claims that "those [fraudulent] households contain nothing they rightly should." He observes that an individual who gains wealth by fraud does so to seek honor "so that people will greet him from afar on bended knee" (*Vox* 213). In medieval London, where status was based on material wealth as much as on birth, wealthy citizens were perceived to be more worthy of higher standing than others (Thrupp 14–15). They also demonstrate their wealth by their dress to provide visual proof to anyone of their status, such as the Physician does in The General Prologue (439–40). Part of the rancor that the Reeve wants to instill in his listeners concerning Symkin and his wife is that they dress to impress while everyone knows Symkin to be a notorious cheat. Gower finds that, even when a peasant, such as Symkin, rises above his station, he is still a peasant (*Vox* 215). Similarly, Symkin pretends to be of higher social standing but behaves only like the churl he is (3925–40). His wife also pretends to be a lady but does not have the status to justify her behavior (3942–68). The wealth they show with their comparatively expensive clothing is ill-gotten, and their honor is hollow.

For both The Reeve's Tale and The Cook's Prologue and Tale, the important point for the students to understand is how commercial deception undermines the communal systems on which London (or any town particularly) is founded. In The Reeve's Tale, no one is on hand who can stop Symkin's manipulation of the milling process. John and Aleyn enact their revenge on him in a way other than trade, which is Symkin's idiom and where Symkin is master. Conversely, the Cook seems to be exposed by Harry, but these revelations have not kept the Cook from being hired by the guildsmen. Chaucer's two texts show that the drive toward wealth and respectability that Symkin and his wife embody tends to compromise quality and should cause all potential buyers significant anxiety when purchasing anything.

A similar corruption affects the exchange of information that is also a falsifiable commodity. In the *Vox*, Gower argues that a figure called the Whisperer undermines the harmony of the city by spreading lies or rumors. Gower concludes that the unregulated tongue can destroy a city (*Vox* 216–19). This passage is useful as a comparison with the tale of Chaucer's Manciple. It is also useful for the description in The Miller's Tale of Absolon, who is concerned with dangerous speech. Absolon is directly engaged in all aspects of town life. He participates in pageants and dances. He also records the achievements of the parish in registering baptisms, weddings, and funerals (3312–36, 3383–85). For him, the destruction of the city would be the destruction of his livelihood. Dangerous speech represents the potential to undermine cities, as Gower argues. Consequently, Absolon is remarkably wary of dangerous speech (3337–38).

In the classroom, however, the portion of this tale that works best with Gower's account of the Whisperer is Nicholas's story of the second Nowell's Flood. Nicholas is not talkative, as from his portrait Absolon must be. He is, though, a liar whose goal is to cause division in the household. Gower says that the Whisperer's weapon is a tongue that, among other things, "loosens marriage bonds, and makes into two what God has declared to be one" (*Vox* 216). The Whisperer is a danger to the community at large and can bring down a city's honor (217). The Whisperer also causes division, which, in the *Confessio Amantis*, Gower says is the worst evil in a community (prologue, lines 971–72).

This far-reaching evil works on the comparatively small stage of John's house in The Miller's Tale because Nicholas's lie divides John from his wife. It will ultimately divide John from his neighbors when they laugh at him for his folly in believing a tale of a world-destroying flood. John's folly also hurts him physically when he breaks his arm falling from the roof of his house with the mistaken belief that Nicholas's cry for "Water" meant that the flood had come.

The fraud perpetrated against John is one that works on his acceptance of Nicholas's words as authoritative because Nicholas is a student of astrology. As with any kind of technical knowledge, such as carpentry or milling, astrology is a skill to learn. John accepts Nicholas's authority in this field because Nicholas appears to have the training in it and John does not. Nicholas, for instance, does not question John's ability to provide the three containers in which they will hide to survive the flood.

Of course, anyone should be able to see through Nicholas's fraud without studying astrology. But the belief that John has in such magic or miracles was commonplace in Chaucer's London. Providing students with two examples of Londoners duped by first a magician and then a false physician from the *Letter-Book H* illustrates to students how people accepted similarly unbelievable claims. The false magician example involves a man named Henry Pot, who alleged that he could find a lost cup by casting a spell over thirty-two white clay balls. His resulting "spell" led to an accusation of theft against a woman named Cristina Freman who was, it turned out, innocent of the crime. Pot confessed to the deceit and was punished in the pillory (Riley 462–63). The false physician example involves Roger Clerk, who knew nothing of medicine and was also illiterate. He convinced a man to tie around his wife's neck a "magic" parchment scroll in which was written a Latin charm. The woman did not get better from this "treatment," the parchment was found to be blank, and Clerk was led through the streets in a procession with the parchment, whetstone, and urinals hung about his neck for lying (464–66).

As with the Cook's bad pasties, Pot's spell, and Clerk's parchment, Nicholas's plan is falsifiable, but only if it is tested. John does not doubt and, therefore, does not believe he needs to test it. His gullibility, as the Miller reports, causes his literal and metaphoric downfall. It also causes John to be rejected by his neighbors, who laugh at the foolishness of his belief. If John had accused Nicholas of fraud, Nicholas would have been exposed to this group as a liar, to the ruin of his reputation. By the public spectacle of Pot's and Clerk's punishment, no one should fall for their frauds again. The potential division in the community that Gower fears would be then stopped. Nicholas's lie works for him in a way that it does not work for Pot and Clerk, and yet Nicholas too is punished (though not exactly for the lie).

Not every commercial transaction in medieval London was tainted by corruption, nor was all technical knowledge professed by its traders and artisans suspect. Yet students should learn that Gower's and Chaucer's texts reveal a definite anxiety in purchasing, particularly in the city. They will see that, in the Middle Ages just as now, buying from a clever seller known to have dubious practices may not be the best policy, food may not be as good as it is advertised, and the people who can best protect them from potential cheaters are themselves.

NOTE

[1] Students read a passage from the *Mirour* in Wilson's translation (330–49), which I quote here, providing page numbers, and the *Vox* in Stockton's translation (214–16), from which I quote here, providing page numbers.

The Hag Transformed:
"The Tale of Florent," Ethical Choice, and Female Desire in Late Medieval England

James M. Dean

A number of Gower's best-known stories appeared in versions by other late medieval authors, notably Geoffrey Chaucer. Gower concerned himself with how individuals can and should relate to the commonwealth—to king, church, institutions, and fellow human beings—and he crafted his verse in what Anne Middleton in "The Idea of Public Poetry in the Reign of Richard II" has characterized as a "public voice," a voice that seeks broad consensus and the common good (107). An accomplished storyteller, Gower provides a treasure trove of questions that modern students can understand and debate despite the often considerable gulfs between medieval and modern attitudes on those questions. Indeed, the differences help sharpen modern positions on, say, exemplary conduct or the role of women in domestic governance. Gower frames his stories along ethical lines, seeking to provide them with broad meaning; and his ethical treatments can best be acknowledged and exploited in comparisons with authors who told the same story. Some of the stories Gower recounts in *Confessio Amantis* appear in Chaucer's *Canterbury Tales,* including Gower's "Tale of Constance" (Chaucer's Man of Law's Tale), the "Tale of Virginia" (Chaucer's Physician's Tale), and the "Tale of Phebus and the Crow" (Chaucer's Manciple's Tale). Gower's "Tale of Florent," a story probably told in its Middle English form first by Gower but subsequently retold by Chaucer as The Wife of Bath's Tale, was revived in the anonymous fifteenth-century *The Wedding of Sir Gawain and Dame Ragnelle.* Students can appreciate Gower's storytelling art by comparing the literary and ethical treatments that give meaning to these stories. A comparative approach reveals Gower's purposes in framing and concluding his twice-told tales, which include but are by no means limited to doing the right thing even when nobody is looking and setting an example in the process.

Gower defines ethics ("etique") as acting according to virtuous principles. He frames his definition as part of rules for kingship, but the rules apply also to any who would understand and engage in right conduct.[1] Ethics, says Genius, teaches "of vertu thilke [this] reule, / Hou that a king himself schal reule / Of his moral condicion / With worthi disposicion / Of good livinge in his persone" (*CA* 7.1653–57). Gower's "Tale of Florent" addresses issues of self-governance when one must adhere to one's word—maintain one's *trouthe*—under trying circumstances. These issues to varying degrees arise in the three versions of the story under consideration here, and a fruitful entrée into the version is to have students, as mine have done, detail the differences in the versions of the tale they are reading.[2] In all three versions a knight must wed a woman who is the archetype of ugliness, the loathly lady. She in turn saves his life by providing him with the correct answer to the question of what "alle wommen most desire," as Gower's tale phrases it (1.1481). These tales immediately raise two ethical issues: the imperatives to follow through on one's word and to conduct oneself gracefully and appropriately under pressure. How should one behave when circumstances oblige one to perform a distasteful task or come to an unpleasant or uncomfortable decision? Gower, Chaucer, and the author of *The Wedding of Sir Gawain and Dame Ragnelle* explore the implications of right conduct in domestic relationships.

Throughout the *Confessio* Gower relates tales under rubrics of sin. The "Tale of Florent" provides an example of the deadly sin of pride in general (the chief subject and organizing principle of *Confessio Amantis*, book 1) and of two species of "Inobedience" in particular, "Murmur and Compleignte" (1345). The issue in "Florent" is grumbling and complaining — "unbuxomnesse" (1394) — against conditions over which one has no control. How should one behave when one's manhood and gentility are tested? Gower makes a point of Florent's virtues and good breeding. He is "worthi" (1408) and, with respect to warfare, "desirous, / Chivalerous and amorous" (1413–14); in the story these are good things. Florent is behaving as he should. But in pursuit of his knightly duties and in self-defense, Florent slays Branchus, himself "[t]he worthieste of al his lond" (1432). Because Florent's reputation for chivalric "worthinesse" and "gentilesse" is so exalted — Florent is related to the emperor — Branchus's relatives cannot exact vengeance immediately, so they leave revenge to Branchus's grandmother, "the slyheste / Of alle that men knewe tho" (1442–43). She devises the question that she expects Florent will not be able to answer about what women most desire; in other words, she concocts a malicious question, devised to entrap and cause the noble knight to fail. If he is unable to deliver the correct answer within a certain date and time, he will be slain. The ethical dilemma for Florent, however, occurs when an old and proverbially ugly woman intervenes to give him the answer to the grandmother's question. The loathly lady explains the terms to Florent — he must marry her if she gives him the right answer — and after initial demurral, offering "[o]f lond, of rente, of park, of plowh" (1566), Florent agrees and gives his word. When he realizes what he is up against — "Or forto take hire to his wif / Or elles forto lese his lif" (1573–74) — he knows his course.

The storytellers or narrators are crucial in Gower's and Chaucer's accounts. In Gower's version, Genius, a priest of Venus, confesses and instructs Amans, the poem's narrative "I," who later on is identified as John Gower. Genius organizes his storytelling and material generally around the seven deadly sins, and the result is that stories are annexed to moral and ethical ideas. In book 1 of *Confessio Amantis*, Genius outlines the five "ministers" of Pride: hypocrisy, inobedience, *surquidry* (presumption), *avantance* (boasting), and vainglory (beginning line 575). These aspects of Pride harmonize with the Parson's "twigs" of Pride in The Parson's Tale from *The Canterbury Tales*. The "twigs," according to the Parson, are "inobedience, avauntynge, ypocrisie, despit, arrogance, in-pudence, swellynge of herte, insolence, elacioun, inpacience, strif, contumacie, presumpcioun, irreverence, pertinacie, veyneglorie, and many another twig that I kan nat declare" (392). All of Genius's ministers find their way into the Parson's list, but the Parson includes others. The storyteller of The Wife of Bath's Tale is of course Alice, the Wife of Bath; the purpose of her telling the story of the knight who consults the loathly lady is quite different from Genius's example of "inobedience" or the Parson's examples in his section on Pride and its remedies. The ostensible purpose of her story is to illustrate her sermonlike point that marriages work out best when the wife is in control—when she exercises "sov-ereignty" in the relationship. The Wife claims that the reformed knight and the transformed hag live happily ever after (1257–58), but then she makes a similar claim for her relationship with her fifth husband, Jankyn, after their contre-temps before the fireplace, when Jankyn, she claims, sees the errors of his mi-sogynistic ways (819–22).

The Wife of Bath's Tale and Prologue share some of the same concerns: power and control in marriage, bigamy (how often may a person legally marry?), and sexuality (is sexual expression allowed or condoned within the marriage bond?). It is not clear whether Chaucer intends for the Wife to occupy a moral position in her storytelling, although at least two ethical issues emerge: the first is justice. King Arthur states that the punishment for the unnamed rapist-knight is death, but the queen transmutes this sanction into a learning experience. The knight has a year and a day to find the correct answer to the question, What is it that women want? If he fails to solve the question, he forfeits his life. The second ethical issue concerns power, manipulation, and dominance in human relation-ships. Students might identify and articulate the dynamic in the relationships the Wife describes. How does the Wife, in her prologue, lose control over her husbands as she ages? How does the loathly damsel gain mastery of the rapist-knight, and is that mastery a good thing? These concerns are ethical rather than moral or spiritual; they touch on universal human truths but not sin, damna-tion, and salvation. A question students can and do debate is, Does the queen's revised punishment fit the crime? The question is especially relevant today in the light of Chaucer's legal entanglements with Cecilia Chaumpaigne and the discovery of a document releasing him from the charge of "raptu" (Crow and Olson 343–47; Cannon, "Raptus" and "Chaucer"). How does Gower's version shift the focus from justice to other ethical issues?

The loathly lady's appearance is very much an issue in Gower's version of the tale. The narrator briefly describes her in lines 1529–32, but later, when Flo-rent must fulfill his end of the bargain and wed her, every detail of her ugliness is related with almost loving relish in a blazon. She is meant to be a folklore figure of nonpareil repulsiveness—a woman so foul that she disrupts and de-stabilizes the knight's chivalric pretensions (Peck, "Folklore" 114–15). She is a "vecke," an old woman or hag (Italian *vecchia*), "Which was the lothlieste what

[thing] / That evere man caste on his yhe" (1675, 1676–77). Although she saves
Florent's life from the evil grandmother's question, she otherwise challenges
the knight's social standing and his reputation. Shakespeare alludes to Gower's
loathly lady when Petruchio will agree to marry any woman of sufficient wealth,
even if she be "as foul as was Florentius' love" (*Taming* 1.2.69). The descriptive
detail usually lavished on a remarkable beauty is, in "Florent," applied to her
loathsome counterpart. The hag is the opposite of the romance heroine both
in her description and in her place in the narrative. She squats, toadlike, in the
position occupied by the lovely lady in more traditional romance narratives.
Florent determines to make a virtue of necessity and to go through with the
marriage, but he hides his wife away from prying eyes and himself ventures
out in public only rarely and with circumspection. Florent comes very close to
falling into "murmur" and "compleignte"—engaging in pride and grumbling
because he expects his reputation to be damaged. Gower's treatment of the
story emphasizes the ethical situation, which Gower crafts to the extreme and
which he shows involves magic; when the loathly lady is released from the evil
stepmother's curse, we see a gender-reversed variant of the folktale modern
readers know as "The Frog Prince."

Students often note that the descriptions of the loathly lady visit cruelty upon
her. Gower goes out of his way to find new language for her ugliness. In addition to the already cited "vecke" and "what," the narrator describes her as "this
foule grete Coise" (1734), defined by the *Middle English Dictionary* as "rump,
haunches" and "figure" and which the *MED* notes is "used disparagingly of an
ugly woman." The narrator compares her with a "More" (1686), a blackamoor,
which is not a compliment. Students can ponder the implications of Gower's
racial and gender insensitivity, typical for his historical era.

Although the riddle-solving loathly lady of Chaucer's Wife of Bath's Tale is
on some level the same archetypal figure as Gower's "vecke," Chaucer devotes
far less space to her physical attributes than Gower does. Chaucer's strategy,
which may in part involve the Wife as storyteller, is to emphasize the agreement
struck between knight and loathly lady. The narrator does say of the hag, "A
fouler wight [creature] ther may no man devyse" (999); moreover, the knight
cries out to her, "Thou art so loothly, and so oold also, / . . . / That litel wonder is thogh I walwe and wynde [wallow and writhe]" (1100–02). This said,
the major alterations to the Wife's tale are that Chaucer sets the story in King
Arthur's time and, more important, that the knight-protagonist rapes a maiden
to set the tale in motion. Far from being the exemplar of chivalric virtue, as in
the "Tale of Florent," the knight of The Wife of Bath's Tale is rash, overbear-
ing, and self-centered. Florent slays the noble knight Branchus while pursuing his chivalric duties and *ethos*; the rapist-knight takes the maidenhood of a
virgin—a capital offense—violently and because he can. Arthur's queen temporarily spares his life, setting him on an ethical quest to learn "what thyng is it
that wommen moost desiren" (905). The knight's quest in all three versions is

the same, but there is special point to the rapist-knight's having to learn what women really want.

The correct answer to the riddle in all three stories is sovereignty in marriage. *Sovereignty* in this signification means "mastery" or "dominion," terms that denote ultimate authority and that have distinct masculine overtones ("soverainte"). This sovereignty refers specifically to say-so in marriage—which spouse gets to dictate the conditions of the relationship and to be in "mais-trie . . . above" (1040). In the three stories, power concerns not who gets to compile the guest list for a feast but how the male spouse will view and judge his wife. In the "Tale of Florent," the hag transforms into the young beauty before Florent decides whether he would have her beautiful by day or by night. If by day, then Florent's society of knights will honor Florent, but he will not be able to enjoy his wife's beauty by night, when they are in bed together, a personal rather than social consideration (Peck, "Folklore" 102–03). If by night, then Florent will be scorned socially but will thrive personally. In a speech that highlights Florent's *gentilesse*, Florent graciously asks the lady to choose for them: "Ches for ous bothen, I you preie" (1829). He emphasizes that he values her powers of discernment and choice:

> Bot evere whil that I may live,
> I wol [desire] that ye be my maistresse,
> For I can noght miselve gesse
> Which is the beste unto my chois [how best to choose].
> (1824–27)

When Florent asks that the lady be his "maistresse," he makes no little concession. Such mastery is precisely what Grisilde of Chaucer's Clerk's Tale repudiates in her relationship with Walter: "I nevere heeld me lady ne maistresse, / But humble servant to youre worthynesse" (823–24). Criseyde, speaking to Troilus, warns him that she will not put up with his exercising mastery over her: "A kynges sone although ye be, ywys, / Ye shal namore han sovereignete / Of me in love, than right in that cas is" (3.170–72). In the "Tale of Florent" the husband shows due deference to his wife, and Genius moralizes that the story illustrates the rewards of obedience. The terms of the relationship as things unfold in the "Tale of Florent" resemble the marriage conditions in Chaucer's Franklin's Tale, where Arveragus is both "servant" and "lord" to Dorigen (792–96). These terms are significant because they underscore the ethical issues of human worth versus societal appearances raised so prominently throughout Gower's version. Florent worries that his status will suffer if the court beholds his repulsive bride—the same woman who rescued him from beheading. The wedding-night terms develop from a similar concern. Would Florent want to make love to a beautiful woman by night but suffer the social consequences of appearing in public with a loathly lady? Or would he prefer to be seen in public with a beautiful woman during the day but suffer at night laboring to pay his marriage debt to the ugliest woman in the world? The choice is daunting for Florent, who cannot decide. Yet Florent's response is gracious, noble, and liberating for the hag:

> O ye, my lyves hele [salvation],
> Sey what you list in my querele [quarrel],
> I not [don't know] what ansuere I schal yive:
> ·
> Thus grante I yow myn hole vois,
> Ches for ous bothen, I you preie;
> And what as evere that ye seie,
> Riht as ye wole so wol I.   (1821–23, 1828–31)

There may be an underlying motif of sovereignty in this speech, as in Gower's tale generally, but the more important issue in Florent's statement and this moment is the nobility Florent exhibits as he gracefully seeks his wife's decision in the matter. He does not concede his choice to her because there seem to be no good choices.

In the "Tale of Florent," consummation of marriage or honoring of spouse is tested. When Florent arranges the wedding ceremony for the dead of night, his integrity comes into question. Gower skillfully sets the scene as he describes how "prive" ("discreet") women prepare the hag for the ceremony. Unlike Grisilde of Chaucer's Clerk's Tale, who appears "translated" into a finer tone when she is invested in rich clothing, the loathly lady appears somehow uglier than she was earlier: "Tho was sche foulere on to se" (1759). Ironically, Florent takes these steps and precautions to maintain his "good name," although in terms of the story and its values he seems less than honorable. His concern is entirely with the damsel's outward appearance and his own reputation — how others might judge him on the basis of his wife's looks. He is worried that others will see her, so he spirits her indoors under the cloak of darkness "in such a wise / That noman myhte hire schappe avise [observe], / Til sche into the chambre cam" (1735–37). (Chaucer's rapist-knight suffers a similar embarrassment, hiding himself away like "an owle" [1081] after the wedding ceremony. Chaucer derives the owl image, though, from Gower.)[3] As a knight, Florent suffers shame and humiliation because of his wife's "shape." In bed on his wedding night, Florent is no model of marital zeal and activity, at least at first. In a coincidental turn of phrase recalling May's attitude toward the wedding night in Chaucer's Merchant's Tale, Florent remains in bed, naked, and "stille as eny ston" (1794) at the prospect of his wedding-night consummation. (May for her part is conducted to the marriage bed "as stille as stoon" [1818].) The phrase has not only biblical resonance (Exodus 15.16) but also proverbial value (Whiting S772a). Chaucer uses the phrase often — five times in Troilus and Criseyde — and usually to convey a sense of ghastly quietude. Florent proves himself, in a way the rapist-knight does not, by overcoming his abhorrence of the damsel's appearance and agreeing to make love to the hag (Yeager, "John Gower" 325). After the hag says they have become, in effect, one flesh as a married couple (1793), the narrator says of Florent, "He herde and understod the bond" (1798), the bond meaning his word that he gave during the marriage ceremony. Only at this point, when Florent affirms the marriage bond, does the hag transform into a maiden.

The hag's transformation occurs at a different moment in The Wife of Bath's Tale—and with far different ethical implications. For that matter, the *terms* of the transformation differ from those in "Florent." The hag asks the rapist-knight whether he would prefer her to be old and foul but faithful or beautiful and potentially unfaithful? The point about *honor* (beauty by day) does not appear in the Wife's tale except annexed to the issue of cuckoldry—"Or elles ye wol han me yong and fair, / And take youre aventure of the repair [visitors] / That shal be to youre hous by cause of me, / Or in som oother place, may wel be" (1223–26). It is unclear from the text if the knight cannot decide because of weariness with the process or because he truly has no opinion, at least at the critical moment. Given his history, one might expect the knight to choose beauty and to let the fidelity issues fall where they may. As the knight asks the hag herself to decide, his words are ambiguous:

> My lady and my love, and wyf so deere,
> I put me in youre wise governance;
> Cheseth youreself which may be moost plesance
> And moost honour to yow and me also.
> I do no fors [I don't care] the wheither of the two,
> For as you liketh, it suffiseth [is sufficient for] me.
> (1230–35)

These crucial lines can be read either as the knight's resignation, with emphasis on "I do no fors the wheither of the two," or as the sentiments of a reformed man. Evidence for the latter include his polite speech, which stresses deference to the hag's wisdom and guidance, and his final statement, "For as you liketh, it suffiseth me." The issue is not so much the hag's transformation as the *knight's* change of heart. Has he learned his lesson about what women desire, or is he unreconstructed and temporarily browbeaten? What students can come to understand is that if Gower in his "Tale of Florent" emphasizes honor and *gentilesse* and turning "inobedience" into "obedience," Chaucer or his storyteller stresses inward transformation and true repentance. Whatever sincerity the knight brings to his wife results in the wife's transformation; she at least takes him at his word, and she understands him to say that he invests her with power in the relationship.

Ethics also come into play in the hag's arguments to the knight about gentility. Does nobility arise from aristocratic lineage and inherited wealth or from noble conduct? Is gentility something outward or something inward? The hag launches into her speech because the knight characterizes her not only as being ugly ("loothly") and "oold" but also as coming from "so lough a kynde" (1100–01), from a poverty-stricken caste. Her social standing is at issue only here, in the marriage bed, because the hag makes it an issue. On the other hand, social status is very much an issue in the "Tale of Florent" and in *The Wedding of Sir Gawain and Dame Ragnelle*, where the hag challenges every courtly sentiment and value with uncouth behavior. The loathly lady's speech in The Wife of Bath's Tale, by contrast, is the picture of gentility. Gower devotes a substantial section in book 4 of the *Confessio* to defining and explaining *gentilesse* according to the common human experiences of the turning of Fortune's wheel, the untitled nobility of Adam and Eve, and death (2204–91).

When the knight in The Wife of Bath's Tale hands over sovereignty to the hag, the lady seizes the opportunity to claim the power in their relationship. There is an element of festive comedy — medieval variety — in her assertion of "maistrie." The hag, after all, has been in charge from the moment she first appeared to the knight "under a forest syde" (990), as if by magic.[4] She controls the knight's destiny: she knows the correct answer to the queen's riddle, and she understands very well that the knight has few choices. She dictates the knight's every move. Another aspect of humor, which The Wife of Bath's Tale emphasizes, is the display of female sexual desire. Female desire occurs in all versions of the tale, but in Gower's story the loathly lady *needs* Florent to release her from the stepmother's curse of hideousness. In the Wife's account, the hag selects the rapist-knight as something like a reclamation project, in the process teaching him about female sexual desire, which does not include sexual mastery, particularly rape. But she chooses the knight because she wants and desires him.

The humorous, topsy-turvy elements receive a full airing in *The Wedding of Sir Gawain and Dame Ragnelle*, a version of the "Tale of Florent" sometimes characterized as a fabliau because of its broad farcical elements. In the Ragnelle story, Gawain stands in for King Arthur, whom Sir Gromer Somer Joure will behead unless he can supply the answer to the riddle about women's desires. The prominent ethical aspect of this account is Gawain's taking the place of the king. Gawain agrees to wed Dame Ragnelle, the loathly lady, and in so doing he manifests the virtue of loyalty to king and kin. The anonymous author goes out of the way to establish Ragnelle as a threat to the courtly and chivalric virtues that Gawain embodies. The description of the loathly lady — the blazon — rivals Gower's portrait. Ragnelle, like her counterpart in other stories, goes beyond grotesque in her features:

> Her tethe hyng [teeth hung] overe her lyppes,
> Her chekys syde [cheeks as broad] as wemens hippes.
> A lute [hump] she bare upon her bak;
> Her nek long and therto greatt;
> Her here cloteryd on an hepe [hair cluttered in a heap];

In the sholders she was a yard brode.
Hangyng pappys [breasts] to be an hors lode [horse's load],
And lyke a barelle she was made.

. . . .
The one tusk went up and the other doun.
A mowthe fulle wyde and fowlle igrown,
With grey herys many on.
Her lyppes laye lumpryd [twisted] on her chyn;
Nek forsothe on her was none iseen —
She was a lothly on!   (235–42, 551–56)

Ragnelle has the greatest impact on the court at the wedding feast, because she threatens to consume everything in sight, perhaps including the overmatched Gawain. Not only is she ugly, she also has atrocious table manners — the opposite of exemplary courtly conduct. She seizes and occupies the place of honor on the dais, and, when the food arrives for the wedding guests, "She ete as moche as six that ther wore; / That mervaylyd many a man" (605–06). As if this were not enough,

She ette [ate] thre capons, and also curlues thre [three curlews],
And greatt bake metes [baked meats] she ete up, perdé [indeed].
Al men therof had mervaylle,
Ther was no mete cam her before
Butt she ete itt up, lesse and more,
That praty [cunning], fowlle dameselle.   (610–15)

Ragnelle surpasses any cultural advice vouchsafed by the late-fourteenth-century *Good Wife's Guide* (also known as the *Ménagier de Paris*), which warns about the fourth branch of gluttony, in which "a person eats his food greedily without chewing and gulps it down in great chunks" (77). The fifth "finger" of the sin gluttony, says the Parson in his Canterbury tale, "is for to eten to gredily" (829). Ragnelle violates just about all the counsel to good breeding advanced in books of advice; but of course she is also under an enchantment, so when she transforms from the loathly lady to the celebrated bride of Gawain, she discards her former self—the socially inappropriate self with a "snotyd" nose (231) and teeth like "borys tuskes" (549).

  The question in all three versions is, What do women really want? But who asks the question and the motives for posing it differ in important ways, which students can discuss. In "Florent" the grandmother formulates the question as revenge for Florent's slaying of Branchus. The grandmother, drawing on a supposed storehouse of secret female lore, believes that Florent will fail to answer the question correctly and so lose his life. When he answers the question successfully, the "grandame" flies into a rage and raises a hue and cry of treason:

"Ha treson, wo thee be, / That hast thus told the privite, / Which alle wommen most desire!" (1659–61). She seems to think that Florent is responsible for the betrayal—that he has brought the "privite" out into the open. The implication is that the loathly lady has initiated Florent into an aspect of female psychology that should remain hidden, and as a result Florent and other males, like Actaeon in the myth, understand things about women that they should not know.[5] In the Wife of Bath's version of the tale, the question originates from Arthur's queen (presumably Guinevere). The rapist-knight, according to law, was going to lose his life for his crime of rape; but when Guinevere and "other ladyes mo" intervene in the legal proceedings, Arthur gives the decision to them. The motive for asking the question seems to be educational: she hopes the knight will be enlightened and that he will solve the riddle. She may also want the learning process to be the ordeal it turns out to be for the knight: he only learns the answer after asking all and sundry and receiving contradictory responses. But whatever Guinevere's motivation, her intervention seems to be benign and helpful, designed to reform an erring courtier. Another possibility is that Guinevere manifests the same pity that the Theban widows or Hippolyta and Emily exhibit in The Knight's Tale, in response to which Chaucer includes his favorite line about pity running soon "in gentil herte" (1761). The motive for the question in *Ragnelle* resembles that in "Florent" except the question originates not with a woman but with the spiteful landowner, Sir Gromer Somer Joure, who has a long-standing dispute with both Arthur and Gawain—Arthur because he gave Sir Gromer's land to Gawain and Gawain because he now "owns" that land. In other words, the cause of quarrel is real estate, not vengeance (as in "Florent") or felonious crime (as in The Wife of Bath's Tale). Sir Gromer has apprehended the king poaching on his lands, and he could slay Arthur on the spot, but he spares Arthur's life for a time until Arthur should return with certain knowledge of "whate wemen love best in feld and town" (91). If there is an educational or ethical lesson in Arthur's quest, it is obscure in Sir Gromer's presentation. Undergraduate students might be encouraged to determine motivation and to sort out the ethical issues involving the three knights' respective quests.

Another important ethical issue involves where and by whom questions are settled, which can entail peer pressure. In Chaucer's tale, the rapist-knight, in despair after a fruitless, inconclusive search, meets the loathly lady in the forest. She not only provides him with the correct answer to the queen's question but accompanies him back to Arthur's court after extracting a "rash promise" that the young man will do whatsoever she demands in return for her life-preserving response. She relies not solely on the rapist-knight's word but also on the ethical persuasion of Arthur's court, for she discloses to everyone the pact that the knight has made with her. She in effect proposes to the knight in open court:

"Bifore the court thanne preye I thee, sir knyght,"
Quod she, "that thou me take unto thy wyf,

For wel thou woost [know] that I have kept [saved] thy lyf.
If I seye fals, sey nay, upon thy fey [word]!"   (1054–57)

Since the knight has proved false to women in the past, the loathly lady's strategy is doubtless well advised. There is no comparable open-court pressure in
Gower's story. The loathly lady makes clear that she relies on Florent's word and
his good faith. She does demand from Florent a "wedd" (1558): a pledge that he
be "trothful." But as Peck puts it, "Florent's truth to his word holds the key to his
tale" (*Kingship* 46). Florent haggles with the damsel, but he eventually relents
on the grounds that his choices boil down to marriage or death. In a low moment, Florent imagines that the old hag will die soon, and he considers placing
his wife to be on a deserted island where nobody can see her (1575–80).[6] This
thought is part of the "murmur and compleignte" formula that helps frame the
exemplary story. Its raison d'être is the sin of pride, to which Amans admits, "in
myn herte I am desesed: / With many a Murmur, god it wot" (1388–89).

Students might also ponder issues of inequality in relationships and the injunction, in modern marriage ceremonies, to love, honor, and obey one's spouse.
Does the loathly lady's mythic ugliness mean that either knight—rapist or Florent—can disregard his marriage vows? What if a spouse is "base born"? The
hag in Chaucer's story seizes particularly on the knight's claim, among other
things he says, that he cannot abide her "low" status. She is not only ugly and
old, but she originates from "so lough a kynde" that the knight writhes in agony
(1101). She does not address the more obvious problem for the knight: her
epic ugliness, which should, one would think, trump lowborn estate for the
terms of their "relationship." The hag instead delivers her lengthy harangue on
the topic of inner virtue versus inherited wealth. The formerly unscrupulous
rapist-knight may well need to hear her set speech, but his evident predicament is his inability or unwillingness to consummate the marriage. The hag's
argument, somewhat "off task" as it is, develops the fourteenth-century ethical concern—also at the heart of Chaucer's lyric poem "Gentilesse" and The
Clerk's Tale—that inner virtue, and not family reputation or inherited wealth,
determines human worth.

A question of agency arises in both Gower's and Chaucer's tales (Peck, "Folklore" 116–21), and agency involves ethical questions. Under whose auspices
do the loathly ladies appear to, give answers to, and wed the knights? Gower's
loathly lady operates under a specific curse placed on her by an evil stepmother
(a folktale type). She is in fact a Sicilian princess who can be released from her
curse only by winning the love and "sovereinete" (1847) of the knight with the
best reputation, or Florent, who remains "trothful" to his wife under the most
trying of circumstances. Gower's loathly lady has a specific reason for seeking
out Florent and wooing him. She has almost as much to gain from the liaison
as Florent, although she reveals her cursed circumstances only after their marriage and only after Florent demonstrates his marital bona fides.

Ragnelle similarly suffers from a "stepdame's" curse; and she makes very clear to Gawain that he has broken the spell of "enchauntement" (693) placed on her when he gave her "sovereynté" of "alle his body and goodes" (697–98). Ragnelle seems to allude to the Virgin Mary's Magnificat when she thanks Gawain for his heroic deed of kindness to her in her identity as the hag: "Gara-mercy, corteys Knight . . . Of alle erthly knyghtes blyssyd mott thou be, / For now am I worshyppyd" (685–87). In the fiction of the story, Gawain, like Flo-rent, has passed a test; he has done the right thing when nobody—not even he—was looking. Ragnelle, like the hag in "Florent," needed the knight to break the spell, and she is glad to reward her now grateful husband. She was enslaved to a curse; now she is free.

The loathly lady in The Wife of Bath's Tale magically appears out of a realm of *faërie*. At one moment, just as the fateful day of decision has arrived, the rapist-knight witnesses twenty-four beautiful maidens in the forest; at the next moment there is only the loathly lady. She knows the situation the knight faces and agrees to help him out of his predicament. We never learn why or how she can transform herself from ugly to beautiful, and seemingly from many and beautiful to solitary and haglike; perhaps the issue does not interest Chaucer. She transforms herself when the knight cannot decide whether he would have her young and beautiful but potentially unfaithful or old, foul, and true. When the knight resigns the decision to the hag, she transmutes to young, beautiful, and faithful. In Chaucer's story the foul hag may be, on some level, a "creature" of the Wife of Bath. Chaucer may have shaped the story to emphasize the hag's autonomy, her ability to plan and act on her own, without the external curse.

Gower and Chaucer both entered public discussions through their poetry and storytelling. Both gave advice to princes and endeavored to influence morality and politics. Gower imagines for himself a "public voice," and his texts, includ-ing *In Praise of Peace, Vox clamantis,* and much of *Confessio Amantis,* consti-tute "entrants," so to speak, in the late-fourteenth-century conversations about public policy. In the first recension of the *Confessio,* Gower praises King Rich-ard II, "In whom hath evere yit be founde / Justice medled with pite, / Largesce forth with charite" (8.2988–90* [p. 469]). He concludes *In Praise of Peace* in a way that recalls Chaucer's "Lenvoy to King Richard": "Kep charite and draugh pite to honde, / Maintene lawe, and so the pes schal stonde" (384–85). If Gower in his story content seeks a "middle weie" between "lust" and "lore" (prologue, lines 17–19), between entertainment and edification, he also consistently keeps his eye on the bigger picture. In the small details—Amans as lover, Genius's in-dividual stories tailored for Amans—he strives to present the rationales for the tales. This method of framing stories was probably first outlined by Augustine in *On Christian Doctrine* when he urges preachers to articulate a larger meaning in "small" things and to speak in a modest or "subdued" manner, which Erich Auerbach identifies as "humble speech" (*sermo humilis*; 72). Augustine says:

> Everything we say is of great importance, even to the extent that pecuni-ary matters, whether they concern loss or gain, or large or small amounts

of money, should not be considered "small" when they are discussed by the Christian teacher. For neither is justice small. . . .   (4.18; 143–44)

Gower's style, composed by a self-proclaimed "burel clerk" (prologue 52) may be humble, but Gower wants to draw larger meaning from his stories related in the vulgar tongue, as he composes his encyclopedic anatomy of love set in a declining world.

Chaucer too composed well-crafted short lyrics on the virtues of reflection, advice, and ethics in public policy. He seems to long for a return to morality in government in his rhyme royal poem "Lak of Stedfastnesse," which concludes, in the "Lenvoy to King Richard," "Dred God, do law, love trouthe and worthinesse, / And wed thy folk agein to stedfastnesse" (p. 654). Chaucer calls for a special "wedding" here: one that unites people generally with their word, which ought to oblige them to make good on what they say; and he wants that virtue to begin at the highest governmental levels. In Chaucer's own Tale of Melibee in *The Canterbury Tales*, Melibeus practices statecraft through advice, especially through the good counsel of his aptly named wife Prudence, who advises deliberation and prudence rather than warfare and revenge, which was Melibeus's initial reflex.[7] Chaucer elsewhere invokes "Solomon's" dictum "Werk al by conseil, and thou shalt nat rewe" (Nicholas to John the carpenter on Noah's flood [MilT 3530]).[8]

The "Tale of Florent" and The Wife of Bath's Tale grapple with ethical circumstances in human relationships. "Florent" interrogates the marriage bond and its larger issues of what it means to be noble and what constitutes right conduct in social relationships. The Wife of Bath's Tale raises questions of who should control—who rules—a marriage, with its issues of governance generally. Few wives or husbands, medieval or modern, will find solutions to marital predicaments through visitations from supernatural beings, but they may have to decide to commit themselves to husbands or wives whose beauty has faded or health has failed over the years; and their decisions may well have larger social consequences. The author of *The Wedding of Sir Gawain and Dame Ragnelle* maintains a certain distance from the ethical issues explored by Gower and Chaucer; but Ragnelle does expose the fragility of courtly virtues. Gawain may be the exemplar of courtliness, the best knight, but he must diverge from his script when confronted by the formidable Ragnelle.

APPENDIX
Comparison of Plot Elements

Rachel Lapp

	"Tale of Florent"	Wife of Bath's Tale	Sir Gawain and Dame Ragnelle
Knight's Crime	Florent kills Branchus in self-defense.	The knight rapes a young virgin.	Gawain himself commits no crime, but he serves Arthur, whom Gromer alleges has hunted on land that is rightfully Gromer's but that Arthur gave to Gawain.
Challenge Issued to Knight	Branchus's grandmother orders Florent to determine what women truly desire.	Guinevere allows the knight to avoid death by ordering him to discover what women truly desire.	Gromer challenges Arthur to determine what women truly desire and to return with the answer within one year's time or face beheading.
Agreement to Challenge	Florent agrees.	The knight is not given the option to agree.	Arthur agrees.
Beginning of the Quest	Florent returns home to ask women what they truly desire but receives no consistent answer.	The knight travels to "every hous and every place" (line 919) and discovers women want different things.	Arthur and Gawain each travel separately to seek the answer, recording responses in a book.
Meeting of the Loathly Lady	Florent meets the lady in the forest under a tree.	In the forest, the knight approaches twenty-four dancing women, who disappear; then he sees the lady nearby.	While riding in Inglewood Forest, Arthur meets the lady, who is sitting on a well-dressed horse.
Loathly Lady's Offer	The lady offers Florent the answer.	The lady offers the knight the answer.	The lady offers to save Arthur's life and explains that only she can do so.
Loathly Lady's Request	The lady asks to marry Florent.	The lady asks that the knight agree to her next request.	The lady asks to marry Gawain.
Knight's Response	Florent is conflicted because the lady is old, and he considers abandoning her but finally consents.	The knight agrees.	Arthur says no and leaves to ask Gawain, who agrees to marry the lady.
Delivering the Answer	The lady provides the answer to Florent, who returns to court to deliver it.	The knight and lady travel to court together to deliver the answer, where the lady then asks the knight to marry her.	Arthur returns to the lady and receives the answer; then he delivers it to Gromer.
The Answer	Women desire to be "sovereign of man's love" (line 1609).	Women desire sovereignty in marriage.	Women desire sovereignty.

APPENDIX (*continued*)
Comparison of Plot Elements

Rachel Lapp

	"TALE OF FLORENT"	WIFE OF BATH'S TALE	SIR GAWAIN AND DAME RAGNELLE
The Wedding	The evening wedding takes place among Florent's most trusted friends.	The morning wedding takes place the day after the couple appears at court.	The grand afternoon wedding is followed by a feast.
Consummation Issues	When Florent agrees to consummate the marriage, he turns over to find the lady transformed from loathly to beautiful.	The marriage is not consummated.	The marriage is consummated at the lady's request, after which the lady is transformed from loathly to beautiful.
The Choice	The lady instructs Florent to choose whether she will be beautiful at night and ugly by day or vice versa.	The lady asks the knight to choose if she will be beautiful and promiscuous or ugly and faithful.	The lady asks Gawain to choose if she will be beautiful at night and ugly by day or vice versa.
How Chosen	The knight yields the decision to the lady.	When the knight yields the decision to the lady, she is transformed.	Gawain yields the decision to the lady.
Reason for the Lady's Loathliness	The lady's loathliness is a curse from her stepmother, from which she is released when she wins the love of the worthy knight.	The lady made herself loathly to test the knight.	The lady's loathliness is a curse from her stepmother, from which she is released when she meets England's finest knight who gives her sovereignty.
Ending	Florent and the lady live happily ever after.	The knight and the lady live happily ever after.	Gawain and Dame Ragnelle do not stay together.

NOTES

[1] For discussions of ethics in Gower, see Alastair Minnis ("John Gower, *Sapiens*") and David Aers ("Reflections," including a bibliographic discussion in note 1). Aers points out contradictions in Gower's ethical stances, but he also notes that Gower mirrors contradictions within Christianity (for example, the crusading ethic versus the "turn the other cheek" injunction).

[2] The table, for example, represents just such a comparison and was compiled by one of my students, Rachel Lapp.

[3] See lines 1727–30: "Bot as an oule fleth be nyhte / Out of alle othre briddes syhte, / Riht so this knyht on daies brode / In clos him hield. . . ."

[4] For the folkloristic space of the forest and the loathly lady as outsider, see Peck, "Folklore" 101.

[5] Gower briefly rehearses the tale of Actaeon in *Confessio*, book 1, but as an example of "mislooking" (lines 333–78).

[6] On these details, see Pearsall, "Gower's Narrative Art" 484.

[7] Contrast Ferster, who argues that "all advice collapses through its self-contradictions" (106).

[8] From Ecclesiasticus (attributed to Solomon) 32.24: "My son, do thou nothing without counsel, and thou shalt not repent when thou hast done" (see *Holy Bible*). Chaucer repeats the sentiment in The Merchant's Tale (1483–86) and The Tale of Melibee (1003). The phrase is ironic in The Miller's and Merchant's Tales but nonironic in The Tale of Melibee.

Teaching the "Tale of Constance" in Context

R. F. Yeager

Gower and Chaucer drew on a common source for the "Tale of Constance" and The Man of Law's Tale: a narrative the Dominican friar Nicholas Trevet (or Trivet) included in his *Chronicle*, composed in Anglo-Norman prose about 1334 for the daughter of Edward I. Robert M. Correale provides a facing-page translation of Trevet's narrative "De la noble femme Constance," edited from Paris, Bibliothèque Nationale MS Français 9687, folios 62vb–69va, along with a discussion of the important bibliography and useful commentary in the *Sources and Analogues of the* Canterbury Tales he and Mary Hamel edited in 2002–05. Margaret Schlauch contributed a version of Trevet to the earlier *Sources and Analogues of Chaucer's* Canterbury Tales, edited in 1941 by W. F. Bryan and Germaine Dempster, where it appears in French with brief summaries of the action in English in the margins. F. J. Furnivall, E. Brock, and W. A. Clouston's *Originals and Analogues of Some of Chaucer's* Canterbury Tales also provides a facing-page edition and translation of Trevet's original.

Although it was once thought that Gower borrowed from Chaucer, this error has been meticulously refuted by Peter Nicholson, who argues that Gower was the first redactor of Trevet; and although Chaucer knew and used both, at times apparently with books by each open simultaneously before him, Gower seems to have done the heavy lifting, simplifying a rambling Trevet to get at the central story and highlighting (or inventing), in the process, many of the tale's most memorable features. As Nicholson notes:

> Gower's version may have been more important to Chaucer than Trevet's was. . . . Gower's tale was shorter, and clearer, and more sharply focused than Trevet's was. Gower had eliminated most of what was extraneous in his source, and had preserved what was most apt. In cutting away . . . he also gave shape: Gower . . . raised Constance above the background of the chronicle account of her life, and . . . the moral and emotional lines of the story above the elaborate account of movements and motivations in Trevet's version. And it was he who first extracted from the mass of detail and episode in Trevet the simple tale of the trials and endurance of the long-suffering heroine and gave it the form by which we know it so well now. . . .　　　　　　　　　　　　　　　("'Man of Law's Tale'" 170)

What Gower saw in Trevet's tale and Chaucer in Gower's was the play of characters pitted, one against another, in a struggle against near-ubiquitous evil, albeit ever beneath the watchful eye of God. Gower's decision to foreground character meant adding dimension to Constance, rounding and humanizing her by enriching her inner life—a process Chaucer extends in some ways, but truncates in others. Foregrounding character demanded significant enhancement of her tormentors' malice as well, to heighten audience response to her innocence, obedience, and undeserving exposure to danger and hardship. Undoubtedly in making these changes to Trevet, Gower was guided by the structural imperatives of the *Confessio Amantis*, where the Constance story appears as an exemplum in book 2, to illustrate Detraction (or "bacbitinge"), a subspecies of Envy. Chaucer, obviously facing no such formal restraint, and despite how closely he adhered to Gower (and to Trevet too, for infrequent details omitted by Gower), elaborated accordingly.

Until very recently, it was Chaucer's elaborations that drew scholarly attention and thus centered classroom discussion whenever the "Tale of Constance" and The Man of Law's Tale were brought together for students' consideration. While doing that will always provide a viable entry into discussing how Chaucer can work wonders, it is no less enlightening for students to have the process reversed. For this there are many profitable approaches. Among the more obvious are comparisons of plot and characters. A clear first choice for such comparison is the three heroines—Trevet's Constance/Custance, Gower's Constance, and Chaucer's Custance, beginning with their names. Trevet (or the scribes) oscillated between "Constance" and "Custance" in the same manuscripts. The fact that, confronted (presumably) with an option in his source, Gower decided on Constance and Chaucer picked Custance can lead to a discussion of what sort of a heroine Gower and Chaucer set out to create—for examples, Is Constance indeed more *constant* than Custance? In what way(s)? If a direct comparison with Trevet's version is to be part of the class, it is worthwhile to call attention to how it differs from Gower's—and Chaucer's, if his is included also.

The most important change Gower made to Trevet—and Chaucer augmented—was to humanize the essentially one-dimensional Constance (as I call her throughout, except when concerned only with Chaucer) Trevet offers. As a historian, Trevet's impulse is to provide "facts": for example, it is exactly seven hundred Saracens, and hired ones, at that ("sept cenz sarazins lowés"; 167) who massacre the Sultan at the feast; Constance is set adrift in a boat with "food, bread called biscuit, peas, beans, sugar, honey, and wine" ("vitaile, de payn quest apele bisquit, et de peis et de feves et de sucre et de meel et de vin"; 167–68). He can include moral judgment ("that member of the devil, the Sultaness" "le member au diable, la soudane"), but his interest in his characters never strays far from describing actions that move the story forward.[1] Gower, like Chaucer, makes his heroine the helpless woman in peril, eliciting the empathetic response such a figure induces in readers. That said, however, Custance and Constance differ in several significant ways—as much sometimes from each other as either does from Trevet. One example must do for all here, but it's proved quite effective over time in classroom discussion.

Gower and Chaucer both make much more of Constance's exile from Northumberland, ostensibly at the order of her husband Allee, than Trevet does. After reporting the people's reaction to the cruel order, Trevet explains with precision just how her boat was set adrift:

everyone lamented her; and although it was not his fault, all cursed King Alla. And after her boat was escorted out onto the high seas, where neither England nor any other land could be seen by them, the sailors with great sadness commended her to God, praying that she might return to land joyously.

toute gentz la weymenteient. E tut ne ust il coupe, al rei Alle touz mauudisoient. E pus qe sa neef par autre nauie estoit ia amene en la haute mere, ou ia en Engleterre ne autre terre lour apparut, lez mariners a grantz dolours la comanderent a dieu, en priaunt qe unquore peust ele a joie a la terre retourner. (175)

It is hardly necessary, however, for students to be aware of the contrast with Trevet's version to be drawn into the moment as rendered in either the *Confessio* or The Man of Law's Tale. The scene in the hands of both English poets is highly emotional: once again Constance is cast adrift to die on the sea, the innocent victim of a heinous plot, her predicament rendered the more heart-wrenching this time by the presence of her infant son, whose youth and vulnerability both play up for effect. (Trevet's comment, in contrast, is almost comical in its understatement: "Maurice, her dear son, who learned seamanship young" ["Moriz soun douce fuitz, qi jeuvenes aprist marinage"; 175].) Both poets add lines for Constance to speak in prayer—as Gower tells it, once she's in the boat; in Chaucer's version, while she's on the beach, before stepping in. These original passages are quite affective. (The Man of Law's, indeed, at times borders on the bathetic.) Adrift at sea, Gower's Constance beseeches God's pity for herself and her son:

> Sche seide, "O hihe mageste,
> Which sest the point of every trowthe,
> Tak of thi wofull womman rowthe [pity]
> And of this child that I schal kepe."
> And with that word sche gan to wepe,
> Swounende [Swooned] as ded [if dead], and ther sche lay. . . .
> (2.1058–63)

Weeping and swooning, Gower's Constance is a purely pitiful figure, for students and for God, too. Chaucer, however, parts company from Gower as well as from Trevet, not only by locating Custance's speech on the shore, but also—and more radically—by delivering mixed emotions. He does this in two ways.

First, Chaucer ratchets up our sense of innocence wronged. Almost like a Greek chorus, the messenger who carried the forged letter regrets his role in bringing tragedy to pass and wonders at God's apparent indulgence of evil ("how may it be / That thou wold suffren innocentz to spille [be destroyed], / And wikked folk regne in prosperitee?"; 814–16); there is an assembled crowd that, choruslike again, "wepen bothe yonge and olde in al that place" (819); Custance herself, after declaring staunchly that God "kan kepe me from harm and eek [also] fro shame / In salte see [salty sea]" (829–30), then kneels to quiet her tiny weeping son, covering the baby's eyes and lulling it, while praying fervently to the Virgin to take pity on the boy (pointedly, not on herself), as a mother who would recognize and identify with her agony. This invocation of the pietà takes two stanzas—fourteen lines (841–54)—and is followed by another stanza (855–61) in which Custance questions why such innocence should be sacrificed and frantically begs the constable to keep her baby ashore, letting her go alone into the boat. The result is the highest level of emotional manipulation in any of the three versions, and it sets us up for what Custance (and Chaucer) does next. Chaucer's real focus here is not the pitifulness but rather how unjustly we treat one another, in stark contrast to the unwavering justice of God, and he drives this home by having Custance momentarily lash out, changing the mood entirely. Getting into the boat, she "looked bakward to the londe, / And seyde, 'Farewel, housbonde routhelees!'" (862–63). Of course she's wrong. Her husband is no less innocent than she. Her condemnation—however mistaken—is itself an injustice, and the keen irony, which we see and she doesn't, only puts a sharper point to Chaucer's thrust.

Many students, and not a few scholars, find Custance's flash of anger psychologically honest and admire Chaucer's insightfulness, which seems to some surprisingly modern—particularly if compared with Gower's "simpler," more "medieval" handling, as it is sometimes deemed. Whatever one's own stance, looking at both versions side by side in class is a fertile teaching moment. It opens doors to topics essential to understanding the *Confessio* (and *The Canterbury Tales*) such as narratorial point of view at the fictive level. Unlike Trevet's historian's voice narrating the *Chronicle*, the story of Custance is, after all, presented as part of a framing fiction by a fictional character, the Man of Law. What tale he tells, and how he tells it, reveals much about him as a character (surely part of Chaucer's design)—and he is an active teller, one of the most intrusive, in fact, in *The Canterbury Tales*. Chaucer has gone to some trouble to foster the illusion that he "speaks for himself." So on one level, we're to see this as "his" story, which makes its emotional depths and altitudes "his" as well. When, however, even the Man of Law confesses to exhaustion in keeping up with the empathetic demands of his own tale (as he does several times [see 874, 1065–71]), it's worth asking, among other questions, precisely what's going on here, and at other planes of authority?

It can be very useful introducing undergraduates, particularly in sophomore surveys, to Gower's Genius in this comparative way. Usually it's not too difficult to bring even entry-level students to see that the Man of Law is not "Chaucer" (whoever *that* is!). But the temptation to mistake Genius (or Amans) for "Gower" seems to be much greater, and consequently harder to banish. Coming to address the problem through the Man of Law ("NOT Chaucer!") can be effective in creating awareness that authorial screens are part of Gower's practice too. "For of course," one can point out, "just as Custance is a creature of the

Man of Law, so Constance equally emanates from Genius," yet another made-up narrative "voice."

A generally successful move from this point can be effected, in two stages. The first stage is centrifugal: refocus on the larger purposes of the "Tale of Constance" in the *Confessio*. It's there to provide the fictional entity Amans, who is more of a concept than a true character (even his name is not a man's but a present participle), with an example of Detraction, a subset of Invidia, so that he can know to confess to it or not. This "confession" takes place, not along a well-marked and well-known road from one actual site in contemporary England to another, in what amounts to "real" time (or in the "historical" England recorded by Trevet), but in an otherworldly setting, perhaps in a dream, perhaps not, in a garden nowhere locatable save in French literary convention. It is important for students to keep in mind the macrofiction of Gower's poem, especially if they are reading only one or two tales in extract. The sole tale spinner in the *Confessio* is the confessor figure Genius (a part of a convention traceable through France back to Rome), and he, unlike the Man of Law, isn't ostensibly trying to win a free dinner at the Southwark Inn; he's attempting to enlighten Amans, a rather naive presence who, for most of Gower's poem, is the only other "real" persona we encounter. Students should be able to perceive that a framing fiction such as Gower's will raise quite different demands—and offer other possibilities, particularly in regard to space, time, and detail in plot and character—than does the quasi verisimilitude of an imaginary pilgrimage with a prize at the end for the one who "telleth in this caas / Tales of best sentence and moost solaas" (GP 797–98). At this juncture, it is worth noting for the students, if they have no means of discovery on their own, that the narrative richness of the "Tale of Constance" is hardly the norm in the *Confessio*, although of course there are others in its class—but that there are reasons for this "simplicity" embedded in Gower's design that must be taken into account in any comparison of his work with Trevet's or Chaucer's. Going outward to the fictive frame permits capture of these essential points; it also serves to clarify when comparison with Chaucer's work—or Trevet's—ceases to be productive and to explain why comparison becomes futile.

The second stage of the move, then, must be centripetal, a deeper dive into "Constance" to reveal what is exclusively and characteristically Gower's. There are too many optional lines of inquiry possible to do more here than suggest a handful and follow one, by way of illustration. Topping the list is the obvious: "Constance" is a tale about faith and love—both human and divine—good and evil, the costs of lust and the unfettered will for power, narrated by a sympathetic but persistent "priest" with a brief to bring a besotted lover to his senses. For those who read the *Confessio* primarily as a political treatise, social issues taken up in the prologue can be shown to resonate in the "Tale of Constance" (e.g., projections of governance, privilege, and betrayal), as can the prologue's tensions between the institutional church and individual faith (e.g., Constance's value as an agent of conversion vs. her personal anguish, as a woman and mother repeatedly endangered, whose sole recourse is faithful prayer) and issues about *imperium* and earthly rule (e.g.; Constance's lineage as daughter of "Tiberie Constantin," emperor of Rome; her treatment of her subjects as King Allee's queen). Psychoanalytic approaches are fruitful too, because they concentrate on Constance's relationships with her father (originally, as Schlauch points out, in her classic study "Accused Queens," Constance's was an incest narrative), with men in whom she kindles unsanctioned desire, and with her mothers-in-law, the one potential (the Sultaness), the other (Domilde) realized.

Yet another approach, involving no comparison with other sources, might focus on (for want of a better descriptor) Gower's "poetics": that is, what does he do with imagery and language and for what purposes? A helpful way to introduce this topic is to call attention to how Genius first describes Envy at the opening of book 2:

> Now after Pride the secounde
> Ther is, which many a woful stounde [attitude]
> Towardes other berth [bears] aboute
> Withinne himself and noght withoute;
> For in his thoght he *brenneth* evere [burns forever],
> Whan that he wot [knows] an other levere [more loved]
> Or more vertuous than he,
> Which passeth him in his degree;
> Therof he takth [is taken with] his maladie:
> That vice is cleped *hot* Envie.   (2.1–10; emphasis added)

Arresting here is the portrayal of Envy as "hot" and the envious as one who "brenneth." Following this lead into the "Tale of Constance" is instructive, since fire and water form the metaphoric and symbolic touchstones of Gower's story — and, indeed, of much of book 2. From the way Gower develops his imagery in the *Confessio* — cumulatively adding layers of resonance one at a time — it seems clear he did not expect his tales to be read in isolation. (Given that most students read Gower's work only in excerpts, it is worth making a point of this disparity.) Images he presents early, in tale, book, or often the poem as a whole, help determine how to read recurring instances. Thus if time permits, it is illustrative to look briefly at how he handles fire and water in "Acis and Galatea," the first tale in book 2, immediately following the introductory lines above. Here he begins to create the context for the reappearance of these elements in the "Tale of Constance." Although "Acis and Galatea" isn't widely anthologized, it is short enough nevertheless — 102 lines — that it can be easily copied and handed out.

"Acis and Galatea" exhibits the tight, economical narrative style at which Gower excelled. Acis and Galathee are in love. As they are enjoying each other "under a banke nyh [near]/ The grete See" (2.144–45), they are discovered by the giant, Polipheme, who also desires Galathee, and, driven mad with envious rage, he buries Acis under a huge chunk of earth. Gower's portrayal of

Poliphemeʼs emotions and actions is notable: "al his herte hath set afire" (149); he becomes "as it were a wilde best" (161), "no reson mihte areste" him, and:

> He ran Ethna the hell [mountain] aboute,
> Wher nevere yit the fyr was oute,
> Fulfild of sorghe [sorrow] and gret desese [distress],
> That he syh [saw] Acis wel at ese.   (163–66)

Interjecting Mount Etna into this story is Gowerʼs inspiration—it doesnʼt appear in his source (Ovid, *Met.* 13.)—and itʼs typical of how Gower often applies his extensive learning. The famous volcano that buried Sicilian towns with molten rock when it exploded provides a spot-on emblem of Poliphemeʼs envious meltdown and his subsequent interment of Acis.

In book 2 of the *Confessio*, however, fire appears most often followed by water, as happens in "Acis and Galatea." Fleeing Polipheme, Galathee is rescued by the sea god Neptune and hidden away. Her unceasing grief "hath the goddes moeved so" that they transform the buried Acis into a spring, so that he could continue:

> With freisshe stremes and with cliere,
> As he whilom [once] with lusti chiere
> Was freissh his love forto qweme [please].   (195–97)

Opposite as suitors of Galathee, Polipheme and Acis are replicated, *mutatis mutandis*, in their opposing emblems: fiery Etna for the envious Polipheme, a well and streams of fresh water for the proper lover Acis, the one destructive, the other quenching, life giving, irenic. At this point, calling studentsʼ attention to the allusive mileage Gower achieves by contrasting the "burials" of Polipheme and Acis is invaluable for seeing into "Acis and Galatea" as well as into the "Tale of Constance" and book 2 as a whole. One set of allusions some students may notice on their own. Gowerʼs gesture toward two of the better-known images of Christ—his resurrection (Acis rises as a spring "in the same place / That he lai ded" [191–92]) and his self-representation as "living water," whose selfless love transcends any magnitude of envy (cf. John 4.14)—remains within most studentsʼ observational reach. Establish that, and then introduce Gowerʼs source for his description of Etna: *Aeneid* 3.570 and following, where Vergil explains that the giant Enceladus, who rebelled against the gods, is punished in the flame beneath Etna and his writhing causes its volcanic instability. Many of Gowerʼs medieval readers would have recognized this story and rapidly connected one criminal giant with another. For them, the decision to bring Etna into Ovidʼs story to emblematize Polipheme could only have been confirmed and enriched—the more so if they knew, as Gower must have, that Enceladusʼs lower body was reptilian, either a single snake or several. Thus if Acis in his way prefigures Christ, so Polipheme—a gigantic man-serpent confined in subterranean flame—suggests Satan, whose defeat Christ's dying and return to life ensure.

In the "Tale of Constance" Gower's treatment of fire as emblematic of Envy and water as its loving antidote builds directly on the foundation established in "Acis and Galatea." Here it is useful to call students' attention to a striking and initially puzzling passage unique in all the versions to Gower:

> Bot whan that thei have hiede take [taken notice],
> And rad [read] that writen is withinne,
> So gret a sorwe [sorrow] thei beginne,
> *As thei here oghne Moder sihen*
> *Brent in a fyr before here yhen*   (1044–48; emphasis mine)

"Thei" are King Allee's servants, reading the letter forged by the envious mother-in-law Domilde commanding Constance and her infant Moris be put out to sea, supposedly as Allee wishes. But in what way can casting adrift conjure a vision, for all the servants simultaneously (Gower's word is *here*, plural third person), of "here oghne Moder" ("their own mother") burning before their eyes? The juxtaposition is startling, and invites—as such conundrums seem intended to do in Gower's work—closer reading.

Some lines later we see further into what Gower is up to. When Allee discovers what his "bacbitinge" mother has wrought, his rage is "lich the fyr which tunder hente [tinder catches]" (1274), and he

> . . . let a fyr do make tho,
> And bad men forto caste hire inne. . . .
> And tho sche was to dethe broght
> And brent tofore hire Sones yhe [her son's eye].   (1286–93)

The servants' odd simile of watching their burning mother thus prefigures the punishment of Domilde, watched by Allee and, we must assume, by those same servants, too. Only in the *Confessio* does Allee's mother die in flame: Trevet has Alla chop her to bits; Chaucer, daintily enough, says only "Alla, out of drede, / His mooder slow [slew]" (MLT 893–94), never specifying the method. But that Gower's handling is unique should not surprise us, given the didactic purpose of his narratives. Envy is fiery in the "Tale of Constance," just as it is in "Acis and Galatea," and Domilde's incineration devolves directly from the nature of her sin, in a context prepared by the earlier tale.

The "Tale of Constance" is a good deal more complex than "Acis and Galatea," however, and pressing this image of Domilde set ablaze in soul and body is effective in showing how. As an envious queen and mother who plots against her son, she recalls the Souldaness of Persia who first puts Constance out to sea—and like the Souldaness, Domilde ratchets up the scale of evil: "O beste of helle," King Allee says of his mother (*CA* 2.1278), echoing "this olde fend, this Sarazine" (705), the Souldaness of Persia—and of course connecting both wicked women with Polipheme, Etna, and Satan himself. Pointing out how this works here is usually eye-opening for students, and it can set up insightful discussion of Gower's artistry later on.

At this juncture it can be productive to call attention to the *contrapasso* of Domilde's fiery end and how it anticipates the subsequent *contrapasso* of the death of the false Steward, drowned in the sea by the hand of God, a direct result of his apostate spurning of the life-giving water of baptism (1120–22). The latter connection is especially important in the "Tale of Constance" because Gower's story has baptism—a water image—as a central concern. Comparing his handling of Constance's royal suitors with Chaucer's illuminates how. In the *Confessio* and The Man of Law's Tale, the Souldan of Persia and King Allee are broadly similar—both have sanguinary mothers, both love the same woman, and neither begins as a Christian—but beyond this they dramatically part company, the one slaughtered by his mother's troops at his wedding feast, the other successfully marrying Constance and fathering her child. What would seem to explain these divergent fates, for Gower and Chaucer both, is the nature of these two royal unbelievers' conversions. Writing on The Man of Law's Tale, Nevill Coghill pointed out many years ago the hollowness of the Souldan's commitment to Christianity, calling it "romantic love, as idolatrous as any he had rejected with his 'Mawmettrie'; he was adopting the love of Christ to gain the love of a woman" (15). It is this false conversion, this feigned love of God, Chaucer suggests, that seals the Souldan's fate.

The same applies in Gower's tale, of course, for the Souldan; and both Chaucer and Gower contrast him with Allee, whose heart becomes fixed on Constance only after he has been moved to turn Christian by the holy miracles she performs. Yet while the process is uncomplicated, even matter-of-fact for Chaucer's Alla, Gower's Allee is more reflective. Observing God's miracles, "He tok it into remembrance / And thoghte more than he seide" (894–95). Gower leaves us to wonder just what went through his king's mind, as typically he does, although usually, as in this case, we can glimpse the deliberative progress in its outcome. Gower makes the baptism of Allee—not his conversion, of some generic kind—the determining issue. Pointedly, Allee lays out what he will do, in rank order:

> Baptesme take and Cristes faith
> Believe, and over that he seith
> He wol hire wedde. . . .   (899–901)

Baptism takes pride of place at the wedding, too:

> And forto make schorte tales,
> Ther cam a Bisshop out of Wales
> Fro [From] Bangor, and Lucie he hihte [was called],

Which thurgh the grace of god almihte
The king with many an other mo [more]
Hath christened, and betwen hem tuo [two]
He hath fulfild the marriage.   (903–09)

Making holy water—baptism—the medium of Allee and Constance's union is powerful on several planes, and it both draws on and consolidates the imagery of fire and water in book 2. Literally, water saves Allee from the Souldan's fate; on levels we might call allegorical and moral it does so as well, opening the door for him into eternal life through the spiritual revivification made possible by Christ and anticipated in Acis's resurrection as "freisshe stremes." The imperfectly converted Souldan, the apostate false Steward, and Domilde, we assume, burn eternally.

Baptism is, surely, the most spiritual water image in book 2, but by far more flexible, and omnipresent, is the sea. In the "Tale of Constance" the sea is linked to baptism through the drowning of the false Steward, whose apostate denial turns what should be living water into a tomb. It is Constance's experiences on, and with, the sea, however, that render the vitality of Gower's use of water readily apparent. For Constance, the sea is not truly a danger, despite how she and all the other characters think of it. In fact, the sea is a locus of safety for her; there she is protected from the Souldaness and Domilde, and there too she lives most fully in and sustained by her faith in a benevolent God. Gower never leaves us in doubt of her safety at sea. When the Souldaness's men "putte [her] upon the wawes [waves] wilde" (713), we learn immediately after this threatening picture:

Bot he which alle thing mai schilde [protect],
Thre yer, til that sche cam to londe,
Hire Schip to stiere hath take in honed.   (714–16)

Similar assurance is extended when she and her child are set adrift from Northumberland. Here a class's attention can be drawn to Gower's uses of "kepe" in these passages. On an immediate level, the several variants of this word illuminate Constance's character and her relationship to God. At the same time—and in some ways more important from a pedagogical perspective—they provide a prime example of how Gower constructs his images through a substantial attentiveness to the nuances of language. This discovery can be developed to broaden understanding of his particular poetic strengths.

"Kepe" appears first in this context as "kepers," for example, the servants of King Allee "That *kepers* weren of the qweene" (941), charged with protecting Constance. They perform their duties in this capacity until the letter forged by Domilde brings them to believe their orders have been changed. It is in this letter that we next find "kepe": the text charges the erstwhile guardians to put Constance and her son into the boat, that they might "Betaketh hire the See to *kepe"* (1027–36; emphasis mine). The irony is palpable and multifaceted. At face value, "kepe," used here in the sense of "hold," implies protection, preservation; but just as her "kepers" have transmuted to become her executioners manqué, so here the holding function of the sea, in Domilde's plot, is to be transformed into Constance's grave. Moreover, since Gower presents the letter as if verbatim, we are left to assume its words are Domilde's own—and hence to suppose her fully aware of the double edge "kepe" acquires in this context. There is, however, a deeper irony here, available not to Domilde but to Gower and to us as readers. Clearly, had Domilde known that in seeking to do the greatest harm she was in fact ensuring Constance's safety, doubtless she would have reconsidered. But we as readers have come to recognize that water is an element friendly to Constance and that the sea especially offers her a place of refuge, fully there in the special care of God.

Gower has Constance herself restore the original meaning of "kepe" when she uses the word in her prayer from aboard ship:

Sche seide, "O hihe mageste,
Which sest the point of every trowthe,
Tak of thi wofull womman rowthe [mercy]
And of this child that I schal *kepe*."
And with that word sche gan to wepe,
Swounende [Swooned] as ded, and ther sche lay;
Bot he which alle thinges may
Conforteth hire. . . .   (1058–65; emphasis mine)

In Constance's prayer, "kepe" means—once again—"protect," without irony. Thereafter what unfolds is a scene of complexity and richness revelatory of Gower's substantial poetic skills. Resonating together in the same passage, Constance's and Domilde's employments of "kepe" starkly emphasize the contrast between them and between the qualities for which they stand: innocence and Envy, nurture (Constance as mother of Moris) and its opposite (Domilde as mother of Allee). This opposition, of mother and mother especially, as "kepers" of their respective sons, anchors Gower's program here, which students can observe as it unfolds:

. . . and ate laste
Sche loketh and hire yhen [eyes] caste
Upon hire child and seide this:
"Of me no maner charge [importance] it is
What sorwe I soffre [suffer], bot of thee
Me thinkth it is a grete pite,
For if I sterve thou schalt deie:
So mot I nedes be that weie[2]
For Moderhed and for tendresse

With al myn hole besinesse [diligence]
Ordeigne me for thilke office [that role],
As sche which schal be thi Norrice [nursemaid]."
Thus was sche strengthened forto stoned [stand];
And tho sche tok hire child in honde
And yaf it sowke [gave it suck], and evere among
Sche wepte, and otherwhile song
To rocke with hire child aslepe:
And thus hire oghne child to *kepe*
Sche hat under the goddes cure.   (1065–83; emphasis mine)

Constance's "Moderhed" [motherhood] and "tendresse" for her child are the antithesis of Domilde's for Allee (and by connection, the Souldaness's for her son the Souldan)—but it is important to have students notice here how subtly they are mirrored by God's treatment of Constance. The connection is made initially in the first half of line 1065, when God "conforteth" Constance, and confirmed by that line's second half, when Constance turns to comfort her child. The relation of the two acts of comfort is macrocosm/microcosm, and Gower's decision to place both in the same line underscores their identicality. At the same time, by heightening the maternal monstrosity of Domilde and the Souldaness, Constance's contrasting presence as a *figura* of innocence, of preservation and protection, emerges more clearly, as does her association with God. The next occurrence of "kepe," in the final lines of the passage, drives home this identification. Just as Constance rocks her sleeping child in her "kepe," so she is rocked herself "under goddes cure," aboard the ship in a sea steadied by God's steering hand. It is worth noting here one more contrast with The Man of Law's Tale: by choosing to put Custance's prayer on the shore rather than in the boat at sea and by adding her angry condemnation of her "housbonde routhelees," Chaucer gains, especially perhaps for readers today, a measure of psychological verisimilitude. But it comes at a cost, nevertheless. By so doing, Chaucer directs the considerable emotive force of a mother and baby thrown into mortal danger away from them and their predicament, to focus it on Alla's behavior. The result is a dimming of Custance's moral luster, precisely to the degree that it humanizes her. The move is characteristically Chaucerian—but Gower's Constance, by design a part of a very different, intentionally exemplary form of narrative, remains more "constant" and loses not an ounce of her integrity or any of her value as a model of obedient virtue.

From a pedagogical point of view, of course, it is precisely this unique, multi-layered exemplarity of Gower's that we strive to teach our students how to see and to appreciate knowledgeably. The approach I offer is likely to achieve this—at least it has thus far for most of the students, undergraduates and graduates alike, with whom I have been fortunate to work. Usually, when students select paper topics after our reading of Gower together in class, a number of them choose to dig deeper into the "Tale of Constance." Often they follow lines of inquiry touched on—but only that!—in the preceding pages. Others find their own directions or ask for guidance toward subjects less obvious and more demanding. A good assignment for those seeking guidance, which builds on the classroom work, can be a closer look at *contrapasso* in "Constance" exclusively or in book 2; another is the larger allegory of Constance/Custance and their boats / the church / the sea / the world as Gower and Chaucer each develop it. Any of the areas noted above make rich and challenging topics as well. Ultimately, though, teaching the "Tale of Constance" alongside Trevet's *Chronicle*, or The Man of Law's Tale is always fruitful. One can scarcely go wrong or regret it.

NOTES

[1] Translations of Trevet are mine.
[2] "So because of that I must."

Gower Teaching Ovid and the Classics

Winthrop Wetherbee

Though Gower was a remarkable Latinist, fluent in several styles of medieval Latin, and a sensitive reader of classical poetry, his major work, the *Confessio Amantis*, can seem to students strikingly unclassical in its view of literary history. Terms like *auctour* and *auctorite*, which commonly denote the canonical status of classical authors, are assigned by Gower to a broad range of figures, classical and medieval, historical and legendary. A Latin poem ("Eneidos Bucolis") found in several important Gower manuscripts, ostensibly a tribute to Gower but likely to have been composed by Gower himself, compares his three major poems favorably with the threefold works of Vergil; and when Gower urges the young King Richard to strive for the renown of Augustus or declares the *Confessio* "a bok for Engelondes sake," he may well be recalling the nationalist vision of the *Aeneid* (Kuczynski). But the Vergil whom he names three times in the *Confessio* is the Vergil of postclassical legend, magician and would-be lover of the emperor's daughter. Gower's Aeneas is the "Eneas" of romance, who conquers Italy and slays Turnus for love of Lavine, and his vision of ancient history, extending from the voyage of the Argonauts to the death of Ulysses, is that of Benoît de Sainte-Maure and Guido delle Colonne. His ancient gods and goddesses commonly appear in the stunted forms assigned them by the moralizing mythographers.

An exception to this apparent disregard of the authentic classical tradition and an exception worth discussing with students is Gower's treatment of "Ovide the poete," the one author whom he dignifies with this title (*poet*) or credits with the production of "poesie" (Schmitz, *Middel Weie* 117–34). The *Vox clamantis*, in which it is hard to find a clear echo of any other classical poet, is studded with allusions to virtually all of Ovid's poems. The *Confessio* mentions Ovid by name more than twenty times, most often as the author of the work that Gower calls "Methamor" and for which "poesie" is virtually an alternative title; at least twenty-five of Gower's tales can be traced, directly or indirectly, to the *Metamorphoses*. Several others are drawn, wholly or in part, from the *Fasti*, the *Heroides*, and the *Ars amatoria*, and the grapplings of Genius and Amans with the problems of love recall the self-dramatizing narrator of the *Amores* (Simpson 134–66).

In several manuscripts of the *Confessio*, Gower's awareness of Ovid appears in the very layout of the pages. The *Metamorphoses*, which descended from antiquity unaccompanied by commentary and was little read in the early medieval period, posed a unique challenge when it surfaced again at the end of the eleventh century. The brief manuscript introductions to Ovid known as *accessus* profess to find in Ovid's poem a profoundly coherent statement about the order of things, but from early on the actual reading of the text involved a process of segmentation, reducing each tale to a self-contained ethical exemplum, as though the cumulative force of Ovid's serial narratives was too overwhelming and too morally ambiguous to be faced directly. Later medieval manuscripts of the *Metamorphoses* often introduce each story with the corresponding couplets from John of Garland's moralizing reading of the *Metamorphoses*, the *Integumenta Ovidii,* and accompany the text with the marginal allegorical glosses of Arnulf of Orleans and others. The Latin head verses and marginal gloss of the *Confessio* (certainly Gower's own and clearly modeled on codices of this sort) seem to assert that his poem, too, possesses an authority and complexity sufficient to justify such ostentatious packaging.

But just as no amount of moralizing can wholly contain Ovid's irony and pathos, so the similar framing of the narratives of the *Confessio* produces a continual tension, and since Gower's apparatus is his own creation, this must reflect a deliberate intention. Though the apparatus by its very presence seems to claim for the *Confessio* something like the moral authority normally attributed to the classical poets, it is so structured as to defy a coherent reading. The marginalia oscillate between the poles of authoritative commentary, placing Gower's tales in a historical and ethico-religious economy, on the one hand, and, on the other, a dogged, schoolmasterly moralism, pompous and often ludicrously irrelevant to the tenor of the vernacular text. The disembodied voice of the head verses offers gnomic pronouncements on love, virtue, and vice, and the calculated ambiguity of this voice often seems designed to point up the limitations of the glossator and anticipates the complex role of *natura*, or "kynde," in Gower's treatment of human love (Wetherbee, "Latin Structure"). The net effect is finally to make clear how fully Gower shares Ovid's vision of a world rendered chronically unstable by ill-governed human desire.

Ovid has often been seen as lacking in compassion, even as sadistic, but his sympathy with the victims of power, be it divine or imperial power or the dominating force of passion, is in fact one of the most frequent, and perhaps the truest, of the many messages his poetry communicates (Kobayashi). Gower is acutely sensitive to this quality. If Genius at times appears comically obtuse in seeking to wrestle an Ovidian tale into yielding the moral he needs, it is often possible to hear in the tone or phrasing of his lesson a hint, such as Ovid himself frequently gives, that such judgment may be beside the point, that a Narcissus, a Canace or Anaxarete, even a Medea, is better viewed with sympathetic understanding.

The end of Gower's "Tale of Narcissus" (1.2275–358) provides a good example of how his version of Ovidian compassion complicates the process of moralization. Gower's Narcissus, who has committed suicide by beating himself against a rock, undergoes no metamorphosis, and the grieving nymphs bury his actual body:

> And thanne out of his sepulture
> Ther sprong anon par aventure

Of floures such a wonder syhte
That men ensample take myhte
Upon the dedes [deeds] whiche he dede [did],
As tho was sene in thilke stede [that place];
For in the wynter freysshe and faire
The floures ben, which is contraire
To kynde, and so was the folie
Which fell of his Surquiderie [presumption].   (1.2349–58)

The moral "ensample" seems plainly drawn, and it is reinforced by a marginal gloss that, after a coldly clinical description of Narcissus's death, waxes vigorously and fatuously alliterative:

Et sic de propria pulcritudine qui fuerat presumptuosus, de propria pulcritudine fatuatus interiit.

and thus he who had been so proud of his personal pulchritude, died of his infatuation with his personal pulchritude.   (my trans.)

But the Narcissus of Gower's vernacular tale had believed that he saw in the "lusty welle" not his own reflection but the face of a nymph (the Latin gloss misinforms us that it was "the nymph whom the Poets call Echo"), a nymph whose beauty was "faie" or magical; he is, as Gower will say in condoning the passion of other youthful lovers, "enchaunted." In despair "he wepth, he crith, he axeth [requests] grace," like any worshipful lover; he has wholly rejected his earlier pride and submitted himself to the law of "kynde" just as Genius would have him do.

Thus Genius's moralizing is at odds with the prevailing tone of the tale and requires an effort that becomes audible in the spluttering energy of the midline shifts from clause to clause as Genius inveighs against the winter flowers — flowers that affirm the sympathy for Narcissus that has already largely preempted Genius's authority. Their blooming, moreover, occurs "par aventure," outside the boundaries of the tale proper, and so outside the sphere of Genius's putative moral authority. At the same time they are in effect Genius's creation, and his attempt to deal with these unruly products of his own imagining in frustrated isolation becomes a burlesque of the plight of Narcissus himself.

In this and other respects Gower's appropriation of Ovidian fable has affinities with Chaucer's, and here is where students can often draw comparisons between the two, separate and apart from the more common comparisons of narrative idiosyncrasies. The comic ineptitude of Genius, so often a foil to Ovidian sympathy, can remind us of the narrator of Chaucer's *Book of the Duchess*, the grumpy insomniac who whiles away a sleepless night reading a tale from Ovid's *Metamorphoses*. In the deceptively simple lines that characterize his book of fables we hear the quiet assertion of an authority very like that of Gower:

> And in this boke were written fables
> That clerkes had in olde tyme,
> And other poetes, put in rime,
> To rede and for to be in minde,
> While men loved the lawe of kinde.   (52–56)

If *The Book of the Duchess* is Chaucer's earliest surviving poem, this is his first reference to books, poets, and reading. In later works Chaucer, like Gower, will assign the name of "poet" almost exclusively to the great poets of Rome. But these lines seem hardly more specific than Gower's prefatory assertion that his poem will be "essampled of these olde wyse" ("with examples drawn from the wise men of old" [*CA*, prologue, line 7; my trans.]). If "clerke" denotes a type of poet and if poets, too, write in rhyme, as the passage suggests, the term must encompass vernacular writers in the tradition of *clergie*—the authors of the *Roman de la Rose*, for example, or Guillaume de Machaut; the pairing of clerk and poet may hint at the growing stature of the vernacular.

But students should also note how time is treated in this passage. That the clerks and other poets evoked wrote "in olde tyme" suggests a literary tradition more ancient and august than that defined by the *Roman de la rose*, scarcely a hundred years old in the late fourteenth century and still sufficiently "modern" to constitute a paradigm-text for clerks like Chaucer and Gower. It is as if Chaucer had been prompted by the idea of "olde tyme" to recognize that the "clerkly" tradition by itself was not precisely what he meant to invoke and had added the more portentous "poetes" as an almost involuntary gloss. And in the last two lines of the passage our perspective is decisively broadened. Poetry is now the substance of thought and memory, an authoritative guide to the laws of nature. And perhaps here too we can see "olde tyme" becoming timeless. The phrase "While men loved the lawe of kinde" has seemed to some commentators to denote the pre-Christian era when pagans and their poets ordered their lives wholly in terms of vital necessity and cosmic process. For others it is a periphrasis for the full span of human existence, historical time itself.

How does poetic tradition inform *The Book of the Duchess*? The poem falls into two main sections, one centered on the legend of Ceyx and Alcyone, the other on the figure of the Man in Black. The two are intimately linked, and the connection expresses an implicit complementarity between vernacular rhyming and classical poetry, courtly idealism and the harsh inevitabilities of the "law of kind" embodied in ancient myth. Gower aims to achieve this complementarity as well in his use of Ovid.

Chaucer's poem is recognizably a *dit amoureuse* in the tradition of Guillaume de Machaut, and Machaut, too, had made Ovid's Alcyone an emblem for love longing, the proper concern of the *dit*. But Chaucer has heard Ovid's voice as well as Machaut's, and the wisdom of the ancient poet has informed his use of clerkly form and motif: the devastating grief of his Alcyone, whose sense of self, like that of Ovid's heroine, is subsumed by her attachment to her husband, takes us well beyond the sorrows of the *dit*. Chaucer's Ovidian tale acknowledges a significant aspect of the work of his French predecessor, but at the same time, by quietly exposing the limitations of Machaut as an Ovidian poet, he defines a program for his own poetry that is also Gower's: nothing less than a marriage of courtly and classical tradition.

Like Chaucer's, Gower's treatments of Ovidian material are free, adding and omitting details to suit his purpose, as with the flowers on the grave of Narcissus. Gower is capable of outrageous parody: where the Dido of Ovid's *Heroides* begins her letter to Aeneas by comparing her words to the death song of the swan, Gower's Dido compares herself to an actual swan who, lovelorn and in despair, thrust a feather into her brain and then lay dying, "sprantlende [sprawling] with hire winges tweye" (4.111). The details, and the egregious mistranslation that conjures them, are absurd, and wholly at odds with the Vergilian suicide that ends the episode. But they carry a step further one of the *Heroides*'s most remarkable tactics, the dethroning of tragic feminine suffering by imagining it from a comic, male-chauvinist perspective, in the light of which Ovid's heroines can seem self-deceived, self-dramatizing, or manipulative. The complex project of the *Heroides* and its ironic reworking of traditional material clearly fascinated Gower: he follows his version of Dido's appeal by rewriting the "heroic epistle" of Ovid's Penelope as a masterpiece of Criseyde-like insinuation, so effective that the homeward journey of the anxious Ulysses can then be contained in a single couplet (4.147–233).

Freewheeling in such cases, Gower can also make a small adjustment of his Ovidian source carry significant meaning. When he ends his tale "Jason and Medea" uncanonically with Medea ascending to "Pallas the Court above" (*CA* 5.4219), he may seem simply to have misread Ovid, who reports that, having murdered her children to avenge Jason's infidelity, she fled to "Palladias arces," or Athens, where King Aegeus later made her his wife (*Met.* 7.399). But he is not misreading when he adds that having gained asylum, she "pleigneth upon love." Gower has rather chosen to add a chapter to the *Heroides*, shifting the emphasis from Medea's cruelty to her grief at Jason's treachery, balancing Ovid's condemnation of her as the worst of mothers with an equally Ovidian reminder that she was the victim of destructive passion.

Again, when Gower's Acteon goes forth to hunt "with Houndes and with grete Hornes" (1.343), we should remember that Ovid, too, mentions horns and hounds at the corresponding point in the story. But while Ovid's *cornua* foretell Acteon's transformation to a stag, Gower's are hunting horns; Ovid's hounds will be "sated with a master's blood," while Gower's are only the companions of the chase. Genius, abetted by the Latin gloss, seeks to draw a moral from Acteon's hapless error, but in Ovid the gods themselves question the justice of his fate;

and this small divergence is the first of several details that show Gower going beyond Ovid in asserting his youthful hero's innocence.

Gower's long retelling of the tale of Tereus, Progne, and Philomene (5.5551– 6029) is in general faithful to Ovid, but while Ovid's narrative ends with the turning of the three into birds, Gower follows Philomene into her new, transformed existence, a wholly original coda to Ovid's tale in which Genius, whose moral focus had been on the "ravyne" of Tereus, reveals a remarkable intuitive sympathy with her tragic fate. Still obsessed with the loss of her virginity, which she had seen as essential to her integrity as a human being, she seeks solace in singing:

> And ek thei seide hou in hir song
> Sche makth gret joie and merthe among,
> And seith, "Ha, now I am a brid,
> Ha, nou mi face mai ben hid:
> Thogh I have lost mi Maidenhede,
> Schal noman se my chekes rede."
> Thus medleth sche with joie wo
> And with hir sorwe merthe also,
> So that of loves maladie
> Sche makth diverse melodie,
> And seith love is a wofull blisse,
> A wisdom which can noman Wisse [know],
> A lusti fievere, a wounde softe:
> This note sche reherceth ofte
> To hem whiche understonde hir tale.   (5.5983–97)

Philomene has experienced love in only its cruellest form. She embodies the suffering to which the passion of love almost inevitably leads, in an Ovidian world where true sympathy and communion between the sexes can seem a virtual impossibility. Her song is like a distillation of the essence of what Gower valued in Ovid. It expresses all that he means by the daunting phrase *naturatus amor* with which the *Confessio* proper begins, and it looks forward to the end of the *Confessio*, where the poet seeks to rise from love poetry to prayer but must resist again and again the tendency to revert to thoughts.

> Of love and of his dedly hele [health],
> Which no phisicien can hele,
> For his nature is so divers.   (8.3155–57)

Gower's only direct engagements with non-Ovidian classical poetry are his accounts of the education of Achilles (4.1963–2019) and Achilles's later recruitment by Ulysses for the Trojan War (5.2961–3218). Both episodes are based on the *Achilleid* of Statius, and though they deal with their source in very different ways, both show Gower adapting his Statian material to his Ovidian concern with aggressive desire. The education of Achilles is conducted "upon the forme of knyhtes lawe" in a wholly male environment (4.1969). At the age of twelve, Achilles is entrusted to the centaur Chiron, whose teaching centers on hunting, and is reduced by Genius to the maxim that "of knihthode the prouesse / Is grounded upon hardinesse" (1965–66). Every day when Achilles returns from the hunt, his mentor inspects his weapons for the trace of blood that will confirm that he has killed, or at least wounded, his prey. Genius assures us that the fearlessness Achilles acquired by this means served him well, but there lurks around the episode the aura of a primitive sexual rite (Zambreno 140–41), and this suggestion becomes clearer when Genius concludes the brief narrative by restating his emblematic maxim:

> That the corage of hardiesce
> Is of knyhthode the prouesce   (4.2015–16)

and then disconcertingly adds that this "prowess"

> . . . is to love sufficant
> Aboven al the remenant [others]
> That unto loves court pursue.   (4.2017–19)

Unto the fierce, it would seem, belong the fair, and we may ask whether the "great need" that Achilles's education is designed to meet is finally martial or sexual.

As if in compensation Genius later tells the tale of Thetis's attempt to forestall Achilles's recruitment for the Trojan War by concealing him among the daughters of King Lichomedes (5.2961–3218). At first this tale seems to report a triumph of *gentilesse*. Once withdrawn from the context of male chivalry, Achilles adapts to life as a girl with uncanonical ease. Statius makes much of the awkward, pseudofeminine posturings of the brawny adolescent, and his Achilles is well aware of the sexual opportunities his concealment will provide. But Gower's Achilles is both graceful and wholly innocent in adapting to his new role. Even Ulysses cannot spot him as he dances with the king's daughters, and we are given no reason to doubt that Achilles has fully assimilated the feminine virtues of his companions as Gower enumerates them: "Honour, servise and reverence" (5.3001). The account of his sexual union with Deidamia conveys no suggestion of the rape frankly described by Statius. It is rather the result of a mutual innocent "stirring" and not the promptings of chivalric "hardiesce" but of the pressure of innocent nature in the total absence of the tensions and constraints chivalric culture would normally have imposed.

But Gower's gently tolerant treatment of the power of "kinde" when the normal barriers between the sexes are removed only serves to set off the power with which the conditioning effect of Achilles's earlier training in "knihthode" reasserts itself when Ulysses confronts him with the spectacle of arms and armor. Instantly his impulses are redirected forcibly toward the male world, and Achilles is effectively transposed to a different genre. Within a few short lines he is on his way to take part in the siege of Troy, and Deidamia is at once relegated to the past.

A similar adaptation of heroic legend to an examination of chivalry as it bears on women is Gower's "Tale of Orestes" (3.1885–2195), based mainly on Benoît's *Roman de Troie*. Throughout Gower's narrative the figure of Orestes is overshadowed by the burden of responsibility imposed on him by a knightly training that points him inexorably toward his unique mission, the matricide that Genius calls "mochel schame" ("much shame") but that Orestes is compelled to carry out.

These examples represent for students the prevailing emphasis of Gower's treatment of Ovidian (and thus of classical) poetry and themes. They enact on the level of history and in terms of medieval social values the drama that is played out more intimately in the dialogue of Genius and his disciple. For the limited power of *courtoisie* to control and dignify the yearnings of Amans reproduces in comic miniature the classically Ovidian problems of disciplining desire and neutralizing the iniquities of power, sexual and social, and the potential for good or ill embodied in cultural institutions.

Gower in the Community College Curriculum

Carole Lynn McKinney

At a two-year institution the pressure for instructors to focus on the basics of the literary canon may prove overwhelming. Numerous sources contribute to this pressure. College transfer requirements are strict, and instructor compliance may be rigorously monitored. Instructors may also be forced to use a prescribed syllabus. Worse, students at community colleges are frequently ill prepared for college-level literature studies. The average level of academic competence in community college populations is often lower than in university populations, as Christopher Oliver notes: "The main attractiveness of the community college is the open-enrollment philosophy . . . allow[ing] students to be accepted into its institution without specific academic prerequisites" (3). Students may have merely a passing acquaintance with only a few of the most prominent authors and works from any given period or region. Finally, the pressure to focus only on the most popular authors and selections in the literary canon is compounded because instructors often have to spend valuable class time reteaching composition and documentation techniques students should already know.

Even the most intelligent and well-prepared community college students tend to be pragmatic; they are frequently beset by strong social and economic pressures demanding that they focus their attention on providing food and shelter for themselves and sometimes also for their families. If such students do not develop an appreciation for the relevance of literature to their lives, their exposure to what they read may provide only limited, short-term benefits. They are likely to cram for examinations and then conveniently forget the material if they do not perceive an immediate connection to their own lives and futures. Nevertheless, taking the time to focus on an interesting lesson or relevant thematic study can help even highly pragmatic students develop a lasting appreciation for literature.

Gower's works may provide community college instructors an excellent opportunity to present a deeply realized, potentially engaging lesson. When used in combination with other medieval writers, Gower's works can illustrate the concept of thematic variance among authors and give students a layered perspective on the political culture of gender relations in the late medieval period. These themes and political issues will be relevant to students' modern experiences, and they can help put other medieval texts in perspective.

Gower and the Community College Student

Some scholars may be frustrated by the choice of the "Tale of Philomene and Tereus" as the selection included in the *Norton Anthology*. As the introductory material in the anthology notes, the tale is one "whose violence entirely overshadows the . . . pursuit of Amans for his lady" (Abrams and Greenblatt 320). However, "The Tale of Philomene and Tereus" examines material that is very relevant to the personal affairs of community college students, especially when used in conjunction with *The Canterbury Tales*, specifically The Wife of Bath's Prologue and Tale. The need to assign responsibility for, deal with the consequences of, and cope with guilt over types of relationship events similar to, if milder than, those discussed in the "Tale of Philomene and Tereus" is a need all too familiar for many community college students.

Because a higher percentage of community college students have created family relationships, both successful and failed, independently from their parents or guardians, many of them have firsthand experience with domestic violence, breaches of marital fidelity, and the consequences that follow. Therefore, the Wife of Bath's violence against her husband and his retribution and Progne's murderous vengeance against her husband are ideal to create instant engagement. Instructors may profit from the exaggerated violence of the tale, which resembles the tabloid and talk-show brand of modern media entertainment that students are familiar with and often find fascinating because it touches on and safely dramatizes their experiences in fictional or sensational form.

Students who normally prefer to remain silent in class frequently become emotionally invested and eager to discuss the "Tale of Philomene and Tereus." They want to debate a variety of questions. Are women justified in committing acts of emotional or domestic violence? Are husbands justified in physical retaliation to those acts? Who has the right to dispense justice? How severe a punishment is appropriate for physical and emotional suffering or infidelity? Certainly this same goal could be achieved by reading Chaucer, and some may argue that assigning Gower's tale is unnecessary. However, including Gower can create a three-dimensional depth to the lesson that is lost when Gower is omitted and only Chaucer is studied. Examining multiple cases by using The Wife of Bath's

Prologue and Tale and contrasting it to Gower's "Tale of Philomene and Tereus" urges students to develop intellectually and ethically, progressing from dualistic thinking toward multiplicity or even contextual relativism (Perry); students are encouraged to internalize the notion that similar crimes may fairly deserve different judgments when an impartial observer considers the nuances of the situations at hand. They grow to acknowledge that culpability usually exists on both sides of an argument and that justice from individuals, governments, and divine agencies alike may prove inadequate to redress the grievances done to husbands, wives, and innocent family members when violence or infidelity occurs in the home. This awareness not only helps students develop emotional and psychological maturity but also enhances their analytic abilities.

Rape is a grave concern for many college students. A survey performed by the United States Department of Justice in 1998 reports, "One in six U.S. women and one in thirty-three U.S. men have been raped" (Armada). Discussing appropriate reactions to and punishment for rape, both in The Wife of Bath's Tale and in the "Tale of Philomene and Tereus," is a pressing issue for students and leads to spirited examination of law and social mores, with positive student outcomes similar to those described above. Questions that are of especial interest in the works of Gower and Chaucer that arise in community college class discussions of rape include whether a husband can rape his wife and whether he has a right to require her sexual services. Students also like to discuss whether women have a right to experience pleasure in sexual activity; how silencing female voices, as Tereus does when he cuts out Philomene's tongue, or denying those voices "auctoritee" creates a climate that fosters male power and privilege; and to what extent men are responsible for governance of the marital relationship. These questions are matched by discussion of women's rights to help decide household affairs, engage in or refuse sexual relationships, and otherwise determine the disposition of their bodies.

Instructors should take special care to make the classroom a safe and unbiased forum for discussing emotionally charged issues of an intimate nature. Some students may find the conversation uncomfortably intense, and discussion of violence or rape may trigger unwanted memories for a few students. It is important that instructors display emotional sensitivity toward an affected student, require other students to behave respectfully regarding that student's distress, and take discreet but prompt action offering to connect the troubled student with appropriate counseling facilities at the college or in the larger community.

Moderating a discussion of gender issues in a classroom that includes vocal students of both genders can be difficult for instructors, especially if students are not accustomed (as many community college students are not) to interrogating gendered issues. How can a teacher work to ensure that both genders experience a respectfully neutral, safe conversation forum? Redirecting the discussion to consider hypothetical abstracts can be a useful tactic for retaining interest while defusing intolerance and resentment. When students attempt to move the argument toward the present and away from textual analysis, they often benefit from leading questions such as, How were standards of conduct different in Gower's time? What would Gower think of this point of contention? What evidence do you find in the text that reveals how he would think? This type of question may deflect off-topic conflict and encourage rational analysis and independent thinking. To help students gain perspective, the instructor can point out that Gower's moral position was largely considered a respectable one by the standards of his time, and then ask, Were those standards in agreement with modern standards? If not, where and why do they differ from ours? Will our modern moral standards be in agreement with the positions held by readers six hundred years in our future?

An instructor need not be a medievalist or a Gower scholar to facilitate useful discussion of Gower. It does require a skillful classroom mediator with an appropriate working knowledge of the authors and texts in question. To gain this knowledge, community college instructors need to become familiar with the authors, texts, and thematic material in the lesson, a concern that is especially pressing for instructors who have not studied the medieval period or the authors in question. For these instructors and for those who seek to supplement their existing approaches to Gower, I would like to outline a set of specific lesson plans that have been useful in a community college setting. The plan below lists supplementary readings that may serve as research resources for both instructors and students and identifies pivotal passages and thematic discussion points for exploration. It also provides essay questions that can be used as an independent writing activity and yield an opportunity for instructor assessment of student performance.

These lessons are arranged chronologically: first Chaucer and The Wife of Bath's Prologue and Tale, then Gower and the "Tale of Philomene and Tereus," and finally a comparative discussion of both. The plan focuses on potential discussion points to help students develop critical skills. Ideally each lesson should occupy at least two hours of class time and could easily expand further. A more detailed version of this assignment is available under Teaching Resources on the International John Gower Society Web site (www.johngower.org/teaching).

Lesson 1: The Wife of Bath's Prologue and Tale

This lesson begins with a class period devoted to the Wife of Bath. The class should start with a reading quiz on the specific material in The Wife of Bath's Prologue and Tale, such as the following: What event made the Wife of Bath lose part of her hearing? Objective questions of this nature should encourage students to do prereadings as assigned. Following the quiz, class discussion should focus on summarizing the plot (since many students still need help understanding its idiosyncrasies) and transitioning to analytic discussion that may focus on some of the following: authority, the female voice, control, "wandring by the waye," rape, bigamy, marital infidelity, or domestic violence.

For example, students should realize that the goal of most of the Wife of Bath's argument is control. The Wife wishes to control her existence, and her prologue demonstrates that she will go to great lengths to do so. The instructor might ask students to identify the arenas of her life (and the lives of her husbands) that the Wife seeks to control. Students may identify elements such as the home, marriage, sexuality, childbearing, money, travel, clothing, and her husbands. If time permits, students may be encouraged to branch out into philosophical discussion, considering questions like these: Is the Wife being reasonable, and should she be given control of everything she wants? Will giving either partner control truly lead to "a bath of blisse" (1253) and "parfit joye" unto "hir lives ende" (1263–64), as she claims at the end of her tale? What alternatives would be preferable to single-partner control? How could the Wife and Janekin negotiate a better alternative?

Students may also enjoy discussing whether it is really rape to require payment of the marital debt; whether the Wife herself is guilty of rape when she requires her husbands to pay their marital debt, especially when they are old and infirm; and whether her husbands are guilty of rape when they obtain her debt though she is not interested in having sex with them. Instructors may offer assistance by pointing out the quotation in which the Wife of Bath says of each of her three old husbands that "I wolde no lenger in the bed abide / If that I felte his arm over my side, / Til he hadde maad his raunson unto me / Thanne wolde I suffre him do his nicetee" (409–12), and contrast it to the quotation in which she boasts about laughing when she thinks "how pitously anight I made hem swinke" (202).

Lesson 2: The "Tale of Philomene and Tereus"

Like the prior class, this class begins with a quiz, leading to plot summary, then to analysis. Instructors may wish to include a discussion or statement pertaining to Gower's mythological sources. The previous discussion of The Wife of Bath's Prologue and Tale should provide a foundation for quick understanding of some of the concepts listed here; for example, it is not necessary to spend time establishing a basis for the wider social-sexual ramifications of Philomene's exit from the implicitly asexual sanctuary of her father's house, since students are already aware of the social consequences and stigma incurred by the Wife of Bath in her decision to leave the domicile of her husband, her designated masculine protector of virtue. And the same topics discussed in the Chaucer class period may be addressed here as well.

For example, although the politics of domestic control do not compose the primary purpose of Gower's narrative as they do the heart of The Wife of Bath's Prologue and Tale, they are nevertheless of concern here, and students may benefit from working to interpret them. As noted above, the instructor may ask who controls the series of events, and students may debate whether Progne bears any blame for the rape as a result of her request that Tereus fetch her sister for a visit. Cynical students, especially those who are growing threatened by prolonged discussion of feminine power and related feminist issues, may suggest that Tereus rapes Philomene to assert his control by demonstrating his independence from his wife's wheedling, or they may suggest similar motives that are not fully supported by the text. More observant students may note that Tereus is not immune to the moral consequences and temptations of wandering: like the Wife of Bath, he succumbs to temptations of opportunity created by leaving the home and abandons his marital virtue. This insight can lead to a discussion of culpability: whose transgression is worse, his or the Wife of Bath's, and why?

The instructor may want to point out that to a medieval audience, Tereus's transgression is a failure of self-control and may be regarded as a failure of personal honor and responsibility as much as a loss of sexual virtue or one of control of his larger household. Tereus fails to uphold the honorable rules of mastery within his extended family and fails to provide a safe space for a female relative by marriage who is entrusted to his care. Thus he is labeled "rude" and a "tyrant raviner," a considerable demotion from his initial status as a worthy king. Students may posit that as a result of his loss of self-control, Tereus loses his right (or at least his ability) to assert control over others. This discussion can lead to further inquiry into medieval expectations for masculine behavior and the penalties for transgression and may serve as a prompt for a research assignment.

After concluding class discussion of Tereus, Philomeme, and Progne, instructors whose classes are still engaged and are not experiencing anxiety or hostility because of the discussion topic may want to call students' attention to the insight regarding control that frames and concludes the "Tale of Philomene and Tereus." Amans declares that he has learned he should prefer terrible punishments rather than let lust overrule his good sense and provoke him to do "any thing or loude or stille, / Which were noght my lady wille" (5.6057–58). Instructors may invite students to compare this conclusion with the Wife of Bath's seemingly identical one to evaluate which of the two is more likely to result in domestic accord and to explain why one may be superior to the other in practical terms.

Identifying the need for a code of behavior for men, above, provides a good transition to discussion of Gower's didactic intent. Instructors may lead students to consider why Gower felt compelled to create an instructive dialogue between Genius and Amans. At this point, they may ask if students think Gower has inserted himself into the frame and question whether they think he plays the role of Genius or that of Amans, and why? This will encourage students to see Gower as a real person, a man who suffered temptation and needed instructive support to foster his own self-control and direct it appropriately.

Lesson 3: Comparative Study

The third lesson allows speculative discussion to develop in depth and thus contains more seeking questions than textual references and interpretive material. As the questions listed below under each key concept are considered, instructors will want to invite frequent direct comparisons between the two authors and their texts, invite students to examine why the similarities and differences they have identified exist, and theorize about what those differences teach about the wider social attitudes toward women in medieval times.

The male voice representing women's issues and women's voices   On the subject of voice, instructors may wish to take up the issue of a male author representing himself as writing a narrative from a female perspective. How does Chaucer's supposedly feminine narrator contrast to Gower's purely masculine representation of narrative? How does Gower represent female voices, positively or negatively? What biases is each author displaying?

Sexuality: shame and reputation   Students may be interested in examining how Chaucer and Gower perceive sexuality as a source of shame. Which gender is more likely to be subject to public shame? How does males' shame differ from females'? Does public knowledge increase shame? Does the Wife of Bath endure shame or a reduction in good reputation because of her sexuality? If so, what sort of shame is it? Can it be found in the text? If not, why not?

Sexual aggression   Tereus and the Wife of Bath are both sexually aggressive characters. What are their motives for sexual aggression, and how are these motives similar and dissimilar? How does each character deal with the motivating influence of lust? Do both feel or experience guilt? If so, where may textual evidence of guilt be found for each character? What sorts of guilt do they feel?

Women's responses to domestic violence   What sort of responses do medieval women make when they are victims of domestic violence? Do the assigned texts show that women have recourse to legal or social support? Is there any evidence in our readings of socially acceptable responses for women to make to domestic violence? Instructors may want to elicit the idea that a lack of recourse to legal or social support may provoke women to respond to violence with violence.

The marital-reproductive contract   The "Tale of Philomene and Tereus" provides a very different perspective on the rights and duties of parties who enter into the marriage contract, both in the couple's relationship to each other and in reference to children. How are the Wife and Progne similar? Instructors may want to suggest that both believe they have a right to keep husbands who do not satisfy them from having children. Some students may make a connection between the Wife's "remedies of love" to Progne's filicide, recognizing that the Wife may have used abortions as well as contraception to avoid reproduction.

The threat of the female voice   Instructors may ask students to identify various vocal threats in The Wife of Bath's Prologue and Tale. How does the Wife use her voice to threaten masculine authority? Why are men threatened by the contents of her statements? How is her voice a subversive threat to her own assumption of authority? Is the Wife really a "noble prechour," as the Pardoner states? If so, how do her evangelical tendencies constitute a threat? What persons or types of social institutions are threatened?

The topics and questions listed in these assignments are, of course, only a sampling of ideas that may be discussed in class. If at all possible, the instructor should reserve time for students to point out other issues they have observed. Often student insights will prove trenchant and may open up areas of discussion the instructor has inadvertently neglected.

Particularly at the community college level, it may be beneficial to supplement students' endeavors in composing challenging critical essays with support outside the classroom. Short mandatory student-teacher conferences over rough drafts are likely to prove particularly successful in improving the quality of final papers. Alternatively, students may be assigned to take drafts to in-house writing labs, or instructors may return final drafts marked with guiding comments and a requirement that they be revised and resubmitted. However, experience indicates that the earlier help is given after initial drafts are attempted, the more valuable it is in improving students' writing performance and reducing their potential frustration with the writing experience. And while secondary research is often limited in community college classrooms, a number of essays can provide useful tools for students addressing the aforementioned topics. I suggest, depending on the focus of the class, Robin Bott's "'O, Keep Me from Their Worse Than Killing Lust'"; Christopher Cannon's "Chaucer and Rape"; Carolyn Dinshaw's "Rivalry, Rape, and Manhood"; Margaret Hallissy's *Clean Maids, True Wives, Steadfast Widows*; Barbara Hanawalt's "*Of Good and Ill Repute*"; Isabelle Mast's "Rape in John Gower's *Confessio Amantis*"; Elizabeth Robertson's "Public Bodies and Psychic Domains"; Christine Rose's "Reading Chaucer Reading Rape"; Corrine Saunders's *Rape and Ravishment in the Literature of Medieval England*; and Angela Jane Weisl's "'Quiting' Eve."

Community college instructors who add Gower to their syllabuses will discover that he is a poet truly worthy of study, one whose works are rich and full of ideas that merit examination and develop his readers' insights and critical inquiry skills in a multitude of ways. They will find that Gower's poetry has the ability to engage young modern readers with relevant social matters and that he is able to hold the attention of many of these readers despite their close acquaintance with the often mindless spectacle and sensationalism of Hollywood entertainment. In fact, students who experience the lessons described above frequently express bafflement when they look up John Gower using *Wikipedia* (as some inevitably do, despite many instructors' efforts to discourage its use as a critical resource) and read there that "his reputation declined [from its original parity with Chaucer's], largely on account of a perceived didacticism and dullness" ("John Gower").

Chaucer by Default?
Difficult Choices and Teaching
the Sophomore British Literature Survey

Susannah M. Chewning

Teaching the early British literature survey class at any college or university is fraught with challenges. Many students arrive at college with little to no experience studying pre–Modern English language or literature, including students who think they cannot read Shakespeare because it is written in "Old English." Of course, such historical errors are easy to correct, but with new editions, such as the No Fear Shakespeare series, which translates Shakespeare's language into more modern, more colloquial English, instructors are faced with students whose understanding and interest in early English language may be limited, at best. While such translations make the text more accessible, they also remove the nuances of the work. *No Fear Shakespeare*'s version of Henry V's famous "Once more unto the breach" speech exemplifies this plight: "Attack the breach in the city wall once more, dear friends, attack it once more — or else let's close it up with English corpses" (3.1.1–2). It is the language of Shakespeare and Gower that makes them worthy of our devotion to them in such survey classes. Their richness is reflected in the difficulty of their language; making their works easier to read is a disservice to the works, to their authors, and ultimately to our students.

This essay considers how to teach Gower's works in a sophomore-level British literature survey class, a class wherein Gower is often not taught but his contemporary, Chaucer, usually is. Although tied to my experience teaching at a two-year college, the approach I suggest can be applied to any sophomore-level literature class. It addresses not merely a problem faced by two-year college students but a wider problem facing higher education in general: the need to find a way to engage modern undergraduates so that the language, context, and historical significance of these early English works is relevant and interesting.

The first time I taught a British literature survey I was, in fact, at a four-year college, a state university in an affluent New Jersey suburb where most students came from good high schools and were prepared to engage with literature at a fairly advanced level. I used the same technique and formula that my own early British literature survey instructor had used when I was a student, some fourteen years before. I taught from the *Norton Anthology of English Literature* and included on my syllabus the main canonical works and figures from *Beowulf* to Thomas Gray. I used *King Lear* as the Shakespeare play because it was in the anthology, and I supplemented the materials very little since there was so much to cover (adding some of the anchoritic works I was myself, at the time, working on, but little else). I attempted that first time to include excerpts from a wide variety of works: the *Fairie Queene* and *Paradise Lost*; The General Prologue, The Miller's Tale, and The Wife of Bath's Tale; Shakespeare's sonnets and *King Lear*; and as much on either end—that is, from *Beowulf* and the *Wanderer* to Pope and Swift—to make me feel that I'd covered as much as I could in a sixteen-week semester. I was proud of the content and of my confidence with the works I taught, and I felt by the end of the semester, though I'd had to cut a few assignments and discussions a bit short, that I had done a good job. However, with overwhelming frequency, the comments on my student evaluations said that there was too much to read. Granted, there is almost no amount of reading we can assign to students that will not be interpreted, by some of them, as too much, but I took the comments to heart, and when I next taught the course, at another suburban four-year campus in New Jersey (this second one a bit more urban), I tried to focus on the texts I thought would be most useful and most accessible to my students.

In the second version of the course, I ordered *Much Ado about Nothing* because I felt a comedy would be more accessible, and less depressing, than *King Lear*. I also cut out Spenser, except for the sonnets, and assigned considerably less Milton than previously. I still included the same amount of Chaucer and Anglo-Saxon material, but this time I didn't use the *Norton Anthology*. It went well, again, but my students still felt overwhelmed by the work they were expected to read, a workload they felt was compounded by the fact that not only were Chaucer's works not translated, but neither were Shakespeare's. I faced what we all face who teach British literature to undergraduates in a survey course: the conflict among trying to cover as much material as possible, assigning manageable amounts of reading for my students, and responding to that almost ubiquitous resistance to early literature in the original language. As my career progressed and I found myself in a tenure-track position at a two-year college, I knew that it was the sophomore-level survey in which I would most likely be teaching early British literature for the foreseeable future. At Union County College, where I now teach, I was, when I was hired, the only person on the full-time faculty who specialized in British literature of any period, so I was (and am) responsible for British Literature I and II, "Beowulf to Virginia Woolf" as it was once described at Yale. Because I teach the courses so frequently, I found very quickly that I had to do something to make the course more accessible to my students and more satisfying for myself. I had to make some difficult choices, and fortunately the *Norton Anthology* came out in a new edition right at the time I was completely remodeling my course.

What follows is the revised version of my British Literature I class as it has evolved over the past ten years. I have omitted some texts that some of my colleagues who read this might consider essential, and I have included some that might be viewed as less significant. But most important, I think I have come to a solution on the matter of Chaucer and Shakespeare that serves as a compromise between my need to raise the bar for my students so they are reading

190 CHAUCER BY DEFAULT?

Middle and early Modern English at a high level of competence (high enough for sophomores) and their need for works that are accessible, interesting, and readable.

When I teach this class, I include a list of required readings and three categories of options, or "threads," for students to continue their reading beyond the minimum requirements. The threads are loosely based on spirituality, love and marriage, and politics. In preparation for most classes, students must complete a required assignment as well as one of the assignments in one of the threads. They can follow one thread throughout the course, which eventually gives them enough information about one of the three threads to write a thoughtful research paper, or they can "read around" among the various optional readings to find what interests them most. I am able, through this structure, to include a number of readings that I could never otherwise cover, and thus I can focus on some works that might not be readily accessible to students outside the context of the course. While this approach means that not all the students in the class have read the same material, it does lead to provocative discussions in class as students contribute ideas based on their various reading experiences and knowledge. The drawback of the approach is that we cannot focus as much on any single author, like Chaucer, as many other survey courses do.

The problem with focusing on Chaucer, like many of the other authors, is that there is so much to cover and so little time to cover it. But if my students transfer to four-year colleges (as many of them do) and if they become English majors (as some of them do), they may at some point take a Chaucer survey or a course that includes more Chaucer and Middle English. So it is important that the students who go from my survey class to an upper-division class in English be prepared for what they will face. On the other hand, many students take these survey classes as humanities or general studies electives, and these students may never be exposed to these works again. So the class must address both of these student populations. Gower's works can serve both kinds of students, and, if his works are not taught in the class, students generally would never have the opportunity to read them. Gower is also accessible given the texts available to us and to students, as the introductory essays in this volume point out. If a primary learning outcome of the British literature survey class is to expose students to a wide range of representative, canonical, uncanonical, and historically relevant literature, then Gower is a perfect choice for inclusion.

The *Confessio Amantis* is a brilliant poem, and it serves as a wonderful opportunity to discuss medieval notions of love and sex (thematic aspects students enjoy discussing). It also reflects a historically relevant poetic structure with Amans seeking solace from Genius. Elsewhere I have argued that teaching the tale of Philomela from Ovid's *Metamorphoses*, Chaucer's *Legend of Good Women*, and Gower's *Confessio Amantis* can provide students with an excellent introduction to the use and interpretation of classical sources by medieval English writers, as well as to the relationship between Chaucer and Gower ("Chaucer and Vernacular Writing"). This discussion is now even easier to initiate in class, given the *Norton Anthology of English Literature*'s recent inclusion of Gower's version of the tale of Philomela from the *Confessio Amantis*. But including such a work in my course necessitated removing other works, and what I deleted was Chaucer. I agree that it would be better to include as much of both Gower and Chaucer as possible, but Gower is as relevant (if not more so) to my class and to its overall thematic connections. So I have made Gower the central Middle English assignment in my British literature survey, and most of Chaucer's texts that are included in other survey classes are now optional. The result of this shift of focus is that most students still recognized and connected with Chaucer even though they spent less time on his work in class, some students ultimately read more of both writers, and all were exposed at least marginally to the works of each author. This wider exposure addresses more closely the function and goals of the survey class at many institutions.

Teaching Gower in my class begins with a discussion of the disastrous world of fourteenth-century England, a topic supported by numerous online materials, including the supplementary materials offered by the *Norton Anthology* site online (www.wwnorton.com/college/english/nael). We discuss the Black Death, the rise of organized labor (something many of my students really do understand), the Peasants' Revolt, and the reign of Edward III. Because of my own interests in the literature of women and in medieval English devotional works, we look at the *Ancrene Wisse*, the works of Julian of Norwich, and excerpts from the *Book of Margery Kempe*, works available in many anthologies and online. In a separate thread we talk about the Arthurian tradition, including excerpts from *Sir Gawain and the Green Knight*. I also spend most of a class period looking at the life of Richard II and his reign and how important Richard was to Chaucer and to Gower (as poets within his court). We discuss how Richard's rule influenced the works of both Chaucer and Gower, and we analyze the supposed meeting between Richard II and Gower on the Thames, as described in the early recensions of the *Confessio Amantis*. Students are particularly interested in discussing Gower's desire to write "Som newe thing . . . That he himself it mighte looke / After the forme of my writing" (*CA*, prologue, lines 51–53), lines. From our discussion of the meeting between Gower and Richard II, our analysis of Gower's later rededication of *Confessio Amantis* to Henry of Lancaster (prologue 81–92), and our recognition of Richard's deposition, students begin to understand what was at stake for both Chaucer and Gower and to see that poetry in the fourteenth century was much more politically motivated than they might otherwise have thought. Students are often ignorant of the relation between politics and artistic production, and Gower's works can exemplify this relation.

Although the passage of Gower that we read focuses on Philomene and her disastrous encounter with Tereus, students come away with a sense that Gower and Chaucer were important players in the political world of their day. It is also within the context of the reigns of Richard II and Henry IV that I present some further ideas associated with both poets: images of their tombs, manuscripts of their works, and their presence in later works, most notably in Shakespeare. Why, I ask, is Gower's tomb so much grander than the tomb of Chaucer? How important were these poets to have had such fully illuminated and detailed manuscripts completed during their lifetimes? Why does Shakespeare represent Gower (going so far as to include Gower as the voice of the chorus of his *Pericles, prince of Tyre*) but not Chaucer, from whom he derived much of his material for works as varied as *Troilus and Cressida, Midsummer Night's Dream, Two Noble Kinsmen*, and *Venus and Adonis*?

Since I use the *Norton Anthology*, I assign the excerpts from *Confessio Amantis* and Gower's tale of Philomene in the text, as well as the excerpts available on the Norton Web site, passages depicting the estates satire in the *Vox clamantis* and the *Miroir de l'omme*. These readings are required, as are several excerpts from Chaucer's General Prologue. I follow these required readings with optional readings: excerpts of Chaucer including The Miller's Tale, The Wife of Bath's Tale, and The Pardoner's Tale. Students are responsible for reading the untranslated excerpts from Gower but may read Chaucer's works in translation (which they can find easily in print and online). They struggle with Gower's works, but no more so than they do with Chaucer's works, and they feel very accomplished for having read what they consider to be so difficult a text. When we do look at some of the Chaucer later on, they find themselves in more familiar territory and are less likely to run to a translation, having persevered through Gower the previous week. The next major reading assignment is Shakespeare's tragedy *Richard II*. We therefore come to the play *Richard II* after some weeks discussing the world of the historical Richard II and his literary representation during the later Middle Ages. We have already discussed his predecessor, Edward III; Richard's troubled reign; his deposition; and his relationships with both Chaucer and Gower.

Because of students' affinity for Jones's humor, I also discuss Terry Jones, R. F. Yeager, Terry Dolan, Alan Fletcher, and Juliette Dor's *Who Murdered Chaucer?*, which may not present a fully convincing argument to all readers but does elaborate on late-fourteenth-century court intrigue and war to help explain the world of the court in the time of Richard II and Henry IV. The Chaucer who emerges from these discussions is not simply the wine-drinking, foul-mouthed court humorist so often envisioned by undergraduates but rather (or perhaps also) a savvy and politically astute member of the court whose work has implications far beyond entertainment at court festivities. Using selections from *Who Murdered Chaucer?*, I try to articulate to my students that, contrary to what they might have heard previously, Chaucer and Shakespeare have little in common. *Richard II* is also an excellent play for explaining the social and political upheaval of Shakespeare's day, and using Michael Wood's film *In Search of Shakespeare*, episode 3, "The Duty of Poets," which discusses the Earl of Essex's rebellion and the performance the night before by Shakespeare and his players of *Richard II*, students begin to see even more of the connections between literary works and authors, political and social events, and the kinds of sensational activities that can easily be related to modern social and political events. For example, Wood recalls the famous moment when Elizabeth evokes Richard II, as the film depicts her remark: "I am Richard II, know ye not that? This tragedy hath been played forty times in open streets and playhouses. In those days, force and arms did prevail, but now the fox is everywhere, and scarcely a faithful or a virtuous man is to be found." Wood points out that the play reinforced for its audience, the night before the earl's rebellion in February 1601, that "a monarch who had lost the trust of the people could be legitimately deposed" (*In Search of Shakespeare*). By this point, students can associate Richard II's reign with Shakespeare's performance of *Richard II* on the eve of the Essex rebellion and revisit the consequences Chaucer and Gower might have paid for their allegiances to Richard II and, in Gower's case, to Henry Bolingbroke.

Gower thus emerges in the context of these assignments as a powerful participant with Chaucer in the literary and political life of the court: Gower the survivor who was important both to Richard and to Henry; Gower the brilliant linguist who, like Chaucer, brought English to a level of poetic power while still giving credit to the other great languages of his culture, French and Latin; Gower the friend and contemporary of Chaucer's and the dedicatee of Chaucer's *Troilus and Criseyde*; Gower the poet of love whose sorrowful Philomene speaks across the centuries as a silenced voice of violence and oppression. I realize reducing the amount of reading of Chaucer's works poses some problems, which I try to work out in the optional readings that go along with the requirements for the course. But I am satisfied that my survey students emerge from the class with a level of facility with the historical, linguistic, social, and literary background to allow them to hold their own in upper-division coursework. And those who do not pursue their studies in literature or the humanities find a moment in literary history that they can connect to their own time and to their other interests.

NOTE

The use of Shakespeare's *Richard II* as a point of connection between Chaucer's and Shakespeare's worlds was first suggested to me by David Roberts, associate professor of English at Bennett College.

Teaching Gower in the Medieval Survey Class: Historical and Cultural Contexts and the Court of Richard II

S. Elizabeth Passmore

A couple of years after being hired as the sole medievalist in the English department of a four-year comprehensive university in the Midwest, I was lucky enough to have the opportunity to teach selections from John Gower's *Confessio Amantis* in an upper-level English course entitled Medieval Courtly Literature. This survey course concentrated on late-fourteenth-century England, with readings from works such as *Sir Gawain and the Green Knight*, *Pearl*, *Richard the Redeless*, *The Travels of Sir John Mandeville*, William Langland's *Piers Plowman*, Jean Froissart's *Chronicles*, and Chaucer's *Book of the Duchess*, as well as from Gower's English poem. Beginning with the choice of course title, I attempted to design this survey of Ricardian poetry and prose to attract the interest of students unfamiliar with most medieval literature, as are many of our students. Moreover, in my advertising campaign to enroll students, I had to consider the fact that our departmental requirements for English majors lacked much opportunity for students to take such "free" electives. In this essay, I discuss my retrospective thoughts on developing this new course and my realizations as the semester unfolded about necessary revisions to improve future versions of the course. Furthermore, I take into account how interpretations of a text such as Gower's *Confessio Amantis* necessarily change in relation to the readers who experience it and how this shifting interpretive process requires openness and flexibility in the planning and unfolding of any course, but perhaps most sensitively in a course on medieval narratives read in the original Middle English.

My approach to teaching Gower's poetry embodies a strongly interdisciplinary emphasis that acknowledges the initial sense of the "foreign" many students encounter on their introduction to medieval writings. By introducing multiple examples of material culture alongside the literary texts, I encouraged students to approach the narratives holistically, familiarizing themselves with the sociohistorical environment alongside the texts inspired by it. In the course of the semester, I regularly brought into class extratextual materials to demonstrate and illustrate the contemporary medieval culture as it was relevant to the readings assigned for each class. These objects helped students understand the medieval environment in which Gower's and other medieval authors' works were created. They included music, artwork (architecture, tapestries, decorative items, illuminated manuscripts), and information about material culture—clothing, food, housing, and so on. This interdisciplinary approach emphasizes the importance and relevance of culture to understanding literary texts, and it represents an accessible approach to the literature, one with which students can identify through awareness of the influences on them of their own sociocultural environments.

The course readings spanned literature from the reign of King Richard II, and the course title, Medieval Courtly Literature, was chosen to attract students, many of whom had never read medieval literature (some, sadly, had never even heard of Chaucer, never mind Gower). At the university where I teach, English majors must choose among several emphases — rhetoric and writing, teaching, creative writing, or literature. After fulfilling the requirements for their concentration, students often have little room in their schedules for open electives — especially since many of them opt for a double major and most are very focused on job-training courses that will enhance their marketability for future employment. It was, therefore, unclear that a course revolving around the literature of late medieval England would attract the ten registered, upper-level students needed. An even greater challenge to garnering a sufficient enrollment was overcoming student fears about the "foreignness" of the medieval language and culture, and so I attempted to pique their curiosity about the time period with audio and visual images.

When the semester began with an enrollment of ten undergraduates, two graduate students, and two auditors, I initially felt much of the battle had been won. However, I found many more challenges to overcome. The course was scheduled in the evening, meeting just once a week for nearly three hours. Since most of the students had either worked or taken classes all day long, their exhaustion was an ongoing challenge, and packing language learning, cultural awareness, and literary interpretations into one evening never ceased to be difficult. About half of the students had never read any medieval literature and were entirely unfamiliar with the appearance of Middle English. The remaining students had either taken a Chaucer course or a history of the English language course in the previous year and so had some familiarity with Middle English. All the students, however, were dedicated to and enthusiastic about learning of and reading literature from this time period. I was definitely lucky to have gathered the committed students who enrolled in the course — they were eager to learn and filled with abundant curiosity about this distant culture they would be encountering.

Because this course focused on texts written during or significant to the Ricardian period, I linked all the texts through an ongoing reading assignment intended to familiarize students with the historical events of the period, assigning one chapter each week of Nigel Saul's *Richard II*. At the beginning of the semester, when we were studying *Sir Gawain and the Green Knight*, students didn't immediately see the relevance of these reading assignments to the literary texts. However, as the semester wore on, their gradually expanding knowledge of the sociopolitical context enabled them to begin to make connections between the historical period and the texts that they read, as well as among the multiple literary texts. For example, as we began reading Gower's prologue to the *Confessio* and I raised the topic of Gower's first-recension explanation for the composition of the poem, students were sufficiently familiar with the events and impressions of Richard II's reign in the late 1380s that the image of Gower and Richard conversing on the Thames seemed to them pregnant with cultural implications.

This layering of historical information and literary works seemed an advantage over merely lecturing students on the cultural context. In effect, students began to relate the multiple facets of the culture in a more amorphous, diffuse way than would have been true if they were imbibing pure lecture. Nevertheless, they had some complaints about Saul's thorough history of Richard II's life and reign. Many of them found his prose style and organization of materials disjointed and confusing, and they ultimately tired of his tendency to shift unexpectedly from one topic to another in a thematic rather than chronological way. In the future, therefore, I may reconsider the use of this text, perhaps drawing on multiple articles and chapters of books. More recently, in a Chaucer course, I assigned the controversial but fascinating *Who Murdered Chaucer? A Medieval Mystery*, by Terry Jones, R. F. Yeager, Terry Dolan, Alan Fletcher, and Juliette Dor. As a way of immersing students in the late-fourteenth-century cultural environment, this book worked fabulously—students loved reading it, and the controversial and circumstantial arguments became the basis for a research project, whereby students hunted down more conventional assumptions about Richard II's reign and contrasted the polemic in that volume with those assumptions.

When I designed the syllabus for Medieval Courtly Literature, I had planned to devote two weeks to Gower's *Confessio Amantis*. In actuality, we spent nearly four weeks on this text, including practice with reading Middle English. Had we met more than the one evening seminar session a week, we might have been able to spend less time overall; however, during the weeks spent discussing Gower's work, students also began to present their cultural research projects, which took up a significant portion of class time.

Since it would have been impossible in a survey course to read Gower's *Confessio Amantis* in its entirety, I had to make some difficult choices about which selections we would study. In the end, I selected enough of the frame narrative to provide students with a sense of the work's design plus several tales (from different books) with biblical, Chaucerian, or Shakespearean analogues—with the idea that these would be the most likely for students to encounter again. Students were assigned to read the whole of the prologue (the discussion of the three estates and "Nebuchadnezzar's Dream"); part of book 1, on Pride (including the beginning of Amans's deliberations with Venus and Genius plus two of the tales: "Tale of Florent"—an analogue to Chaucer's Wife of Bath's Tale—and "Nebuchadnezzar's Punishment," which correlates to "Nebuchadnezzar's Dream" from the prologue); selected stories from book 3, on Wrath (the "Tale of Pyramus and Thisbe"—also told by Chaucer and in Shakespeare's *Midsummer Night's Dream*); and book 4, on Sloth, including the "Tale of Aeneas and Dido" (cf. the story in Vergil's *Aeneid*) and the "Tale of Ceix and Alceone" (cf. the version in Chaucer's *Book of the Duchess*); all book 7 (which includes Aristotle's instruction of Alexander; the "Tale of Tarquin, Aruns, and Lucrece," which is an analogue to Chaucer's *Legend of Good Women*; the "Tale of Virginia," an analogue to Chaucer's Physician's Tale; the "Tale of Tobias and Sara"—from the Old Testament Book of Tobias); and book 8 (except for the "Tale of Apollonius of Tyre"), most notable for the resolution of Amans's instruction by Genius. Book 7 of Gower's *Confessio Amantis* is perhaps the most important section of the poem, with its "mirror of princes" theme of counsel and kingship existing in numerous medieval analogues. Through brief lectures and discussion, students became aware of the relevance of late-fourteenth-century social and political events to understanding how book 7 is significant to the construction and theme of the entire poetic narrative.

The students responded well to Gower's poem, to the tales, and to Amans's predicament, identifying especially with the "lovelorn" hero and his unrequited infatuation. Most, however, did not immediately perceive the significance of the broader sociopolitical context—that of Amans's experience as an allegory of King Richard's reign and of England itself. In retrospect, I believe that *Who Murdered Chaucer?* would have been invaluable as a tool for discussion, particularly in regard to Gower's revisions to the frame narrative in later recensions. Students soon were able, even so, to draw on their own growing knowledge (from previous literary and historical assignments and discussions of other texts from the same time period) to discuss cultural concerns raised in the narrative.

The week before we began discussing Gower's *Confessio*, we devoted a portion of the evening to language practice, using a handout of the first ninety lines of the prologue. Students took turns translating lines and discussing Gower's writing style as well as the differences between Middle English and Modern English syntax. In anticipation of the following week's reading assignment, I spoke about the conventional medieval tripartite division of society into different estates and how this would figure, along with the concept of multiple ages of the world, in the content of the prologue.

During the second evening, I introduced the overall purpose of Gower's *Confessio Amantis* at the level of the individual (Amans), the society (ruler, church, Commons), and the country (kingdom). We discussed King Richard II's reign and the political and social events of the 1380s, pondering the purpose of their implicit reflection in the *Confessio*. Students were curious about the structure and organization—the division into eight books, six of which specifically name a deadly sin as its theme. Students were also intrigued by the lack of a separate book explicitly devoted to the sin of lechery, and we reviewed scholarly debates examining the purpose of this omission. I brought into class images of facsimiles of Gower's manuscripts, including an illuminated leaf illustrating Nebuchadnezzar's dreams, which led students to think about the implications of text-image relations in a manuscript culture.

By the third week, students felt sufficiently comfortable with Gower's language and the structure and purpose of the *Confessio* that we could focus more narrowly on individual tales and their relation to their sources or analogues (Chaucer, biblical, and classical as well as later Shakespearean uses). We focused particularly on the reasons for retelling tales familiar to the contemporary audience—including concepts of history, memory devices, and the use of the confession and dream-vision genres as primary structural devices and modes of instruction. Since we read selections from the books on the sins of pride, wrath, and sloth, we concentrated on examining the connection of the stories we read to each book's thematic sin. Discussion during this evening led inevitably to connections with today's political and economic situations—the dissolution of common profit, the rise of greed, and the connection of both to the apparent inevitability of war. Students marveled at Gower's ability to pinpoint troubles in society, which still remain unsolved today, and a lively debate ensued between the merits of *Piers Plowman* and the *Confessio Amantis*.

Our discussion of the *Confessio* concluded with the relation of the significance of book 7 (as a manual of instructions for rulers) to the overall structure. We also discussed the differences between, especially, the first and third recensions and the implications of these revisions for contemporary cultural events. Students were fascinated by the image of Gower and Richard II conversing on the Thames and were deeply curious about the fact that Gower, eight years before Richard's deposition, had changed his dedication from Richard to Henry of Derby. Again, it would be interesting, in the future, to bring in the suggestion in *Who Murdered Chaucer?* of a retrospective revision, from the early years of Henry IV's reign, to this potentially propagandistic change.

One of the biggest challenges in teaching Gower's *Confessio Amantis* was making the Middle English language accessible to my students. This is not a challenge specific to Gower, of course—it is simply the greatest barrier between modern students and any medieval literature read in its original language. Half of the students in the course had never read Middle English before; however, with every text we'd studied that had been translated from Middle English, I had students examine excerpts from the original, either reading to them in Middle English or using tapes of others' reciting portions of the works. With several of these texts—*Sir Gawain and the Green Knight*, *Piers Plowman*, *The Travels of Sir John Mandeville*—we compared available modern translations of the Middle English and discussed choices made by each translator as well as the effect of these choices on our interpretations of the literary texts.

Similar to my use of Saul's *Richard II* as a way of easing students into knowledge of the time period, my introduction of samples of Middle English over a number of weeks was intended to assist students in becoming gradually more familiar with the language in a comparatively stress-free environment. My hope was that, by the time they read Gower's *Confessio Amantis* in its original Middle English, the language would already seem familiar and understandable to them. While this approach worked to a certain extent, it could have been more effective if I had incorporated a couple of other techniques into the plan. First, we could have spent some class time each week actually translating parts of the

Middle English texts, as we eventually did with Gower's prologue. Second, it would help to provide students at the beginning of the semester with a brief glossary of commonly used Middle English words and their Modern English translations, especially the false friends, the words that look like Modern English but have changed in meaning. It might, in fact, have been useful to require a text such as Simon Horobin and Jeremy Smith's *An Introduction to Middle English*, which I have used more recently (to great success) in another medieval literature course. Some formal practice in medieval grammar and vocabulary, even in a literary course, seems increasingly necessary, at least with the students I have taught.

I should also, in retrospect, have required a different edition of Gower's English work. For Medieval Courtly Literature, I had students purchase the MART edition (Medieval Academy Reprints for Teaching, ed. Peck, 1997) of the *Confessio Amantis* because I wanted them to gain a sense of the whole poem by drawing from all parts of it. I believed that this wouldn't be possible with the TEAMS edition (ed. Peck, 2002–06) because I couldn't expect students to purchase all three volumes, particularly for a survey course in which they had other texts to purchase. I realized in the process of teaching the poem, however, that it is virtually impossible to give a sense of the whole *Confessio Amantis* through selective reading assignments, simply because of its sheer length and complexity. Moreover, the MART edition lacked an overall glossary that, combined with fairly skimpy on-page glosses, made for greater student challenges in reading the Middle English. I had originally thought that the combination of translations and Middle English text in the MART edition would serve as a stepping-stone transition from reading translated texts (as we did in the first half of the semester) to reading the original Middle English texts in the latter part of the semester (Gower, Chaucer, *Pearl*, and *Richard the Redeless*). Student reaction, however, was not universally positive—students found the process of switching back and forth between Modern and Middle English disconcerting and distracting and felt that it would have been preferable to have read just the Middle English (but with more extensive glosses).

In the future, I would require students to obtain volume 1 of the TEAMS edition (which includes the prologue as well as books 1 and 8 in their entirety), and I would supplement this volume with selections from the TEAMS full text of the *Confessio Amantis* available online. By providing an edition with more comprehensive glosses and notes, this solution would solve many of the problems my students encountered. At the same time, it would allow me to introduce students to a broader sense of the whole work since parts of the work aren't summarized, as they are in the MART edition.

In the course of the semester, I created assignments intended to spark students' curiosity and creativity as well as to engage their abilities to connect medieval cultural information with their interpretations of the literary texts. One assignment was based on my conviction that the educational process works best by creating questions. Students kept an ongoing journal of questions they thought of in the process of reading and discussing texts in class. Twice each semester, students chose from among their questions a selection that focused either on single or on multiple texts (considering especially topics of character, theme, and composition), and they submitted these sets of questions as a written assignment. I then drew on these questions to create yet another assignment—a take-home study-question project—that gave them the opportunity to work together outside class, exploring further possibilities for understanding the texts in ways that extended beyond the ability of class lecture and discussion to address.

Another assignment encouraged students to delve more deeply into the cultural environment of late-fourteenth-century England through a research presentation project, for which students chose some aspect of medieval material or social culture to explore and share with their classmates. They were encouraged to approach this research and their presentation using multiple media—music, art, material culture. Students researched topics such as architecture, knighthood, aspects of daily life, or games and supplemented their projects with a one- or two-page handout and slides (including, sometimes, video or audio clips). Presentations were expected to take ten or fifteen minutes of class time, though students often became so enthralled with their topic that they found it a challenge to fit their mass of researched material within the time limit.

This research presentation could also become the foundation of a cultural studies interpretation of one or more of the literary texts studied. However, I offered multiple approaches for the final literary research paper to reflect the wide disparity of student abilities. I have students who are working at advanced levels of sophisticated interpretive research as well as students who have never done any independent library research. Because of the students' wide range of intellectual sophistication, it seemed expedient to offer multiple approaches to discussions of the text. All approaches required library research, but not all required independent interpretations. For example, students could write essays in the style of a critical "book review," assessing the value of several thematically related journal articles or book chapters. Alternatively, they could create a bibliographic essay reviewing a wide range of materials available on a particular literary text. Finally, they could apply their own interpretive approach, using scholarly support, to one or more literary texts. While I am happy to provide specific approaches and topics to students who require them, I prefer to offer students the opportunity to discover how their own curiosity can lead to particular approaches, and this freedom generally leads to an excitement and enthusiasm in the students' research, which is infectious for the whole class.

While many of my paper and research assignments for Medieval Courtly Literature were not limited to teaching Gower's *Confessio Amantis* specifically, I found in teaching this particular work that students were deeply drawn to the poem, in part because they encountered the work after having already become familiar with Gower's cultural environment. I was impressed and pleased at how much students enjoyed reading Gower. They immediately recognized how different his style and approach were compared with other contemporary poets, but the less flashy nature of his writing did not leave them uninterested. Instead, they found Gower's style and narrative content both endearing and compelling. One student commented that, in comparison with Chaucer, Gower's writing seemed "rather dry" but had a sincerity that gave an impression "almost like a soul journey." Moreover, he opined that Gower had "some of the BEST lines—the kind you should be reading on Web sites for inspirational quotes." My experience, overall, in teaching John Gower's *Confessio Amantis* indicated that this medieval poet's voice has the power to speak to students of the twenty-first century, and it is well worth the effort to overcome hurdles of cultural and linguistic unfamiliarity to do so.

Gower in Seminar:
The *Confessio Amantis* as
Publishing Opportunity for Graduate Students

Peter G. Beidler

For teachers fortunate enough to teach at a university with a graduate program in English, John Gower's *Confessio Amantis* provides an opportunity not only to teach the work of a fine medieval writer but also to help fledgling graduate students find their way into the brave new world of academic publication. In my own medieval research life I am mostly a Chaucerian. While I have found some new things to say about Chaucer, the standard Chaucerian works have been pretty well picked over in the past hundred years, and I have despaired of helping graduate students who are just learning the field to find publishable things to say about Chaucer. But with Gower, it is different. Because Gower studies is in its relative infancy, Gower presents novice medievalists with a refreshing variety of research topics. With a little help from a professor, graduate students can not only learn about John Gower's works but also contribute new criticism to the field.

Because Lehigh University has only a small graduate program in English, the rotation of graduate courses in any period is relatively infrequent. When their turn does come around, faculty members are discouraged from offering single-author seminars, even on major writers like Chaucer, Shakespeare, Milton, and James. As a result, I could not offer a graduate seminar just on Gower, even if I felt inclined to do so and even if I thought graduate students would take such a course in sufficient numbers to make it float. Thus I have been able to teach Gower only in conjunction with other writers. Because I enjoy helping graduate students think of themselves as serious scholars as well as merely pupils, on those occasions where I got to teach a graduate seminar, I tried to plan at least one activity that got my students directly involved in a joint project that could, if all went well, lead to a conference presentation or to a publication. For example, a few years ago in a seminar on medieval comedy, my eight graduate students wrote, under my guidance, coordinated papers on a French fabliau called *The Gelded Lady*. Later they all presented at a small one-day conference in nearby New Jersey (the New Jersey College English Association) and then with my help published their papers jointly in *ANQ* as "*The Gelded Lady*, An Old French Fabliau: New Views and a New Translation."

The first time I included Gower in a seminar—back in 1980—I crowded him into a course with the *Pearl* poet and Langland. In getting ready for that seminar, I noticed in reading through G. C. Macaulay's notes to Gower's *Complete Works* that a large number of the tales in the *Confessio Amantis* had sources in Ovid's *Metamorphoses*. I decided to have my students read a translation of selected tales in the *Metamorphoses* in conjunction with the tales' counterparts in the *Confessio.* The comparisons were so revealing of Gower's methods and altered emphases that I decided to assign each of my seven students papers on two of the pairs of tales. I selected two of the pairs of tales myself and wrote essays for my students to read and use as rough models for their own two essays. Modeling such essays is crucial when helping graduate students prepare for their publishing careers. When we were finished revising our sixteen papers, I wrote a summarizing introduction, arranged for a couple more pieces on Gower to be written, and sent the collection off to the University Press of America (UPA). The UPA eventually published the short book *John Gower's Literary Transformations in the* Confessio Amantis*: Original Articles and Translations* (1982). It is not a brilliant achievement, but it is still useful, and in any case it stands as one of the first books of criticism devoted to Gower.

The last time I taught Gower—in fall 2005—I combined him in a graduate seminar with Chaucer, Boccaccio, and Nicholas Trevet. In the rest of this essay I describe that course in some detail, focusing on the project that resulted in a 122-page publication on the John Gower Society Web site (www.johngower.org).

The course, Chaucer's Tales and Their Sources, was described in the catalog of course offerings as a comparison of several of the narratives in the *Canterbury Tales* with their literary sources and analogues, particularly those in John Gower's *Confessio Amantis.* The purpose of the comparisons was to help modern readers understand Chaucer's purposes, emphases, originality, and comparative modernity. Examples included comparing The Knight's Tale with Boccaccio's *Teseida,* The Wife of Bath's Tale with Gower's "Tale of Florent," The Man of Law's Tale with Trevet's *Anglo-Norman Chronicle* and Gower's "Tale of Constance," The Physician's Tale with Gower's "Tale of Virginia," and The Manciple's Tale with Gower's "Tale of Phebus and Cornide." The description announced that students would be encouraged to work at least one of their papers involving Gower into a possible conference presentation or publication.

Note that I name Chaucer in the course title. Because most graduate students have never heard of Gower, that naming gave the course some sticker appeal, but I emphasized Gower in the course description and in the last sentence, which mentioned a research paper with possible conference presentation and publication. Graduate students have already gotten the message that they will one day be competing for jobs with candidates who already have several conference presentations and publications on their CVs. I thought it would appeal to students that I offered them the possibility for something beyond the traditional graded-and-filed-away term paper. It did appeal, and a full dozen students signed up.

After an introductory seminar session, I prepared for our focal work on the various versions of the Constance story by spending weeks 2–4 on the "Tale of Florent" and The Wife of Bath's Tale, then weeks 5–7 on the *Teseida* and The Knight's Tale. Halfway through the seminar, in week 7, the students selected, from a list I provided, a plot element from Trevet's *Of the Noble Lady*

Constance, which we were to read the following week. The list also gave them a quick overview of the tale they were to read:

1. The Heathen Merchants (lines 1–49)
2. The Marriage Negotiations (50–72)
3. The Murder of the Christians (73–99)
4. The Voyage to Northumberland (100–51)
5. The Blind Man (152–209)
6. The False Knight (210–52)
7. The King's Marriage (253–65; 305–17)
8. The Substitute Letters (266–304)
9. The Second Exile (318–59)
10. The Attempted Rape (360–94)
11. The Return to Rome (433–83)
12. The Reunion with Alla (395–432)
13. The Tying of Loose Ends (484–598)

The students made their selection. As a member of the seminar I too made a selection. My area was to be number 10, the attempted rape of Constance. I assigned Trevet's *Of the Noble Lady Constance* in translation, which appears in Robert M. Correale and Mary Hamel's *Sources and Analogues* (2: 296–329). I asked students to look at the accompanying Old French text on the facing right-hand pages and to come to class prepared to lead a discussion on the narrative unit they selected. They were to think about why Trevet made the choices he made about emphases, characterization, and narrative alternatives and about how they would retell the part of the story they selected if they were authors writing after Trevet and for a different audience.

Since it had yet to appear in print, I was most fortunate to have secured the permission of Bob Correale to let my students use draft copies of his edition of *Of the Noble Lady Constance* with its facing-page translation. He had generously sent me the corrected proofs from his upcoming chapter on the sources of The Man of Law's Tale in volume 2 of *Sources and Analogues*. We were able, then, to have prepublication access to the first and only full translation of Trevet's story, a real boon for our project. Chaucer and Gower scholars knew about Trevet's work, of course, but it had been mostly a closed book to all but the few who were fluent in Old French.

During class the students gave oral reports on their area of Trevet's *Constance* story. Each student talked and invited the rest of us to talk about interesting, problematic, contradictory, or unclear elements of the story. I had my own list of questions or concerns to help guide their thinking if necessary. When my turn came, I talked about item 10, the attempted rape of Constance. Then we were ready for the following week's assignment: students were to read Gower's "Tale of Constance" and to think about their chosen narrative unit, particularly about the changes Gower made in the passages they were assigned. They were also to prepare to ask classmates questions about what elements Gower kept, what he altered, and why. This session would be an opportunity for students to pretest some of their own ideas and to receive from classmates other ideas that would help them write their papers. The discussions that resulted from this assignment were the best of the term, perhaps because the students, having come to see what comparative narrative analysis was all about, had specific areas to be responsible for. Perhaps it was that they knew that an important paper was coming up and hoped to get some help with their topic.

Thinking of the possibility for publication, I had written to Bob Yeager about our Constance project. He was kind enough to encourage me to go forward and submit the project for possible publication on the John Gower Society Web site, just then about to be launched by Brian Gastle. While online publications are still met with skepticism in some scholarly communities, they are becoming more and more common. Online publication often does not carry the same prestige as a traditional peer-reviewed print publication, but original scholarly material posted to the John Gower Society Web site is reviewed and represents an alternative publication forum quite appropriate for both young and experienced scholars.

For the following week the students wrote drafts of their papers—eight pages, more or less—on Gower's alterations of Trevet. To guide my students as they wrote their papers, I drafted my own essay on the attempted rape of Constance. If our group project was to have any integrity as a unified piece, there needed to be some commonality of approach. My essay was designed specifically to be a rough model for the work of my students. It had an informative introductory paragraph, brief summaries of the rape incidents as they appeared in the two versions, and a detailed analysis of the changes Gower made. I give here only the introduction to that paper on the attempted rape of Constance in Trevet's *Noble Lady Constance* (lines 360–94) and Gower's *Confessio Amantis* (2.1084–125):

As Constance drifts back toward Rome from Northumberland in Trevet's version of the story of Constance, Telous, a renegade Christian in Spain boards her boat. The scene runs to nearly 450 words, which I give here in summary:

When God guides Constance's boat under a castle on the eastern shore of Spain, the local heathen emir has Constance and Maurice brought to his castle and instructs his seneschal, a former Christian named Telous, to take charge of them. Telous takes pity on her and gives her good food and drink. He offers her lodging ashore, but she refuses, feeling better protected by God on the sea than ashore on heathen lands. Telous is ordered by the emir to make sure she is not ill-treated by anyone. Telous, delighted with that task, carries down to Constance's boat in the dead of night a sizable treasure of valuable jewels, silver, and gold. Then he tells Constance that he had been greatly at fault for forgetting his Christian religion among the heathens and begs her to let him accompany her back to a Christian land where he can reclaim his Christian faith. Then with the help of his close friends, he casts off and the boat soon comes to the high seas. There the devil moves the knight to try to seduce Constance. God, of course, will not allow her to consent, and when Telous tries to force her, Constance restrains his folly by arguing that the child Maurice, then two years old, might understand and remember his mother's sexual encounter. She asks Telous to look out on all sides to see if he might spy any land, promising that if they find a good place to land she will satisfy the renegade's desires in a suitably private place there. Telous likes this proposal and stands in the front of the ship looking all around to see if he can see land. While he looks so attentively, Constance sneaks up behind him and pushes Telous into the sea, where he drowns.

Gower renders the scene rather differently in some 275 words:

> By chance, after a year of drifting on the seas, Constance's ship is driven by the winds of God eastward to Spain under the castle wall of a heathen admiral. This admiral has a steward named Theloüs, a false knight and a corrupt renegade who goes out to check on the condition of the ship. There he finds the lady with a child in her arms. He takes a good look at her, sees that she is beautiful, and plans that night to have his way with her. Taking care that no other men will see her, he lets her lie there in the ship. Constance has no idea what he is planning. That night Theloüs takes a boat and rides out to her ship again, thinking to gratify his lust. He swears that if she resists him, he will kill her. Seeing that there is no other way, Constance says that she will comfort him well, but asks Theloüs first to look out the door to make sure no one is near enough to observe them. Theloüs is happy to do so and goes to the door. Then Constance prays to God for help. God hears her prayer and quickly throws Theloüs out of the ship, drowning him. Then God sends a wind to blow the ship away from that land. Thus has mighty God protected Constance.

Although the incidents in the two versions of the story of Constance are broadly similar, Gower makes a number of important changes. He gives Constance less agency, makes Maurice younger, makes the would-be rapist more evil, and makes God more powerful.

To save space, I do not reproduce here the whole paper, but to help my students I went on in the rest of my paper to discuss in much greater detail each of those four changes. Along with my model paper on the attempted rape, I gave my students a list of specific guidelines for their essays. Such detail in an assignment is crucial if students are to learn the nuances of scholarship in a particular field or within a particular scholarly genre. In my guidelines I told them that the opening paragraph should give narrative summaries of the two versions of their assigned section, as in my example, and end with a thumbnail summary or outline of their argument. They were to make no reference to Chaucer here or elsewhere in the paper. They were to provide no footnotes or endnotes, at least at this stage. I told them that if the project was to develop into actual publication, I would write an introduction including references. To identify quotations, they were to use the abbreviation *NLC* for Trevet's *Of the Noble Lady Constance* and *CA* for Gower's *Confessio Amantis*; follow my examples for commas, parentheses, and so on; and use shorter rather than longer quotations. For Trevet, they needed to find line numbers in the French text and quote in the Old French first, then provide, in brackets, Correale's English translation. They were to quote Gower in Middle English. I even gave instructions about how to spell the names of characters and what tense to use for the plot summaries. Fledgling scholars need detailed instructions, especially in a collaborative effort like ours. Blending the thirteen papers into one scholarly production would have been virtually impossible without such guidelines up front.

During class the following week, the students discussed their research findings and turned in their essays. With a view to the summarizing introduction that I would write, my students and I, toward the end of that class, compiled a list of the kinds of changes Gower made to Trevet's story of Constance. I had each student indicate which items on the list applied to the plot element that he or she had worked on. Here is the numerical summary, with the bracketed numbers indicating how many plot elements featured each type of change:

Gower shortens the story. [4]
Gower cuts or reduces minor characters and events. [5]
Gower gives fewer numbers (people converted, soldiers killed, etc.). [3]
Gower is less interested in history, more in morality. [4]
Gower focuses less on Christian conversions. [5]
Gower gives God a more active role in protecting and punishing. [4]
Gower focuses more on envy and slanderous backbiting (detraction). [5]
Gower makes Constance more passive. [3]
Gower makes Constance more emotional. [3]
Gower makes Constance more secular. [5]
Gower makes Constance more motherly. [3]
Gower focuses less on Moris's origins and life story. [3]
Gower makes Allee kinder, more respected by his own people. [4]
Gower gives the devil a reduced role. [5]

Before ending that class, we talked about the disadvantages of Web publication (less prestige) and advantages (ease of access for users, speed of publication) and decided that we would give the John Gower Society Web site a try. I walked out of that class with the students' papers. I set to work reading them and writing extensive comments on them. My comments were designed less to evaluate the students' work than to guide them in their revisions for our joint publication project.

The following week, we read Chaucer's Man of Law's Tale, for which Chaucer drew from both Trevet and Gower. I did not want my students to read Chaucer's version before they wrote their papers, because it was hard enough to keep two versions separate, let alone three. Having read and written on the first two, however, my students were now ready to read and discuss a third, and to do so with opened eyes ready to notice the ways Chaucer made the tale his own. In the coming weeks we read some more pairs of Gower-Chaucer tales—Gower's "Tale of Virginia" and Chaucer's Physician's Tale, Gower's "Tale of Phoebus and Cornide" and Chaucer's Manciple's Tale—but the students' main focus as the semester wound down was revising their Constance papers for publication.

After the students turned in their rewritten papers in the final class, there was of course more work for me to do. I made final edits and put the thirteen pieces together, smoothed transitions, composed the introductory summary, proofread for style and accuracy, and so on. Then I shipped the whole composite piece electronically off to Brian Gastle, the editor of the John Gower Web site, who eventually made it available online (Beidler, *John Gower's Transformation*).

I encourage readers of this essay to find and read our combined essay. It gives the names of the students, and it makes, we proudly feel, a new and significant contribution to the growing field of Gower studies. It was important to me, and of course to my students, that each section appear with its own title and author so that the students could mention their individual publications in their CVs. I close with a return to my central point: that a graduate course involving John Gower gives faculty members an opportunity to introduce their students to the pleasures and reward of original and publishable scholarship. The student work detailed here is just one example of such a project and could be replicated with any number of other issues in Gower's poetry. Such a project, of course, necessitates a certain level of faculty mentorship and guidance to initiate students into the intricacies of scholarly work on the literature of the medieval period.

NOTES ON CONTRIBUTORS

Peter G. Beidler is Lucy G. Moses Professor of English emeritus at Lehigh University and now lives in Seattle. He has published on Chaucer and other medieval writers as well as on Henry James and contemporary Native American novelists. He was named CASE National Professor of the Year in 1983. He coedited the MLA's *Approaches to Teaching Henry James's* Daisy Miller *and* The Turn of the Screw. His two most recent books are *Chaucer's Canterbury Comedies: Origins and Originality* and *A Student Guide to Chaucer's Middle English*.

Craig E. Bertolet is associate professor of English at Auburn University. His research on Gower has appeared in *John Gower: Manuscripts, Readers, Contexts*; *On John Gower: Essays at the Millennium*; and *Philological Quarterly*, and he has published on other medieval literature in *Studies in Philology* and the *Chaucer Review*. His work focuses on commerce, trade, and urban culture in medieval literature, and he is researching a book-length project on commerce in the works of Chaucer and Gower.

Andreea Boboc is assistant professor in the English department at the University of the Pacific, where she teaches medieval literature, linguistics, history of the English language, and courses on law and literature. She has written articles on Chaucer, Gower, law and literature, and medieval drama and is completing a monograph called "Justice and Self in Late Middle English Literary Trials."

María Bullón-Fernández is associate professor of English at Seattle University, where she teaches and conducts research on Chaucer, Gower, feminist and literary theory, medieval women's writings, Arthurian romance, and England and Iberia in the Middle Ages. She is the author of *Fathers and Daughters in Gower's* Confessio Amantis: *Authority, Family, State, and Writing* as well as essays and articles on Gower and Chaucer. She is the editor of *England and Iberia in the Middle Ages, 12th–15th Century* and is working on poverty, property, and notions of the self in medieval literature.

Susannah M. Chewning is associate professor of English at Union County College. She is the editor of *Intersections of Sexuality and the Divine in the Middle Ages: The Word Made Flesh* and *The Milieu and Context of the Wohunge Group*. Her research focuses on women's literature and anchoritic literature of the Middle Ages and has appeared in several collections, including *Straight Writ Queer* and *Anchorites, Wombs, and Tombs*. Her next edited collection, "Anchoritic Spirituality: Enclosure, Authority, Transcendence," is forthcoming.

Joyce Coleman is Rudolph C. Bambas Professor of Medieval English Literature and Culture at the University of Oklahoma. She has published on late medieval literary reception, performance, and patronage, including *Public Reading and the Reading Public in Late Medieval England and France* and articles in anthologies such as *On John Gower: Essays at the Millennium* and in journals such as *Speculum, Studies in the Age of Chaucer*, and the *British Library Journal*. Her current focus is on the "iconography of the book," the cultural conceptions of literature encoded in manuscript illuminations.

James M. Dean is professor of English at the University of Delaware. He has written or edited seven books on Gower, Chaucer, and Middle English writings, including *The World Grown Old in Later Medieval Literature*; he has published articles on those subjects in *PMLA, Speculum, ELH, Philological Quarterly, Studies in Philology*, and others. Currently he is coediting Chaucer's *Troilus and Criseyde* for Broadview Press and is pursuing two main areas of research: Gower, Chaucer, and the Bible, as well as the meaning and value of undergraduate research.

Georgiana Donavin is professor of English at Westminster College, where she teaches literature from *Beowulf* to Virginia Woolf, as well as Latin. Her research focuses on the history of medieval rhetoric, Arthurian studies, and gender studies. She is the author of *Incest Narratives and the Structure of Gower's* Confessio Amantis and articles in *Domestic Violence in Medieval Texts*, in *On John Gower: Essays at the Millennium*, and in *John Gower: Manuscripts, Readers, Contexts*. She is the coeditor of Disputatio. Her forthcoming book is titled "Scribit Mater: Mary and the Language Arts in the Literature of Medieval England."

Siân Echard is professor of English and Distinguished University Scholar at the University of British Columbia. Her book-length works include *Printing the Middle Ages*; *Arthurian Narrative in the Latin Tradition*; and *A Companion to Gower*. She has translated (with Claire Fanger) *The Latin Verses in John Gower's* Confessio Amantis: *An Annotated Translation*, and her articles on Gower have appeared in *Studies in the Age of Chaucer, Journal of Medieval and Early Modern Studies, Studies in Philology*, and *Medium Aevum*.

Brian W. Gastle is the department head and associate dean of the graduate school and associate professor of English at Western Carolina University, where he teaches both medieval literature and professional / technical / Web writing. He has published on Gower, Chaucer, Margerey Kempe, and the Pastons, and he has prepared print, online, and multimedia pedagogical materials for the North Carolina Department of Public Instruction and PBS. He serves as the Web master for the International John Gower Society.

Erick Kelemen is visiting assistant professor at Fordham University. His scholarship focuses on textual criticism and Middle English literature, and his most recent work is *Textual Editing and Criticism: An Introduction*.

Leonard Koff teaches English and humanities and is an associate of the Center for Medieval and Renaissance Studies at UCLA. He is the author of *Chaucer and the Art of Storytelling* and co-editor of *The* Decameron *and the* Canterbury Tales: *New Essays on an Old Question*. He has written essays on medieval literature, medievalism, Ricardian literary associations, and Chaucer's *trecento* connections. His current project is a study of medieval and Renaissance conversion narratives, tentatively entitled, "Does the Body Have a Mind of Its Own?"

Steven F. Kruger is professor of English and medieval studies at Queens College and the Graduate Center, City University of New York. His book-length publications include *Dreaming in the Middle Ages*; *AIDS Narratives: Gender and Sexuality, Fiction and Science*; *The Spectral Jew: Conversion and Embodiment in Medieval Europe*; *Approaching the Millennium: Essays on* Angels in America (edited with Deborah R. Geis); and *Queering the Middle Ages* (edited with Glenn Burger). His teaching and scholarship focus on Middle English literature and culture, medieval Jewish and Christian inter-action, religious conversion, critical theory, and contemporary LGBTQ literature and culture.

Scott Lightsey is associate professor of English at Georgia State University. He is a member of the International John Gower Society and teaches the poet's work in a vari-ety of graduate and undergraduate courses on Middle English, Chaucer, and medieval literature and culture. His research interests revolve around the transmission of wonders in medieval texts and material culture, and his recent publications include *Manmade Marvels in Medieval Culture and Literature*.

Carole Lynn McKinney is professor of English at Mayland Community College in Spruce Pine, North Carolina, where she teaches developmental English, freshman com-position, business writing, and literature courses. She is the coordinator for and a tutor in Mayland's writing-skills lab. Her areas of research include medieval feminist studies, Chaucer, and Tolkien.

J. Allan Mitchell is associate professor of English at the University of Victoria. He is the author of *Ethics and Exemplary Narrative in Chaucer and Gower* and *Ethics and Eventfulness in Middle English Literature*. His current research interests include medie-val forms of rhetoric, practical ethics, medical science, embodiment, and ecology.

Peter Nicholson is professor of English at the University of Hawai'i at Mānoa. He has served as bibliographic editor and reviewer for the *John Gower Newsletter* and has pub-lished *An Annotated Index to the Commentary on Gower's* Confessio Amantis, *Gower's* Confessio Amantis: *A Critical Anthology* (ed.), and *Love and Ethics in Gower's* Confes-sio Amantis.

James M. Palmer is associate professor of English at Prairie View A&M University, where his teaching and research focuses on medieval and Renaissance literature, medi-eval libraries, and the history of medicine. His scholarship has appeared in the *Chaucer Review*, *Neophilologus*, *Teaching English in the Two-Year College*, *Companion to Pre-1600 British Poetry*, *Gender Scripts in Medicine and Narrative*, and *Early Modern Liter-ary Studies*, and he has recorded for the Chaucer Studio.

S. Elizabeth Passmore is associate professor of English at the University of South-ern Indiana, where she teaches medieval literature, history of the English language, and British surveys. Her research focuses on medieval romances and the image of the loathly lady; she is the editor (with Susan Carter) of *The English "Loathly Lady" Tales: Boundaries, Traditions, Motifs*, and her essays have appeared in the *Medieval Femi-nist Forum*, *Misconceptions about the Middle Ages*, and *Essays on the Early Irish King Tales*.

Derek Pearsall became Gurney Professor of English emeritus at Harvard University in 1985 after teaching for twenty years at the University of York, where he helped found the Centre for Medieval Studies. His published work includes a biography of John Lydgate; *Old English and Middle English Poetry*; a critical study of the *Canterbury Tales*; *Geoffrey Chaucer: A Critical Biography*; *Arthurian Literature: An Introduction*; *Gothic Europe*; and a fully annotated edition, newly revised, of the C-Text of Langland's *Piers Plowman*. He is the author of essays on medieval romance, fifteenth-century literature, *Sir Gawain and the Green Knight*, Gower, as well as on Chaucer, Lydgate, and Langland.

Russell A. Peck is John Hall Deane Professor of English at the University of Rochester, where he teaches Gower, Chaucer, Langland, medieval drama, Arthurian literature, and medieval romance. His publications include the three-volume Medieval Institute edition of the *Confessio Amantis* and *Kingship and Common Profit in Gower's* Confessio Amantis. He serves as general editor of the Middle English Texts Series.

Winthrop Wetherbee is professor emeritus at Cornell University and the author of works on medieval literature and classical Latin poetry. His book-length projects include *Chaucer:* The Canterbury Tales and *The Ancient Flame: Dante and the Poets.* He is working on translations of medieval Latin philosophical poetry.

R. F. Yeager is professor of English and chair of the Department of English and Foreign Languages at the University of West Florida. He has written and edited on Gower, Chaucer, and Old and Middle English literatures and has translated Gower's shorter Latin poetry, the *Traitié pour essampler les amantz marietz* and the *Cinkante balades*, both for TEAMS. He is president of the International John Gower Society and edits the *John Gower Newsletter*.

SURVEY PARTICIPANTS

The editors would like to thank the following teachers and scholars for responding to either the print or online survey questionnaire on teaching the works of John Gower. Much of this volume reflects both the practices submitted and the pedagogical issues raised by them, and their contributions to teaching and studying John Gower's works has been invaluable.

Arthur Bahr, *Massachusetts Institute of Technology*
Candace Barrington, *Central Connecticut State University*
Christopher Baswell, *University of California, Los Angeles*
Peter G. Beidler, *Lehigh University*
Craig E. Bertolet, *Auburn University*
Kristin Bovaird-Abbo, *University of Kansas*
María Bullón-Fernández, *Seattle University*
David R. Carlson, *University of Ottawa*
Joyce Coleman, *University of Oklahoma*
Margaret Connolly, *University of Saint Andrews*
Rita Copeland, *University of Pennsylvania*
Rebecca Dark, *Dallas Baptist University*
James M. Dean, *University of Delaware*
Georgiana Donavin, *Westminster College*
Martha W. Driver, *Pace University*
Christina Fitzgerald, *University of Toledo*
Helen Fulton, *University of Wales, Swansea*
Alison Ganze, *Valparaiso University*
Matthew Boyd Goldie, *Rider University*
R. James Goldstein, *Auburn University*
C. Marie Harker, *Truman State University*
Jonathan Hsy, *George Washington University*
Alexander L. Kaufman, *Auburn University, Montgomery*
Erick Kelemen, *Fordham University*
Teresa Kennedy, *University of Mary Washington*
Lisa J. Kiser, *Ohio State University*
Jo Koster, *Winthrop University*
Miriamne Ara Krummel, *University of Dayton*
Roger A. Ladd, *University of North Carolina, Pembroke*
Ross Leasure, *Salisbury University*
Scott Lightsey, *Georgia State University*
B. W. Lindeboom, *unaffiliated*
Arthur Lindley, *University of Birmingham*
Thomas R. Liszke, *Pennsylania State University, Altoona*
Michael Livingston, *The Citadel*
Brian Merrilees, *University of Toronto*
Allan Metcalf, *MacMurray College*

Linne Mooney, *University of York*
Maura Nolan, *University of California, Berkeley*
Steele Nowlin, *Hampden-Sydney College*
James M. Palmer, *Prairie View A&M University*
S. Elizabeth Passmore, *University of Southern Indiana*
Tison Pugh, *University of Central Florida*
David A. Roberts, *Bennett College*
William Robins, *University of Toronto*
E. C. Ronquist, *Concordia University*
Martha Rust, *New York University*
Elizabeth Scala, *University of Texas, Austin*
Misty Schieberle, *University of Kansas*
Andrea Schutz, *Saint Thomas University*
James Simpson, *Harvard University*
Ameer Sohrawardy, *Rutgers University*
A. C. Spearing, *University of Virginia*
Glenn A. Steinberg, *The College of New Jersey*
Theodore Steinberg, *State University of New York, Fredonia*
Emily Steiner, *University of Pennsylvania*
Paul E. Szarmach, *Medieval Academy of America*
Karen Harrod Townsend, *Pensacola Junior College*
Malte Urban, *Queens University, Belfast*
Winthrop Wetherbee, *Cornell University*
Suzanne Yeager, *Fordham University*

WORKS CITED

Abrams, M. H. *A Glossary of Literary Terms*. 7th ed. Boston: Heinle, 1999. Print.

Abrams, M. H., and Stephen Greenblatt, gen. eds. *The Norton Anthology of English Literature*. 8th ed. Vol. 1. New York: Norton, 2006. Print.

Aers, David. *Literary Theory: A Reintroduction*. Oxford: Blackwell, 2008. Print.

———. "Reflections on Gower as '*Sapiens* in Ethics and Politics.'" Yeager, *Re-Visioning Gower* 185–201.

———. "Representations of the 'Third Estate': Social Conflict and Its Milieu around 1381." *Southern Review* [Australia] 16.3 (1983): 335–49. Print.

Agamben, Giorgio. *The Coming Community*. Trans. Michael Hardt. Minneapolis: U of Minnesota P, 1993. Print.

———. *Homo Sacer: Sovereign Power and Bare Life*. Trans. Daniel Heller-Roazen. Stanford: Stanford UP, 1995. Print.

———. *The State of Exception*. Trans. Kevin Attell. Chicago: U of Chicago P, 2005. Print.

Alford, John. "Law and Literature in Medieval England." *PMLA* 92.5 (1977): 941–51. Print.

Allen, Elizabeth. *False Fables and Exemplary Truth in Later Middle English Literature*. New York: Palgrave, 2005. Print.

Allen, Judson B. *The Ethical Poetic of the Later Middle Ages: A Decorum of Convenient Distinctions*. Toronto: U of Toronto P, 1982. Print.

Amis and Amiloun. Amis and Amiloun, Robert of Cisyle, *and* Sir Amadace. Ed. Edward E. Forster. 1997. Kalamazoo: Medieval Inst. Pubs., 2007. TEAMS Middle English Texts. *TEAMS Middle English Texts Series*. U of Rochester, 2007. Web. 5 Nov. 2010.

Anderson, Benedict. *Imagined Communities: Reflections on the Origin and Spread of Nationalism*. New York: Verso, 1991. Print.

Archibald, Elizabeth. *Incest and the Medieval Imagination*. Oxford: Oxford UP, 2001. Print.

Arderne, John. *Treatises of Fistula in Ano, Haemorrhoids, and Clysters*. Ed. D'Arcy Power. London: Kegan Paul, 1910. Print. EETS 139.

Armada, Jacey. "Rape in America: The Recent Statistics Are Startling: What Can We Do as a Nation?" 28 June 2007. Web. 27 Nov. 2010.

Attridge, Derek. *The Singularity of Literature*. London: Routledge, 2004. Print.

Auerbach, Erich. *Mimesis: The Representation of Reality in Western Literature*. Trans. Willard R. Trask. Princeton: Princeton UP, 1953. Print.

Augustine. *On Christian Doctrine*. Trans. D. W. Robertson, Jr. Indianapolis: Bobbs-Merrill, 1958. Print. Lib. of the Liberal Arts.

Austin, J. L. *How to Do Things with Words*. 2nd ed. Cambridge: Harvard UP, 1975. Print.

Bakalian, Ellen Shaw. *Aspects of Love in John Gower's* Confessio Amantis. New York: Routledge, 2004. Print. Studies in Medieval History and Culture 25.

Baker, J. H. *An Introduction to English Legal History.* 4th ed. Bath: Butterworth, 2001. Print.

Bakhtin, Mikhail M. *The Dialogic Imagination.* Ed. Michael Holquist. Trans. Caryl Emerson and Holquist. Austin: U of Texas P, 1981. Print.

Barthes, Roland. *Roland Barthes by Roland Barthes.* Trans. Richard Howard. Berkeley: U of California P, 1977. Print.

Bartholomaeus Anglicus. *De proprietatibus rerum.* Ed. Christel Meier et al. 6 vols. Turnhout: Brepols, 2007. Print.

Bauman, Richard. *Verbal Art as Performance.* Prospect Heights: Waveland, 1977. Print.

Beidler, Peter G., ed. "*The Gelded Lady,* An Old French Fabliau: New Views and a New Translation." *ANQ: A Quarterly Journal of Short Articles, Notes, and Reviews* 17.4 (2004): 3–37. Print.

———, ed. *Geoffrey Chaucer: The Wife of Bath.* New York: Bedford, 1996. Print. Case Studies in Contemporary Criticism.

———, ed. *John Gower's Literary Transformations in the* Confessio Amantis: *Original Articles and Translations.* Washington: UP of Amer., 1982. Print.

———, ed. *John Gower's Transformation of the "Tale of Constance" from Nicholas Trevet's "Of the Noble Lady Constance."* International John Gower Society. Intl. John Gower Soc., 2006. Web. 20 May 2010.

———. "Transformations in Gower's 'Tale of Florent' and Chaucer's 'Wife of Bath's Tale.'" Yeager, *Chaucer and Gower* 100–14.

Benjamin, Walter. "The Storyteller." *Illuminations.* Trans. Harry Zohn. New York: Schocken, 1969. 83–110. Print.

Bennett, J. A. W. "Gower's 'Honeste Love.'" *Patterns of Love and Courtesy: Essays in Memory of C. S. Lewis.* Ed. John Lawlor. London: Arnold, 1966. 107–21. Print.

Bennett, Judith. "The Tie That Binds: Peasant Marriages and Families in Late Medieval England." Neel 214–33.

Berger, Maurice, Brian Wallis, and Simon Watson, eds. *Constructing Masculinity.* New York: Routledge, 1995. Print.

Bhabha, Homi K. *The Location of Culture.* New York: Routledge, 1994. Print.

Black's Law Dictionary. Ed. Bryan Garner. Saint Paul: Thompson-West, 2004. Print.

Blackstone, William. *Commentaries on the Laws of England.* Ed. James DeWitt Andrews. 4th ed. 4 vols. Chicago: Callaghan, 1899. Print.

Bloch, Howard. *Etymologies and Genealogies: A Literary Anthropology of the French Middle Ages.* Chicago: U of Chicago P, 1983. Print.

Boswell, John Eastburn. "*Expositio* and *Oblatio*: The Abandonment of Children and the Ancient and Medieval Family." Neel 234–72.

Bott, Robin L. "'O, Keep Me from Their Worse Than Killing Lust': Ideologies of Rape and Mutilation in Chaucer's 'Physician's Tale' and Shakespeare's *Titus Andronicus.*" Robertson and Rose 189–211.

Bourdieu, Pierre. *Distinctions: A Social Critique of the Judgment of Taste.* Trans. Richard Nice. Cambridge: Harvard UP, 1984. Print.

—. *The Field of Cultural Production: Essays on Art and Literature*. Ed. Randal Johnson. New York: Columbia UP, 1993. Print.

—. *Outline of a Theory of Practice*. Trans. Richard Nice. Cambridge: Harvard UP, 1977. Print.

—. *Practical Reason: On the Theory of Action*. Stanford: Stanford UP, 1998. Print.

—. *The Rules of Art: Genesis and Structure of the Literary Field*. Trans. Susan Emanuel. Stanford: Stanford UP, 1996. Print.

Braswell, Christopher, and Anne Howland Schotter, eds. *The Middle Ages*. Vol. 1A of *The Longman Anthology of British Literature*. 2nd ed. Ed. David Damrosch. New York: Addison, 2003. Print.

Bryan, W. F., and Germaine Dempster, eds. *Sources and Analogues of Chaucer's* Canterbury Tales. Chicago: U of Chicago P, 1941. Print.

Bryant, John. *The Fluid Text: A Theory of Revision and Editing for Book and Screen*. Ann Arbor: U of Michigan P, 2002. Print.

Bullón-Fernández, María. "Confining the Daughter: Gower's 'Tale of Canace and Machaire' and the Politics of the Body." *Essays in Medieval Studies* 11 (1994): 75–85. Print.

—, ed. *England and Iberia in the Middle Ages, 12th–15th Century: Cultural, Literary, and Political Exchanges*. New York: Palgrave, 2007. Print.

—. *Fathers and Daughters in Gower's* Confessio Amantis: *Authority, Family, State, and Writing*. Cambridge: Brewer, 2000. Print. Publications of the John Gower Soc. 5.

Burger, Glenn. *Chaucer's Queer Nation*. Minneapolis: U of Minnesota P, 2003. Print.

Burger, Glenn, and Steven F. Kruger, eds. *Queering the Middle Ages*. Minneapolis: U of Minnesota P, 2001. Print.

Burrow, John. "The Portrayal of Amans in *Confessio Amantis*." *Gower's* Confessio Amantis: *Responses and Reassessments*. Ed. A. J. Minnis. Cambridge: Brewer, 1983. 5–24. Print.

—. *Ricardian Poetry: Chaucer, Gower, Langland, and the "Gawain" Poet*. New Haven: Yale UP, 1971. Print.

Butler, Judith. *Antigone's Claim: Kinship between Life and Death*. New York: Columbia UP, 2000. Print.

—. *Bodies That Matter: On the Discursive Limits of "Sex."* New York: Routledge, 1993. Print.

—. *Gender Trouble: Feminism and the Subversion of Identity*. New York: Routledge, 1993. Print.

—. *The Psychic Life of Power: Theories in Subjection*. Stanford: Stanford UP, 1997. Print.

—. *Undoing Gender*. New York: Routledge, 2004. Print.

Butler, Sara M. "A Case of Indifference? Child Murder in Later Medieval England." *Journal of Women's History* 19.4 (2007): 59–82. Print.

Butterfield, Ardis. "*Confessio Amantis* and the French Tradition." Echard, *Companion* 165–80.

Cambridge Univ. Lib. *British Literary Manuscripts from Cambridge University Library, Series One, the Medieval Age, 1150–1500*. Brighton: Harvester P Microform Pubs., 1984. Print.

218   WORKS CITED

Cannon, Christopher. "Chaucer and Rape: Uncertainty's Certainties." *Studies in the Age of Chaucer* 22 (2000): 67–92. Rpt. in Robertson and Rose 255–79.

———. "'Raptus' in the Chaumpaigne Release and a Newly Discovered Document concerning the Life of Geoffrey Chaucer." *Speculum* 68.1 (1993): 74–94. Print.

Caxton, William. *Book of Curtesye*. Ed. Frederick James Furnivall. London: Oxford UP, 1868. Print. EETS es 3.

Chakrabarty, Dipesh. *Provincializing Europe: Postcolonial Thought and Historical Difference*. Princeton: Princeton UP, 2000. Print.

Chaucer, Geoffrey. *The Riverside Chaucer*. Gen. ed. Larry D. Benson. 3rd ed. Boston: Houghton, 1987. Print.

Cherniss, Michael D. *Boethian Apocalypse: Studies in Middle English Vision Poetry*. Norman: Pilgrim, 1987. Print.

Chewning, Susannah M. "Chaucer and Vernacular Writing." *Approaches to Teaching Chaucer's* Troilus and Criseyde *and the Shorter Poems*. Ed. Tison Pugh and Angela Jane Weisl. New York: MLA, 2007. 50–55. Print.

Chow, Rey. *The Age of the World Target: Self-Referentiality in War, Theory, and Comparative Work*. Durham: Duke UP, 2006. Print.

Chrétien de Troyes. *Perceval; or, The Story of the Grail*. Trans. Ruth Harwood Cline. Atlanta: U of Georgia P, 1985. Print.

Cicero, Marcus Tullius. *De inventione*. Trans. H. M. Hubbell. 1949. Cambridge: Harvard UP, 1960. Print. Loeb Classical Lib.

Clarke, Edwin, and Kenneth Dewhurst. *An Illustrated History of Brain Function: Imaging the Brain from Antiquity to the Present*. 2nd ed. San Francisco: Norman, 1996. Print.

Coghill, Nevill. Introduction. Coghill and Tolkien 6–57.

Coghill, Nevill, and Christopher Tolkien, eds. *The Man of Law's Tale*. London: Harrap, 1969. Print.

Cohen, Jeffrey J., ed. *Cultural Diversity in the British Middle Ages: Archipelago, Island, England*. New York: Palgrave, 2008. Print.

———. *Of Giants: Sex, Monsters, and the Middle Ages*. Minneapolis: U of Minnesota P, 1999. Print. Medieval Cultures 17.

———, ed. *The Postcolonial Middle Ages*. New York: St. Martin's, 2000. Print.

"Coise." *Middle English Dictionary*. 2001. U of Michigan. Middle English Compendium. 1 Aug. 2008. Web. 4 Aug. 2010.

Coleman, Janet. *Medieval Readers and Writers, 1450–1500*. New York: Columbia UP, 1981. Print.

Coleman, Joyce. "'A Bok for King Richardes Sake': Royal Patronage, the *Confessio*, and the *Legend of Good Women*." Yeager, *On John Gower* 104–23.

———. "Lay Readers and Hard Latin: How Gower May Have Intended the *Confessio Amantis* to Be Read." *Studies in the Age of Chaucer* 24 (2002): 209–35. Print.

———. "Philippa of Lancaster, Queen of Portugal—and Patron of the Gower Translations?" Bullón-Fernández 135–66.

———. *Public Reading and the Reading Public in Late Medieval England and France*. Cambridge: Cambridge UP, 1996. Print.

The Complete Works of the Pearl *Poet*. Ed. and trans. Casey Finch. Berkeley: U of California P, 1993. Print.

Copeland, Rita. *Rhetoric, Hermeneutics, and Translation in the Middle Ages: Academic Traditions and Vernacular Texts*. Cambridge: Cambridge UP, 1991. Print.

Correale, Robert M., and Mary Hamel, eds. *Sources and Analogues of the* Canterbury Tales. 2 vols. Cambridge: Brewer, 2002–05. Print.

Crow, Martin M., and Claire C. Olson, eds. *Chaucer Life-Records*. Austin: U of Texas P, 1966. Print.

Cuffel, Alexandra. *Gendering Disgust in Medieval Religious Polemic*. Notre Dame: U of Notre Dame P, 2007. Print.

Dalton-Puffer, Christiane. "Middle English as a Creole and Its Opposite: On the Value of Plausible Speculation." *Linguistic Change under Contact Conditions*. Ed. Jacek Fisiak. Berlin: Gruyter, 1995. 35–50. Print.

Dane, Joseph. *Who Is Buried in Chaucer's Tomb? Studies in the Reception of Chaucer's Book*. East Lansing: Michigan State UP, 1998. Print.

Dean, James M., ed. *Medieval English Political Writings.* Kalamazoo: Medieval Inst. Pubs., 1996. *TEAMs Middle English Texts Series.* U of Rochester, 1996. Web. 20 May 2010.

———, ed. *Six Ecclesiastical Satires.* Kalamazoo: Medieval Inst. Pubs., 1991. *TEAMS Middle English Texts Series*. U of Rochester, 1991. Web. 20 May 2010.

Deleuze, Gilles, and Félix Guattari. *Kafka: Toward a Minor Literature*. Trans. Dana Polan. Minneapolis: U of Minnesota P, 1986. Print.

———. *A Thousand Plateaus: Capitalism and Schizophrenia.* Trans. Brian Massumi. London: Continuum, 1987. Print.

Derrida, Jacques. *Archive Fever: A Freudian Impression*. Trans. Eric Prenowitz. Chicago: U of Chicago P, 1996. Print.

———. "Force of Law: The 'Mystical Foundation of Authority.'" *Acts of Religion*. Ed. Gil Anidjar. New York: Routledge, 2002. 228–98. Print.

———. *On the Name*. Trans. David Wood et al. Stanford: Stanford UP, 1995. Print.

———. *Specters of Marx: The State of the Debt, the Work of Mourning, and the New International.* Trans. Peggy Kamuf. London: Routledge, 1994. Print.

———. *The Truth in Painting*. Trans. Geoffrey Bennington and Ian McLeod. Chicago: U of Chicago P, 1987. Print.

Dijk, Conrad van. "Giving Each His Due: Gower, Langland, and the Question of Equity." *Journal of English and Germanic Philology* 108.3 (2009): 310–35. Print.

Dinshaw, Carolyn. *Getting Medieval: Sexualities and Communities, Pre- and Postmodern*. Durham: Duke UP, 1999. Print.

———. "Rivalry, Rape, and Manhood: Gower and Chaucer." Yeager, *Chaucer and Gower* 130–52. Rpt. in *Violence against Women in Medieval Texts*. Ed. Anna Roberts. Gainesville: UP of Florida, 1998. 137–60. Print.

Donavin, Georgiana. *Incest Narratives and the Structure of Gower's* Confessio Amantis. Victoria: U of Victoria P, 1993. Print.

———. "Rhetorical Gower: Aristotelianism in the *Confessio Amantis*'s Treatment of 'Rethorique.'" *John Gower: Manuscripts, Readers, Contexts*. Ed. Malte Urban. Turnhout: Brepols, 2009. 155–73. Print.

————. "Taboo and Transgression in Gower's 'Apollonius of Tyre.'" *Domestic Violence in Medieval Texts*. Ed. Eve Salisbury, Donavin, and Merrall Llewelyn Price. Gainesville: UP of Florida, 2002. 94–121. Print.

————. "'When Reson Torneth into Rage': Violence in Book III of the *Confessio Amantis*." Yeager, *On John Gower* 216–34. Print.

Dunbar, William. *The Golden Targe*. *The Complete Works*. Ed. John Conlee. Kalamazoo: Medieval Inst. Pubs., 2004. TEAMS Middle English Texts. *TEAMS Middle English Texts Series.* U of Rochester, n.d. Web. 14 Mar. 2011.

Echard, Siân, ed. *A Companion to Gower*. Cambridge: Brewer, 2004. Print.

————. "Gower's 'Bokes of Latin': Language, Politics, and Poetry." *Studies in the Age of Chaucer* 25 (2003): 123–56. Print.

————. Introduction. Echard, *Companion* 1–22.

————. "The John Gower Page." U of British Columbia, 14 Nov. 2008. Web. 20 May 2010.

————. "Last Words: Latin at the End of the *Confessio Amantis*." *Interstices: Studies in Late Middle English and Anglo-Latin in Honour of A. G. Rigg*. Ed. Richard Firth Green and Linne R. Mooney. Toronto: U of Toronto P, 2004. 99–121. Print.

————. *Printing the Middle Ages*. Philadelphia: U of Pennsylvania P, 2008. Print.

————. "With Carmen's Help: Latin Authorities in the *Confessio Amantis*." *Studies in Philology* 95 (1998): 1–40. Print.

Echard, Siân, and Claire Fanger. *The Latin Verses in the* Confessio Amantis. East Lansing: Colleagues, 1991. Print.

Economou, George. "The Character Genius in Alain de Lille, Jean de Meun, and John Gower." *Chaucer Review* 4.3 (1970): 203–10. Print.

Edelman, Lee. *No Future: Queer Theory and the Death Drive*. Durham: Duke UP, 2004. Print.

Emmerson, Richard. "Reading Gower in a Manuscript Culture: Latin and English in Illustrated Manuscripts of the *Confessio Amantis*." *Studies in the Age of Chaucer* 21 (1999): 143–86. Print.

Epstein, Robert. "London, Southwark, Westminster: Gower's Urban Contexts." Echard, *Companion* 43–60.

Evans, G. R. *Law and Theology in the Middle Ages*. New York: Routledge, 2002. Print.

Ferster, Judith. *Fictions of Advice: The Literature and Politics of Counsel in Late Medieval England*. Philadelphia: U of Pennsylvania P, 1996. Print.

Fish, Stanley. "Literature in the Reader: Affective Stylistics." *New Literary History* 2.1 (1970): 123–62. Print.

Fisher, John H. *John Gower: Moral Philosopher and Friend of Chaucer*. New York: New York UP, 1964. Print.

Forni, Kathleen, ed. *Chaucerian Apocrypha: Selections*. Kalamazoo: Medieval Inst. Pubs., 2005. Print.

Foucault, Michel. *The Archaeology of Knowledge*. Trans. A. M. Sheridan Smith. London: Tavistock, 1972. Print.

————. *The History of Sexuality*. Vol. 1. Trans. Robert Hurley. New York: Vintage, 1990. Print.

———. *The Order of Things: An Archaeology of the Human Sciences*. New York: Routledge, 1989. Print.

———. "What Is an Author?" *Language, Counter-memory, Practice*. Ithaca: Cornell UP, 1977. 124–27. Print.

Fradenburg, Louise, Carla Freccero, and Kathy Lavezzo, eds. *Premodern Sexualities*. New York: Routledge, 1996. Print.

Freccero, Carla. *Queer/Early/Modern*. Durham: Duke UP, 2006. Print.

Furnivall, F. J., E. Brock, and W. A. Clouston, eds. *Originals and Analogues of Some of Chaucer's* Canterbury Tales. London: Trübner, 1872–78. Print. Chaucer Soc., 2nd ser., 7, 10, 15, 20, 22.

Fuss, Diana. *Identification Papers*. New York: Routledge, 1995. Print.

Gallacher, Patrick J. *Love, the Word, and Mercury: A Reading of John Gower's* Confessio Amantis. Albuquerque: U of New Mexico P, 1975. Print.

Galloway, Andrew. "Latin England." Lavezzo 41–95.

———. "The Literature of 1388 and the Politics of Pity in Gower's *Confessio Amantis*." Steiner and Barrington 67–104.

Geertz, Clifford. *Local Knowledge*. New York: Basic, 1983. Print.

Geoffrey Chaucer. Harvard U. and the President and Fellows of Harvard Coll., 17 Nov. 2008. Web. 14 Dec. 2008.

Geoffrey of Vinsauf. *The New Poetics [Poetria Nova]*. Trans. Jane Baltzell Kopp. Ed. James J. Murphy. *Three Medieval Rhetorical Arts*. Berkeley: U of California P, 1971. Print.

Gillespie, Alexandra. *Print Culture and the Medieval Author: Chaucer, Lydgate, and Their Books, 1473–1557*. Oxford: Oxford UP, 2006. Print.

The Good Wife's Guide (Le Ménagier de Paris): A Medieval Household Book. Trans Gina L. Greco and Christine M. Rose. Ithaca: Cornell UP, 2009. Print.

Görlach, Manfred. "Middle English: A Creole?" *Linguistics across Historical and Geographical Boundaries*. Ed. Dieter Kastovsky, A. J. Szwedek, Barbara Płoczińska, and Jacek Fisiak. Berlin: Gruyter, 1986. 329–44. Print.

Gower Bibliography. Ed. Mark Allen. John Gower Society, the Dept. of English at UTSA, and the UTSA Lib., n.d. Web. 20 May 2010.

Gower, John. *The Complete Works of John Gower*. Ed. G. C. Macaulay. 4 vols. Oxford: Clarendon, 1899–1902. Print. Vol. 1: *French Works*. Vol. 2: *English Works*. Vol. 3: *English Works*. Vol. 4: *Latin Works*.

———. *Confessio Amantis*. Ed. Russell A. Peck. Latin trans. Andrew Galloway. 3 vols. 2000–04. Kalamazoo: Medieval Inst. Pubs., 2002–06. TEAMS Middle English Texts. *TEAMS Middle English Texts Series*. U of Rochester, 2002–06. Web. 20 May 2010.

———. *Confessio Amantis*. Ed. and trans. Masayoshi Itô. 2nd ed. Tokyo: Shinozaki Shorin, 1988. Print.

———. *Confessio Amantis*. Ed. Russell A. Peck. 1980. Toronto: U of Toronto P, 1997. Print. Medieval Acad. Rpts. for Teaching 9. Rpt. of *Confessio Amantis*. Ed. Peck. New York: Holt, 1968.

———. *The French Balades*. Ed. and trans. R. F. Yeager. Kalamazoo: Medieval Inst. Pubs., 2010. Print. Middle English Texts.

———. *In Praise of Peace*. Ed. Michael Livingston. Kalamazoo: Medieval Inst. Pubs., 2005. TEAMS Middle English Texts. *TEAMS Middle English Texts Series*. U of Rochester, 2005. Web. 21 May 2010.

———. *The Major Latin Works of John Gower: The Voice of One Crying and The Tripartite Chronicle*. Trans. Eric W. Stockton. Seattle: U of Washington P, 1962. Print.

———. *The Minor Latin Works*. Ed. and trans. R. F. Yeager. With *In Praise of Peace*. Ed. Michael Livingston. Kalamazoo: Medieval Inst. Pubs., 2005. TEAMS Middle English Texts. *TEAMS Middle English Texts Series*. U of Rochester, 2005. Web. 21 May 2010.

———. *Mirour de l'omme*. Trans. William Burton Wilson. East Lansing: Colleagues, 1992. Print.

———. *Selections from John Gower*. Ed. J. A. W. Bennett. Oxford: Clarendon, 1968. Print. Medieval and Tudor Ser.

———. *Traitié ... pour essampler les amantz marietz*. Ed. Tamara O'Callaghan and Brian Merrilees. U of Toronto, n.d. Web. 26 May 2010.

The Gower Project. Ed. Malte Urban. N.p., 16 Feb. 2010. Web. 21 May 2010.

Green, Richard F. *A Crisis of Truth: Literature and Law in Ricardian England*. Philadelphia: U of Pennsylvania P, 1999. Print.

———. "Medieval Literature and Law." Wallace 407–31. Print.

Green, Thomas A. *Verdict according to Conscience: Perspectives on the English Criminal Trial Jury, 1200–1800*. Chicago: U of Chicago P, 1985. Print.

Greene, Robert. "The Description of John Gower." *The Plays and Poems of Robert Greene*. Ed. J. Churton Collins. Vol. 2. Oxford: Clarendon, 1905. 321–22. Print.

Grinnell, Natalie. "Medea's Humanity and John Gower's Romance." *Medieval Perspectives* 14 (1999): 70–83. Print.

Guy de Chauliac. *The Cyrurgie of Guy de Chauliac*. Ed. Margaret S. Ogden. London: Oxford UP, 1971. Print. EETS 265.

Halberstam, Judith. *In a Queer Time and Place: Transgender Bodies, Subcultural Lives*. New York: New York UP, 2005. Print.

Hallissy, Margaret. *Clean Maids, True Wives, Steadfast Widows: Chaucer's Women and Medieval Codes of Conduct*. Westport: Greenwood, 1993. Print.

Hanawalt, Barbara. "The Female Felon in Fourteenth-Century England." *Viator* 5 (1974): 253–68. Print.

———. "*Of Good and Ill Repute*": Gender and Social Control in Medieval England. New York: Oxford UP, 1998. Print.

———. *The Ties That Bound: Peasant Families in Medieval England*. Oxford: Oxford UP, 1986. Print.

Harding, Alan. *The Law Courts of Medieval England*. London: Allen, 1973. Print.

Hardt, Michael, and Antonio Negri. *Empire*. Cambridge: Harvard UP, 2000. Print.

Hatton, Thomas J. "John Gower's Use of Ovid in Book III of the *Confessio Amantis*." *Mediaevalia* 13 (1989): 257–74. Print.

Heldris de Cornuälles. *Silence: A Thirteenth-Century French Romance*. Ed. and trans. Sarah Roche-Mahdi. East Lansing: Colleagues, 1992. Print.

Helmholz, Richard H. "Infanticide in the Province of Canterbury during the Fifteenth Century." *History of Childhood Quarterly* 2 (1975): 379–90. Print.

Herlihy, David. *Medieval Households*. Cambridge: Harvard UP, 1985. Print.

Hines, John, Nathalie Cohen, and Simon Roffey. "*Johannes Gower, Armiger, Poeta*: Records and Memorials of His Life and Death." Echard, *Companion* 23–42.

Hiscoe, David W. "Heavenly Sign and Comic Design in Gower's *Confessio Amantis*." *Sign, Sentence, Discourse: Language in Medieval Thought and Literature*. Ed. Julian N. Wasserman and Lois Roney. Syracuse: Syracuse UP, 1989. 228–44. Print.

Hoccleve, Thomas. *The Regiment of Princes*. Ed. Charles R. Blyth. Kalamazoo: Medieval Inst. Pubs., 1999. *TEAMS Middle English Texts Series*. U of Rochester, 1999. Web. 21 May 2010.

Holsinger, Bruce. *The Premodern Condition: Medievalism and the Making of Theory*. Chicago: U of Chicago P, 2005. Print.

———. "Vernacular Legality: The English Jurisdiction of *The Owl and the Nightingale*." Steiner and Barrington 154–84.

Holy Bible: Translated from the Latin Vulgate. Rockford: Tan, 1971. Print.

Horobin, Simon, and Jeremy Smith. *An Introduction to Middle English*. Oxford: Oxford UP, 2002. Print.

Hsy, Jonathan. "Middle English as Catalyst: Postcolonial Theory and Gower's Multilingualism." First International Congress of the Intl. John Gower Soc., Queen Mary U, London. July 2008. Address.

Hunter, Kathryn Montgomery. *Doctors' Stories: The Narrative Structure of Medical Knowledge*. Princeton: Princeton UP, 1991. Print.

Ingham, Patricia Clare, and Michelle R. Warren, eds. *Postcolonial Moves: Medieval through Modern*. New York: Palgrave, 2003. Print.

In Search of Shakespeare. Writ. Michael Wood. Narr. Wood. Dir. David Wallace. PBS, 2003. DVD/Video.

Iser, Wolfgang. *The Act of Reading: A Theory of Aesthetic Response*. Baltimore: Johns Hopkins UP, 1978. Print.

Itnyre, Cathy Jorgensen, ed. *Medieval Family Roles: A Book of Essays*. New York: Garland, 1996. Print.

Itô, Masayoshi. *John Gower, the Medieval Poet*. Tokyo: Shinozaki Shorin, 1976. Print.

"John Gower." *Wikipedia*. Wikimedia, 5 Mar. 2010. Web. 20 Aug. 2010.

John Gower Society. "Audio-Readings Gower Texts." Read by Brian W. Gastle. *International John Gower Society*. Intl. John Gower Soc., n.d. Web. 21 May 2010.

Jones, Terry, R. F. Yeager, Terry Dolan, Alan Fletcher, and Juliette Dor. *Who Murdered Chaucer? A Medieval Mystery*. New York: St. Martin's, 2003. Print.

Julian of Norwich. *The Writings of Julian of Norwich: A Vision Showed to a Devout Woman and A Revelation of Love*. Ed. Nicholas Watson and Jacqueline Jenkins. University Park: Pennsylvania State UP, 2006. Print.

Kabir, Ananya Jahanara, and Deanne Williams, eds. *Postcolonial Approaches to the European Middle Ages: Translating Cultures*. Cambridge: Cambridge UP, 2005. Print.

Kanno, Masahiko. *Studies in John Gower, with Special References to His Words*. Tokyo: Eihōsa, 2007. Print.

Karras, Ruth Mazo. *Sexuality in Medieval Europe: Doing unto Others*. New York: Routledge, 2005. Print.

Karras, Ruth Mazo, and David Lorenzo Boyd. "'Ut cum muliere': A Male Transvestite Prostitute in Fourteenth Century London." Fradenburg and Freccero 101–16.

Kelemen, Erick, ed. *Textual Editing and Criticism: An Introduction*. New York: Norton, 2008. Print.

Kellum, Barbara A. "Infanticide in England in the Later Middle Ages." *History of Childhood Quarterly* 1 (1974): 367–88. Print.

Kelly, Henry A. *Love and Marriage in the Age of Chaucer*. Ithaca: Cornell UP, 1975. Print.

Kempe, Margery. *The Book of Margery Kempe*. Trans. and ed. Lynn Staley. New York: Norton, 2001. Print.

Kendall, Elliot. *Lordship and Literature: John Gower and the Politics of the Great Household*. Oxford: Clarendon, 2008. Print.

Kobayashi, Yoshiko. "*Principis Umbra*: Kingship, Justice, and Pity in John Gower's Poetry." Yeager, *On John Gower* 71–103.

Kristeva, Julia. *Powers of Horror: An Essay on Abjection*. New York: Columbia UP, 1984. Print.

Kruger, Steven F. "Gower's Mediterranean." Yeager, *On John Gower* 3–19.

Kuczynski, Michael P. "Gower's Virgil." Yeager, *On John Gower* 161–87.

Langland, William. *The Vision of Piers Plowman: A Complete Edition of the B-Text*. Ed. A. V. C. Schmidt. London: Dent, 1991. Print.

Latini, Brunetto. *Li livres du Trésor*. Ed. Francis J. Carmody. Berkeley: U of California P, 1948. Print. U of California Pubs. in Mod. Philology.

Lavezzo, Kathy, ed. *Imagining a Medieval English Nation*. Minneapolis: U of Minnesota P, 2004. Print.

Lévi-Strauss, Claude. *The Elementary Structures of Kinship*. Ed. and trans. James Harle Bell, John Richard von Sturmer, and Rodney Needham. Rev. ed. London: Eyre, 1969. Print.

Lewis, C. S. *The Allegory of Love: A Study in Medieval Tradition*. 1936. London: Oxford UP, 1977. Print.

Lim, Gary. "Familiar Estrangements: Reading 'Family' in Middle English Romance." Diss. City U of New York, Graduate Center, 2009. Print.

Livingston, Michael. Introduction. *In Praise of Peace*. Gower, *Minor Latin Works* 89–105.

Lochrie, Karma. *Covert Operations: The Medieval Uses of Secrecy*. Philadelphia: U of Pennsylvania P, 1999. Print.

———. *Heterosyncrasies: Female Sexuality When Normal Wasn't*. Minneapolis: U of Minnesota P, 2005. Print.

Lubet, Steven, and Jill Trumbull-Harris. *Mock Trials: Preparing, Presenting, and Winning Your Case*. Louisville: Natl. Inst. for Trial Advocacy, 2001. Print.

Lydgate, John. *The Fall of Princes*. Ed. Henry Bergen. 1924. London: Oxford UP, 1927. Print. EETS es 121–24.

Lynch, Kathryn. *The High Medieval Dream Vision: Poetry, Philosophy, and Literary Form.* Stanford: Stanford UP, 1988. Print.

Macaulay, G. C. Introduction. Gower, *Complete Works* 1: xi–lxxxvii.

———. Introduction. Gower, *Complete Works* 2: vii–clxxiv.

Machan, Tim William. "Medieval Multilingualism and Gower's Literary Practice." *Studies in Philology* 103.1 (2006): 1–25. Print.

Mahoney, Dhira B. "Gower's Two Prologues to *Confessio Amantis*." Yeager, *Re-Visioning Gower* 17–37.

Marcus, Leah. *Unediting the Renaissance: Shakespeare, Marlowe, and Milton.* New York: Routledge, 1996. Print.

Masschaele, James. *Jury, State, and Society in Medieval England.* New York: Palgrave, 2008. Print.

Mast, Isabelle. "Rape in John Gower's *Confessio Amantis* and Other Related Works." *Young Medieval Women.* Ed. Katherine J. Lewis, Noël James Menuge, and Kim M. Phillips. New York: St. Martin's, 1999. 103–32. Print.

Matthews, David. *The Making of Middle English, 1765–1910.* Minneapolis: U of Minnesota P, 1999. Print.

McCarren, Vincent, and Douglas Moffat. "A Bibliographical Essay on Editing Methods and Authorial and Scribal Intention." *A Guide to Editing Middle English.* Ed. McCarren and Moffat. Ann Arbor: U of Michigan P, 1998. 25–57. Print.

McClintock, Anne. *Imperial Leather: Race, Gender, and Sexuality in the Colonial Contest.* New York: Routledge, 1995. Print.

McLeod, Randall. "Un 'Editing' Shak-speare." *Substance* 33-34 (1981–82): 26–55. Print.

McIntosh, Marjorie. *Controlling Misbehavior in England, 1370–1600.* Cambridge: Cambridge UP, 1998. Print.

Menand, Louis. *The Marketplace of Ideas: Reform and Resistance in the American Academy.* New York: Norton, 2010. Print.

Meyers, Diana Tietjens, Kenneth Kipnis, and Cornelius F. Murphy, Jr., eds. *Kindred Matters: Rethinking the Philosophy of the Family.* Ithaca: Cornell UP, 1993. Print.

Middleton, Anne. "The Idea of Public Poetry in the Reign of Richard II." *Speculum* 53.1 (1978): 94–114. Print.

Miller, William Ian. *The Anatomy of Disgust.* Cambridge: Harvard UP, 2007. Print.

Minnis, Alastair J., ed. *Gower's* Confessio Amantis: *Responses and Reassessments.* Cambridge: Brewer, 1983. Print.

———. "John Gower, *Sapiens* in Ethics and Politics." *Medium Aevum* 49.2 (1980): 207–29. Print.

———. *Magister Amoris:* The Roman de la rose *and Vernacular Hermeneutics.* New York: Oxford UP, 2001. Print.

———. "Moral Gower and Medieval Literary Theory." Minnis, *Gower's* Confessio 50–78.

Mitchell, J. Allan. *Ethics and Exemplary Narrative in Chaucer and Gower.* Cambridge: Brewer, 2004. Print. Chaucer Studies 33.

Mohanty, Chandra Talpade. *Feminism without Borders: Decolonizing Theory, Practicing Solidarity.* Durham: Duke UP, 2003. Print.

Mohl, Ruth. *The Three Estates in Medieval and Renaissance Literature*. New York: Columbia UP, 1933. Print.

Moi, Toril. *Sexual/Textual Politics: Feminist Literary Theory*. 1985. New York: Routledge, 2003. Print.

Murfin, Ross C. "The New Historicism and the Wife of Bath." Beidler, *Geoffrey Chaucer* 115–31.

Murphy, James J. "John Gower's *Confessio Amantis* and the First Discussion of Rhetoric in the English Language." *Philological Quarterly* 41 (1962): 401–11. Print.

Musson, Anthony. *Medieval Law in Context: The Growth of Legal Consciousness from Magna Carta to the Peasants' Revolt*. Manchester: Manchester UP, 2001. Print.

Musson, Anthony, and Edward Powell, trans. and eds. *Crime, Law, and Society in the Later Middle Ages*. Manchester: Manchester UP, 2009. Print.

Myrc, John. *Instructions for Parish Priests*. Ed. Edward Peacock. London: Oxford UP, 1868. Print. EETS os 31.

Neel, Carol, ed. *Medieval Families: Perspectives on Marriage, Household, and Children*. Medieval Acad. of Amer. Toronto: U of Toronto P, 2004. Print.

Ngũgĩ wa Thiong'o. *Decolonising the Mind: The Politics of Language in African Literature*. London: Currey; Portsmouth: Heinemann, 1986. Print.

Nicholson, Peter. *An Annotated Index to the Commentary on John Gower's* Confessio Amantis. Binghamton: Center for Medieval and Early Renaissance Studies, 1989. Print. Medieval and Renaissance Texts and Studies 62.

———. "The Dedications of Gower's *Confessio Amantis*." *Mediaevalia* 10 (1988): 159–80. Print.

———, ed. *Gower's* Confessio Amantis: *A Critical Anthology*. Cambridge: Brewer, 1991. Print. Publs. of the John Gower Soc. 3.

———. "Gower's Revisions in the *Confessio Amantis*." *Chaucer Review* 19.2 (1984): 123–43. Print.

———. *Love and Ethics in Gower's* Confessio Amantis. Ann Arbor: U of Michigan P, 2005. Print.

———. "The 'Man of Law's Tale': What Chaucer Really Owed to Gower." *Chaucer Review* 26.2 (1991): 153–74. Print.

———. "Poet and Scribe in the Manuscripts of Gower's *Confessio Amantis*." *Manuscripts and Texts: Editorial Problems in Later Middle English Literature*. Ed. Derek Pearsall. Cambridge: Brewer, 1987. 130–42. Print.

Nowlin, Steele. "Narratives of Incest and Incestuous Narrative: Memory, Process, and the *Confessio Amantis*'s 'Middel Weie.'" *Journal of Medieval and Early Modern Studies* 35.2 (2005): 217–44. Print.

Nussbaum, Martha. *Hiding from Humanity: Disgust, Shame, and the Law*. Princeton: Princeton UP, 2004. Print.

———. *Upheavals of Thought: The Intelligence of Emotions*. Cambridge: Cambridge UP, 2001. Print.

O'Callaghan, Tamara, trans. *John Gower's "Traitié."* French text ed. Brian Merrilees. Gower Project, 1 Aug. 2008. Web.

Old English Homilies and Homiletic Treatises. Ed. and trans. Richard Morris. London: Trübner, 1868. Print. EETS 29.

Oliver, Christopher. "The Community College Open-Door Philosophy: What Negative Outcomes Have Developed?" *Viewpoints* 120 (1995): 1–24. Print.

Olsen, Alexandra Hennessey. *"Betwene Ernest and Game": The Literary Artistry of the* Confessio Amantis. New York: Lang, 1990. Print. American U Studies 4: English Lang. and Lit. 110.

Olsson, Kurt. *John Gower and the Structures of Conversion: A Reading of the* Confessio Amantis. Cambridge: Brewer, 1992. Print.

———. "John Gower's *Vox Clamantis* and the Medieval Idea of Place." *Studies in Philology* 84.2 (1987): 134–58. Print.

———. "Reading, Transgression, and Judgment: Gower's Case of Paris and Helen." Yeager, *Re-Visioning Gower* 67–92.

Ovid. *Metamorphoses*. Trans. Rolfe Humphries. Bloomington: Indiana UP, 1955. Print.

———. *Metamorphoses*. Trans. A. D. Melville. Oxford: Oxford UP, 1986. Print.

———. Metamorphoses, *Books I–VIII*. Trans. Frank Justus Miller. 1916. Ed. and trans. G. P. Goold. 3rd rev. ed. Cambridge: Harvard UP, 1977. Print. Loeb Classical Lib.

The Parliament Rolls of Medieval England. Ed. C. Given-Wilson et al. Woodbridge: Boydell, 2005. CD-ROM. Scholarly Digital Eds.

Passmore, S. Elizabeth, and Susan Carter, eds. *The English "Loathly Lady" Tales: Boundaries, Traditions, Motifs*. Kalamazoo: Medieval Inst. Pubs., 2007. Print. Studies in Medieval Culture 48.

Pearsall, Derek. "Chaucer's Tomb: The Politics of Reburial." *Medium Ævum* 64.1 (1995): 51–73. Print.

———. "Gower's Narrative Art." *PMLA* 81.7 (1966): 475–84. Print.

———. "The Gower Tradition." Minnis, *Gower's* Confessio Amantis 179–97.

———. "The Idea of Englishness in the Fifteenth Century." *Nation, Court, and Culture: New Essays on Fifteenth-Century English Poetry*. Ed. Helen Cooney. Dublin: Four Courts, 2001. 15–27. Print.

———. "The Manuscripts and Illustrations of Gower's Work." *A Companion to Gower*. Ed. Siân Echard. Cambridge: Brewer, 2004. 73–97. Print.

Peck, Russell A. "Folklore and Powerful Women in Gower's 'Tale of Florent.'" Passmore and Carter 100–45.

———. "John Gower." *Old and Middle English Literature*. Ed. Jeffrey Helferman and Jerome Mitchell. Detroit: Gale, 1994. 178–90. Print. Vol. 146 of *Dictionary of Literary Biography*.

———. "John Gower and the Book of Daniel." Yeager, *John Gower: Recent Readings* 159–87.

———. "John Gower: Reader, Editor, and Geometrician." *John Gower: Manuscripts, Readers, Contexts*. Ed. Malte Urban. Turnhout: Brepols, 2009. 11–37. Print.

———. *Kingship and Common Profit in Gower's* Confessio Amantis." Carbondale: Southern Illinois UP, 1978. Print.

———. "The Phenomenology of Make Believe in Gower's *Confessio Amantis.*" *Studies in Philology* 91.3 (1994): 250–69. Print.

———. "The Problematics of Irony in Gower's *Confessio Amantis.*" *Mediaevalia* 15 (1993): 207–29. Print.

Perry, William G., Jr. *Forms of Intellectual and Ethical Development: A Scheme.* New York: Holt, 1970. Print.

Peters, Julie Stone. "Law, Literature, and the Vanishing Real: On the Future of an Interdisciplinary Illusion." *PMLA* 120.2 (2005): 442–53. Print.

Pickles, J. D., and J. L. Dawson, eds. *A Concordance to John Gower's* Confessio Amantis. Cambridge: Brewer, 1987. Print. Pubs. of the John Gower Soc. 1.

Pollock, Frederick, and Frederic W. Maitland. *History of the English Law.* 2 vols. 2nd ed. Cambridge: Cambridge UP, 1968. Print.

Porter, Elizabeth. "Gower's Ethical Microcosm and Political Macrocosm." Minnis, *Gower's* Confessio Amantis 134–62.

Prendergast, Thomas. *Chaucer's Dead Body.* New York: Routledge, 2004. Print.

Prosser, Jay. *Second Skins: The Body Narratives of Transsexuality.* New York: Columbia UP, 1998. Print.

Reynolds, Suzanne. *Medieval Reading.* Cambridge: Cambridge UP, 1996. Print. Cambridge Studies in Medieval Lit. 27.

Rhetorica ad Herennium. Trans. Harry Caplan. Cambridge: Harvard UP, 1954. Print. Loeb Classical Lib.

Richter, David H., ed. *Falling into Theory: Conflicting Views of Reading Literature.* 2nd ed. New York: Bedford, 1999. Print.

Ricks, Christopher. "Metamorphosis in Other Words." Minnis, *Gower's* Confessio 25–49.

Rigg, A. G., and Edward S. Moore. "The Latin Works: Politics, Lament, and Praise." Echard, *Companion* 153–64.

Riley, Henry Thomas, ed. *Memorials of London and London Life in the XIIIth, XIVth, and XVth Centuries.* London: Longmans, 1868. Print.

Robertson, Elizabeth. "Public Bodies and Psychic Domains: Rape, Consent, and Female Subjectivity in Geoffrey Chaucer's *Troilus and Criseyde.*" Robertson and Rose 281–310.

Robertson, Elizabeth, and Christine Rose, eds. *Representing Rape in Medieval and Early Modern Literature.* New York: Palgrave, 2001. Print.

Rose, Christine M. "Reading Chaucer Reading Rape." Robertson and Rose 21–60.

Rose, Jonathan. "English Legal History and Interdisciplinary Legal Studies." *Boundaries of the Law: Geography, Gender, and Jurisdiction in Medieval and Modern Europe.* Ed. Anthony Musson. Burlington: Ashgate, 2005. 169–86. Print.

Rothwell, William. "The Trilingual England of Geoffrey Chaucer." *Studies in the Age of Chaucer* 16 (1994): 45–67. Print.

Rubin, Gayle. "The Traffic in Women: Notes on the 'Political Economy of Sex.'" *Toward an Anthropology of Women.* Ed. Rayna R. Reiter. New York: Monthly Review, 1975. 157–210. Print.

Saul, Nigel. *Richard II.* New Haven: Yale UP, 1997. Print. Yale English Monarchs.

Saunders, Corrine. *Rape and Ravishment in the Literature of Medieval England*. Cambridge: Brewer, 2001. Print.

Scanlon, Larry. *Narrative, Authority, and Power: The Medieval Exemplum and the Chaucerian Tradition*. Cambridge: Cambridge UP, 1994. Print. Cambridge Studies in Medieval Literature 20.

———. "The Riddle of Incest: John Gower and the Problem of Medieval Sexuality." Yeager, *Re-Visioning Gower* 93–127.

Schlauch, Margaret. *Chaucer's Constance and Accused Queens*. New York: New York UP, 1927. Print.

Schmitz, Götz. *The Middel Weie: Stil- und Aufbauformen in John Gower's* Confessio Amantis. Bonn: Grundmann, 1974. Print.

———. "Rhetoric and Fiction: Gower's Comments on Eloquence and Courtly Poetry." Nicholson, *Gower's* Confessio Amantis 117–42.

Sedgwick, Eve Kosofsky. *Between Men: English Literature and Male Homosocial Desire*. New York: Columbia UP, 1985. Print.

———. *Epistemology of the Closet*. Berkeley: U of California P, 1990. Print.

"Seduction." *The Oxford English Dictionary*. 2nd ed. 1989. Print.

Shakespeare, William. *Henry V*. New York: Sparknotes, 2004. Print. No Fear Shakespeare.

———. *A Midsummer Night's Dream.* Shakespeare, *Riverside Shakespeare* 1: 251–83.

———. *Pericles, Prince of Tyre*. Shakespeare, *Riverside Shakespeare* 2: 1527–64.

———. *The Riverside Shakespeare*. G. Blakemore Evans, gen. ed. 2nd ed. 2 vols. Boston: Houghton, 1997. Print.

———. *The Taming of the Shrew*. Shakespeare, *Riverside Shakespeare* 1: 106–42.

Sheingorn, Pamela. "Appropriating the Holy Kinship: Gender and Family History." Neel, *Medieval Families* 273–301.

Simpson, James. *Sciences and the Self in Medieval Poetry: Alan of Lille's* Anticlaudianus *and John Gower's* Confessio Amantis. Cambridge: Cambridge UP, 1995. Print.

Skelton, John. *Garland of Laurel. The Poetical Works of John Skelton*. Vol 1. Ed. Alexander Dyce. London: Rodd, 1843. 361–424. Print.

Sobecki, Sebastian. *The Sea and Medieval English Literature*. Cambridge: Brewer, 2008. Print.

"Soverainte." *Middle English Dictionary*. 2001. U of Michigan. Middle English Compendium. 1 Aug. 2008. Web. 4 Aug. 2010.

Spivak, Gayatri Chakravorty. "Can the Subaltern Speak?" *Marxism and the Interpretation of Cultures*. Ed. Cary Nelson and Lawrence Grossberg. Urbana: U of Illinois P, 1988. 271–313. Print.

———. *Death of a Discipline*. New York: Columbia UP, 2003. Print.

———. *The Spivak Reader: Selected Works of Gayatri Chakravorty Spivak*. Ed. Donna Landry and Gerald MacLean. New York: Routledge, 1996. Print.

Steiner, Emily, and Candace Barrington. Introduction. Steiner and Barrington, *Letter* 1–11.

———, eds. *The Letter of the Law: Legal Practice and Literary Production*. Ithaca: Cornell UP, 2002. Print.

Stephanus. *Commentary on Galen's Therapeutics to Glaucon*. Ed. and trans. Keith Dickson. Leiden: Brill, 1998. Print.

Strohm, Paul. "Chaucer's Audience(s): Fictional, Implied, Intended, Actual." *Chaucer Review* 18.2 (1983): 137–45. Print.

———. "Form and Social Statement in *Confessio Amantis* and the *Canterbury Tales*." *Studies in the Age of Chaucer* 1 (1979): 17–40. Print.

Suleiman, Susan. *Authoritarian Fictions: The Ideological Novel as a Literary Genre*. New York. Columbia UP, 1983. Print.

Sylvester, Louise. "Reading Narratives of Rape: The Story of Lucretia in Chaucer, Gower and Christine de Pizan." *Leeds Studies in English* 31 (2000): 115–44. Print.

Thomas, A. H., ed. *Calendar of Select Pleas and Memoranda of the City of London Preserved among the Archives of the Corporation of the City of London at the Guildhall, A.D. 1381–1412*. Vol. 3. Cambridge: Cambridge UP, 1932. Print.

Thompson, Stith. *The Folktale*. Berkeley: U of California P, 1977. Print.

Thrupp, Sylvia. *The Merchant Class in Medieval London, 1300–1500*. 1948. Ann Arbor: U of Michigan P, 1989. Print.

Tinkle, Theresa. *Medieval Venuses and Cupids: Sexuality, Hermeneutics, and English Poetry*. Stanford: Stanford UP, 1996. Print.

Todd, Henry J. *Illustrations of the Lives and Writings of Gower and Chaucer Collected from Authentick Documents*. London: Rivington, 1810. Print.

Trevet, Nicholas. *Of the Noble Lady Constance*. Trans. Robert M. Correale. Correale and Hamel 2: 296–329.

———. "Trivet's Life of Constance." Bryan and Dempster 165–81.

Turville-Petre, Thorlac. *England the Nation: Language, Literature and National Identity, 1290–1340*. Oxford: Oxford UP, 1996. Print.

Tyrwhitt, Thomas, ed. *Geoffrey Chaucer: The Canterbury Tales*. 1775–78. 5 vols. London: Pickering, 1830. Print.

Vitz, Evelyn Birge. "Teaching Arthur through Performance." *Arthuriana* 15.4 (2005): 31–36.

Wallace, David, ed. *The Cambridge History of Medieval English Literature*. Cambridge: Cambridge UP, 1999. Print.

Warton, Thomas. *The History of English Poetry, from the Close of the Eleventh to the Commencement of the Eighteenth Century*. 3 vols. London: Dodsley, 1774–81. *Eighteenth Century Collections Online*. Web. 1 Aug. 2008.

Watt, Diane. *Amoral Gower: Language, Sex, and Politics*. Minneapolis: U of Minnesota P, 2003. Print. Studies in Medieval Cultures 38.

The Wedding of Sir Gawain and Dame Ragnelle. *Sir Gawain: Eleven Romances and Tales*. Ed. Thomas Hahn. Kalamazoo: Medieval Inst. Pubs., 1995. Print.

Weisl, Angela Jane. "'Quiting' Eve: Violence against Women in *The Canterbury Tales*." *Violence against Women in Medieval Texts*. Ed. Anna Roberts. Gainesville: UP of Florida, 1998. 115–36. Print.

Wetherbee, Winthrop. "John Gower." Wallace 589–609.

———. "Latin Structure and Vernacular Space: Gower, Chaucer and the Boethian Tradition." Yeager, *Chaucer and Gower* 7–35.

White, Hayden. *The Content of the Form: Narrative Discourse and Historical Representation.* Baltimore: Johns Hopkins UP, 1990. Print.

White, Hugh. *Nature, Sex, and Goodness in a Medieval Literary Tradition.* Oxford: Oxford UP, 2000. Print.

Whiting, B. J. *Proverbs, Sentences, and Proverbial Phrases; from English Writings Mainly before 1500.* Cambridge: Belknap–Harvard UP, 1968. Print.

Wickert, Maria. *Studien zu John Gower.* 1953. Trans. Robert J. Meindl. Washington: UP of Amer., 1981. Print.

Williams, Deanne. "Gower's Monster." Kabir and Williams 127–50.

Wimsatt, James I, ed. *Chaucer and the Poems of "Ch."* Rev. ed. U of Rochester, 2009. Web. 26 May 2010. TEAMS Middle English Texts.

"The World of Chaucer: Medieval Books and Manuscripts." Hunterian Museum. U of Glasgow, n.d. Web. 24 May 2010.

Yeager, R. F., ed. *Chaucer and Gower: Difference, Mutuality, Exchange.* Victoria: U of Victoria P, 1991. Print.

———. "Gower's Lancastrian Affinity: The Iberian Connection." *Viator* 35 (2004): 483–515. Print.

———. Introduction to *Cinkante balades.* Gower, *French Balades* 49–55.

———. Introduction to the *Traitié.* Gower, *French Balades* 5–10.

———. "John Gower's French." Echard, *Companion* 137–51.

———. "John Gower and the *Exemplum* Form: Tale Models in the *Confessio Amantis.*" *Mediaevalia* 8 (1982): 307–35. Print.

———. *John Gower Materials: A Bibliography through 1979.* New York: Garland, 1981. Print.

———, ed. *John Gower: Recent Readings. Papers Presented at the Meetings of the John Gower Society at the International Congress on Medieval Studies, Western Michigan University, 1983–88.* Kalamazoo: Western Michigan UP, 1989. Print. Studies in Medieval Culture 26.

———. "John Gower's Audience: The Ballades." *Chaucer Review* 40.1 (2005): 81–105. Print.

———. "John Gower's French." Echard, *Companion* 137–51.

———. "John Gower's Images: 'The Tale of Constance' and 'The Man of Law's Tale.'" *Speaking Images: Essays in Honor of V. A. Kolve.* Ed. Robert F. Yeager and Charlotte C. Morse. Asheville: Pegasus, 2001. 525–57. Print.

———. *John Gower's Poetic: The Search for a New Arion.* Cambridge: Brewer, 1990. Print.

———, ed. *On John Gower: Essays at the Millennium.* Kalamazoo: Medieval Inst. Pubs., 2007. Print.

———. "Pax Poetica: On the Pacifism of Chaucer and Gower." *Studies in the Age of Chaucer* 9 (1987): 97–121. Print.

———, ed. *Re-Visioning Gower.* Asheville: Pegasus, 1998. Print.

Yeager, R. F., Mark West, Robin L. Hinson, and Adrienne Hollifield. *A Concordance to the French Poetry and Prose of John Gower.* East Lansing: Michigan State UP, 1997. Print. Medieval Texts and Studies 17.

Young, Robert J. C. *Colonial Desire: Hybridity in Theory, Culture, and Race*. New York: Routledge, 1995. Print.

Zambreno, Mary Frances. "Gower's *Confessio Amantis* IV, 1963–2013: The Education of Achilles." *Proceedings of the Illinois Medieval Association* 3 (1986): 131–48. Print.

Zimmermann, Reinhard. *The Law of Obligations: Roman Foundations of the Civilian Resources*. Oxford: Oxford UP, 1996. Print.

INDEX

Modern Language Association of America
Approaches to Teaching World Literature

Eliot's Middlemarch. Ed. Kathleen Blake. 1990.
Eliot's Poetry and Plays. Ed. Jewel Spears Brooker. 1988.
Shorter Elizabethan Poetry. Ed. Patrick Cheney and Anne Lake Prescott. 2000.
Ellison's Invisible Man. Ed. Susan Resneck Parr and Pancho Savery. 1989.
English Renaissance Drama. Ed. Karen Bamford and Alexander Leggatt. 2002.
Works of Louise Erdrich. Ed. Gregg Sarris, Connie A. Jacobs, and
    James R. Giles. 2004.
Dramas of Euripides. Ed. Robin Mitchell-Boyask. 2002.
Faulkner's As I Lay Dying. Ed. Patrick O'Donnell and Lynda Zwinger. 2011.
Faulkner's The Sound and the Fury. Ed. Stephen Hahn and Arthur F. Kinney. 1996.
Fitzgerald's The Great Gatsby. Ed. Jackson R. Bryer and Nancy P. VanArsdale. 2009.
Flaubert's Madame Bovary. Ed. Laurence M. Porter and Eugene F. Gray. 1995.
García Márquez's One Hundred Years of Solitude. Ed. María Elena de Valdés and
    Mario J. Valdés. 1990.
Gilman's "The Yellow Wall-Paper" and Herland. Ed. Denise D. Knight and
    Cynthia J. Davis. 2003.
Goethe's Faust. Ed. Douglas J. McMillan. 1987.
Gothic Fiction: The British and American Traditions. Ed. Diane Long Hoeveler
    and Tamar Heller. 2003.
Poetry of John Gower. Ed. R. F. Yeager and Brian W. Gastle. 2011.
Grass's The Tin Drum. Ed. Monika Shafi. 2008.
Hebrew Bible as Literature in Translation. Ed. Barry N. Olshen and
    Yael S. Feldman. 1989.
Homer's Iliad *and* Odyssey. Ed. Kostas Myrsiades. 1987.
Hurston's Their Eyes Were Watching God *and Other Works.* Ed. John Lowe. 2009.
Ibsen's A Doll House. Ed. Yvonne Shafer. 1985.
Henry James's Daisy Miller *and* The Turn of the Screw. Ed. Kimberly C. Reed and
    Peter G. Beidler. 2005.
Works of Samuel Johnson. Ed. David R. Anderson and Gwin J. Kolb. 1993.
Joyce's Ulysses. Ed. Kathleen McCormick and Erwin R. Steinberg. 1993.
Works of Sor Juana Inés de la Cruz. Ed. Emilie L. Bergmann and Stacey Schlau. 2007.
Kafka's Short Fiction. Ed. Richard T. Gray. 1995.
Keats's Poetry. Ed. Walter H. Evert and Jack W. Rhodes. 1991.
Kingston's The Woman Warrior. Ed. Shirley Geok-lin Lim. 1991.
Lafayette's The Princess of Clèves. Ed. Faith E. Beasley and
    Katharine Ann Jensen. 1998.
Works of D. H. Lawrence. Ed. M. Elizabeth Sargent and Garry Watson. 2001.
Lazarillo de Tormes *and the Picaresque Tradition.* Ed. Anne J. Cruz. 2009.
Lessing's The Golden Notebook. Ed. Carey Kaplan and Ellen Cronan Rose. 1989.
Mann's Death in Venice *and Other Short Fiction.* Ed. Jeffrey B. Berlin. 1992.
Marguerite de Navarre's Heptameron. Ed. Colette H. Winn. 2007.
Medieval English Drama. Ed. Richard K. Emmerson. 1990.
Melville's Moby-Dick. Ed. Martin Bickman. 1985.

Metaphysical Poets. Ed. Sidney Gottlieb. 1990.
Miller's Death of a Salesman. Ed. Matthew C. Roudané. 1995.
Milton's Paradise Lost. Ed. Galbraith M. Crump. 1986.
Milton's Shorter Poetry and Prose. Ed. Peter C. Herman. 2007.
Molière's Tartuffe *and Other Plays.* Ed. James F. Gaines and
    Michael S. Koppisch. 1995.
Momaday's The Way to Rainy Mountain. Ed. Kenneth M. Roemer. 1988.
Montaigne's Essays. Ed. Patrick Henry. 1994.
Novels of Toni Morrison. Ed. Nellie Y. McKay and Kathryn Earle. 1997.
Murasaki Shikibu's The Tale of Genji. Ed. Edward Kamens. 1993.
Nabokov's Lolita. Ed. Zoran Kuzmanovich and Galya Diment. 2008.
Works of Tim O'Brien. Ed. Alex Vernon and Catherine Calloway. 2010.
Works of Ovid and the Ovidian Tradition. Ed. Barbara Weiden Boyd and
    Cora Fox. 2010.
Poe's Prose and Poetry. Ed. Jeffrey Andrew Weinstock and Tony Magistrale. 2008.
Pope's Poetry. Ed. Wallace Jackson and R. Paul Yoder. 1993.
Proust's Fiction and Criticism. Ed. Elyane Dezon-Jones and
    Inge Crosman Wimmers. 2003.
Puig's Kiss of the Spider Woman. Ed. Daniel Balderston and Francine Masiello. 2007.
Pynchon's The Crying of Lot 49 *and Other Works.* Ed. Thomas H. Schaub. 2008.
Novels of Samuel Richardson. Ed. Lisa Zunshine and Jocelyn Harris. 2006.
Rousseau's Confessions *and* Reveries of the Solitary Walker. Ed. John C. O'Neal
    and Ourida Mostefai. 2003.
Scott's Waverley Novels. Ed. Evan Gottlieb and Ian Duncan. 2009.
Shakespeare's Hamlet. Ed. Bernice W. Kliman. 2001.
Shakespeare's King Lear. Ed. Robert H. Ray. 1986.
Shakespeare's Othello. Ed. Peter Erickson and Maurice Hunt. 2005.
Shakespeare's Romeo and Juliet. Ed. Maurice Hunt. 2000.
Shakespeare's The Tempest *and Other Late Romances.* Ed. Maurice Hunt. 1992.
Shelley's Frankenstein. Ed. Stephen C. Behrendt. 1990.
Shelley's Poetry. Ed. Spencer Hall. 1990.
Sir Gawain and the Green Knight. Ed. Miriam Youngerman Miller and
    Jane Chance. 1986.
Song of Roland. Ed. William W. Kibler and Leslie Zarker Morgan. 2006.
Spenser's Faerie Queene. Ed. David Lee Miller and Alexander Dunlop. 1994.
Stendhal's The Red and the Black. Ed. Dean de la Motte and Stirling Haig. 1999.
Sterne's Tristram Shandy. Ed. Melvyn New. 1989.
Stowe's Uncle Tom's Cabin. Ed. Elizabeth Ammons and Susan Belasco. 2000.
Swift's Gulliver's Travels. Ed. Edward J. Rielly. 1988.
Teresa of Ávila and the Spanish Mystics. Ed. Alison Weber. 2009.
Thoreau's Walden *and Other Works.* Ed. Richard J. Schneider. 1996.
Tolstoy's Anna Karenina. Ed. Liza Knapp and Amy Mandelker. 2003.
Vergil's Aeneid. Ed. William S. Anderson and Lorina N. Quartarone. 2002.

Voltaire's Candide. Ed. Renée Waldinger. 1987.
Whitman's Leaves of Grass. Ed. Donald D. Kummings. 1990.
Wiesel's Night. Ed. Alan Rosen. 2007.
Works of Oscar Wilde. Ed. Philip E. Smith II. 2008.
Woolf's Mrs. Dalloway. Ed. Eileen Barrett and Ruth O. Saxton. 2009.
Woolf's To the Lighthouse. Ed. Beth Rigel Daugherty and Mary Beth Pringle. 2001.
Wordsworth's Poetry. Ed. Spencer Hall, with Jonathan Ramsey. 1986.
Wright's Native Son. Ed. James A. Miller. 1997.